DATE DUE

More Praise for *Building a World-Class Compliance Program:*

"For those who benefited from reading Martin's first book, *Executive Roadmap to Fraud Prevention and Internal Control*, you now have the 'Atlas' on ethics and compliance. The compliance insights, poignant case studies, and best practices provide a significant value-added read for executives who must set the 'tone at the top' and for those who struggle day-to-day to establish and maintain ethical and compliant behavior within their organizations. A must-read for faculty and particularly students, for whom the lessons so expertly presented here will shape the ethical compass of future careers."

—George E. Curtis, J.D.

Associate Professor and former Director of Economic Crime Programs, Utica College

"Building a World-Class Compliance Program is essential reading for in-house executives of all stripes. Boards, management, legal counsel, HR, and compliance officers all will find this 'how to' guide filled with practical advice and tips. For all people interested in how to avoid their company becoming the next Enron, this book is a must-read. It chronicles real-life examples of corporate malfeasance ripped from the headlines and offers sage measures to enhance corporate compliance programs so as to detect and deter such conduct. Given the expertise of the author—with years of experience in both law enforcement and in-house compliance—this is the preeminent guide to corporate fraud prevention."

—Andrew Weissmann

Partner, Jenner & Block and former director, U.S. Department of Justice Enron Task Force

"The globalization of business and communications presents an unprecedented opportunity for successful growth in many industries and for companies large and small. Conversely, the compliance challenges faced by businesses worldwide have never been more challenging. The urgency to develop a world class compliance program has never been greater. This book is a must for all companies facing today and tomorrow's compliance challenge."

—John Connors

CFO, Microsoft Corporation (Retired) & Partner at Ignition Partners (Current)

"Unbiased, well-researched, comprehensive, and interesting. A great resource for compliance professionals and a great read for CEOs, management and board members who care about doing the right thing. I have been involved with the production of over 150 compliance articles, books, magazines, and newsletters and Martin's work is amongst the best I have seen."
—Roy Snell,
CEO, Society of Corporate Compliance and Ethics

"Martin slices through the confusion surrounding corporate compliance and offers not only useful guidelines, but a step-by-step approach to establishing an effective program. *Building a World-Class Compliance Program* is essential for anyone concerned with compliance and ethics within organizations."
—James D. Ratley, CFE
President, Association of Certified Fraud Examiners

"Martin and Daniel Biegelman provide business people with an exceptionally important book in *Building a World-Class Compliance Program: Best Practices and Strategies for Success*. They demonstrate how value is added to companies who get it right in this vital aspect of business. Each chapter contains concrete examples of best practices ensuring compliance, backed by solid supporting examples. We hear from some of the best authorities in this field, drawing from experience as a federal law enforcement agent, and now as experienced executives."
—Edward M. Stroz
Co-President of Stroz Friedberg, LLC and former FBI Special Agent

"Gone are the days when compliance programs were optional or companies could just have faith that none of their employees would go astray. Today's organizations need compliance programs and strategies in place. Martin and Daniel Biegelman have written the consummate guide."
—Joel Bartow, CFE, CPP
Director of Fraud Prevention & Investigations, Sitel Corporation

Building a World-Class Compliance Program

Building a World-Class Compliance Program

Best Practices and Strategies
for Success

MARTIN T. BIEGELMAN
with DANIEL R. BIEGELMAN

WILEY

John Wiley & Sons, Inc.

This book is printed on acid-free paper. ∞

Copyright © 2008 by John Wiley & Sons, Inc. All rights reserved.

Published by John Wiley & Sons, Inc., Hoboken, New Jersey.

Published simultaneously in Canada.

For general information on our other products and services or for technical support, please contact our Customer Care Department within the United States at (800) 762-2974, outside the United States at (317) 572-3993 or fax (317) 572-4002.

Wiley also publishes its books in a variety of electronic formats. Some content that appears in print may not be available in electronic books. For more information about Wiley products, visit our Web site at www.wiley.com.

Library of Congress Cataloging-in-Publication Data:

Biegelman, Martin T.
  Building a world-class compliance program : best practices and strategies for success / Martin T. Biegelman, Daniel R. Biegelman.
    p. cm.
  Includes index.
  ISBN 978-0-470-11478-0   (cloth)
  1. Compilance auditing. 2. Auditing, Internal. 3. Corporations—Corrupt practices—Prevention. 4. Business ethics. I. Biegelman, Daniel R. II. Title.
  HF5668.25.B54 2008
  657'.45—dc22
                                        2007039390

Printed in the United States of America

10   9   8   7   6   5   4   3   2   1

For Joseph T. Wells:

*As founder and Chairman of the Association of
Certified Fraud Examiners, he has worked tirelessly
to promote fraud prevention as a key component of a
world-class compliance program.*

Contents

Foreword   xi

Preface   xiii

Acknowledgments   xvii

About the Author   xix

CHAPTER 1
Why Ethics and Compliance Will Always Matter   1

CHAPTER 2
Tone at the Top and Throughout   25

CHAPTER 3
The Growth and Evolution of Compliance   45

CHAPTER 4
Caremark and Sarbanes-Oxley: Enhancing Compliance   71

CHAPTER 5
CA's Compliance Rebirth: Don't Lie, Don't Cheat, Don't Steal   87

CHAPTER 6
The International Landscape of Compliance   107

CHAPTER 7
Compliance Programs and Anti-Money Laundering Efforts   131
By Marc B. Sherman, Laura Connor, and David Meilstrup
About the Chapter Authors   148

CHAPTER 8
Interview with an Ethics and Compliance Thought Leader   149

CHAPTER 9
Building a World-Class Compliance Program: The Seven Steps
in Practice (Part I)   163

CHAPTER 10
Building a World-Class Compliance Program: The Seven Steps
in Practice (Part II)   191

CHAPTER 11
Recognizing Compliance Excellence: Premier, Inc. and Winning the
Baldrige Award   219

CHAPTER 12
Designing Robust Fraud Prevention Policies: The Airservices
Australia Fraud Control Plan   233

CHAPTER 13
The Skunk in the Room   257

Appendix A: Summary of the 2004 Federal Sentencing Guidelines
            Amendments and Recommended Action Steps   269

Appendix B: Sample Compliance Program Charter   277

Appendix C: Resources for Compliance Professionals   283

Index   291

Foreword

By Caren Gordon and Ronnie Kann*

AN EVOLVING FUNCTION

The corporate compliance and ethics function has grown rapidly in the last few years in response to high profile governance failures and subsequent regulatory reforms. Companies have made unprecedented investments in compliance and ethics, launching new compliance organizations, building risk management systems, and rolling out more comprehensive mandatory training. This phenomenon has struck companies across a diverse set of industries, even those that have traditionally received less regulatory attention.

Now that most companies have established some basic level of compliance and ethics infrastructure, many are also beginning to evaluate whether that infrastructure is sufficient. Or, in some cases, they are simply transitioning into maintenance mode: solidifying their oversight and monitoring capabilities, building permanent structures, and ensuring ongoing awareness of compliance and ethics obligations.

A FALSE SENSE OF SECURITY

Despite these dedicated efforts, many organizations may have lulled themselves into a false sense of security. Recent analysis indicates that current control and training activities hardly seem to impact the outcomes that truly matter: (1) decreasing the likelihood of business misconduct and (2) reducing the fear of retaliation and discomfort raising concerns. In truth, employees are skeptical about their company cultures and their colleagues.

---

*Caren Gordon is Executive Director of the Legal and Governance Practice at the Corporate Executive Board. Ronnie Kann is Senior Director of the Compliance and Ethics Leadership Council at the Corporate Executive Board. Both are based in Washington, DC.

Simply put, there continues to be more widespread misconduct and less willingness to report or discuss that misconduct than anyone thought when the global wave of corporate scandals began with Enron in 2001. It occurs at all levels of the company, in all regions of the world, and it appears in organizations of all kinds. We live in a society not unlike the mythical town of "Lake Wobegon" where everyone believes that compliance and ethics at their company is "above average." And, yet, that cannot possibly be true. The result—the culture of integrity, which regulators and Boards of Directors want to see displayed—is at best inconsistent in most corporations.

HIGH STAKES

Unfortunately, this inconsistency in establishing a culture of integrity is problematic and masks significant potential costs from compliance and ethics failures. Indeed, the implied costs from compliance and ethics gaps are staggering in terms of both direct and indirect expenses. Elevated misconduct levels undermine employee engagement and morale and are the source of increasing legal and reputation liability. Moreover, there is a vicious cycle that has emerged between legal and reputation risk. Legal issues give rise to reputation risk, and reputation issues give rise to legal issues.

The bottom line is that companies are more vulnerable—and the stakes are higher—than ever before. It is no longer a matter of paying fines, but rather of protecting the company, its senior executives, and the employee population from significant harm.

SUPPORT FOR THIS ENDEAVOR

While daunting in its scope, the challenge that exists for most organizations is not insurmountable. Many have made substantial progress in taking compliance and ethics to the next level and demonstrating that there are different ways to approach compliance and ethics. It is not necessary for companies to start from scratch or conform to a one-size-fits-all method. Rather, the last few years have given rise to a variety of principles and guidelines, tactics and initiatives that facilitate efforts to safeguard the company.

This book sets forth a host of these solutions, illustrated with rich examples of best practices, sample programs, and individual reports from the front. This ready-to-use set of ideas and tools provide significant support as organizations determine what is right for them and set their course for pursuing an ethical culture.

Preface

When I wrote my first book, *Executive Roadmap to Fraud Prevention and Internal Control: Creating a Culture of Compliance*, co-authored with Joel Bartow, there was a common theme running throughout the work. It was that fraud, abuse, and non-compliance with policies and laws would always be concerns for all organizations, large or small, public or private, foreign or domestic. Yet, much could be done in the way of program development, robust fraud prevention, compliance oversight, and executive leadership to dramatically lessen compliance failures. In many ways, this book is a companion to that book in that it continues and expands on many of these themes.

Although the corporate scandals of Enron, WorldCom, Tyco, Adelphia, and others are mostly history now, we said that other frauds and compliance issues would continue to rear their ugly heads. It didn't take long for our prophecy to come true. Backdating of stock options, bribery and corruption, insider trading, corporate spying, and pretexting scandals have all made global headlines over the last few years. As of the writing of this book, more than 140 corporations are under investigation by the Securities and Exchange Commission and Department of Justice in the United States, as well as subject to internal probes for backdating stock options. Corporate executives have been removed and some have been prosecuted and convicted. As New York Yankee great Yogi Berra has said, "It seems like déjà vu all over again."

Early in my career, I realized the importance of prevention techniques and strategies to lessen compliance failures. As a federal agent with the United States Postal Inspection Service, I arrested hundreds of fraudsters. But no matter how many I arrested and sent to prison, others quickly surfaced to take their places. Prosecutions didn't return the financial losses to businesses and consumers. Few cases ever resulted in full restitution to victims. It was even harder to restore lost reputations to organizations crippled by fraud allegations. I grasped the need to do more than just react when a compliance failure was discovered. Even more important was preventing these abuses from occurring in the first place.

Following my career in federal law enforcement, I joined a professional services firm as an investigative consultant in their fraud investigation and litigation services practice. My clients included public and private companies, both foreign and domestic. I saw firsthand how compliance worked but more often than not, how and why it didn't. I was shocked at the number of companies of all types and sizes that had either no compliance programs or poorly conceived ones. My clients never thought they would be victims of fraud or involved in committing a fraud. The compliance failures they faced were a wake-up call for them. Few had ever taken Ben Franklin's often repeated quote to heart: "An ounce of prevention is worth a pound of cure."

After leaving consulting, I joined Microsoft to create and lead the Financial Integrity Unit, a worldwide fraud detection, investigation, prevention, and recovery program based within Internal Audit. We built a fraud prevention and compliance program from the ground up and staffed it with some of the best people in the field. My interaction with my team and others at Microsoft as well as counterparts at companies worldwide, has given me great insight into best practices and strategies for success that I will share with you. I will also share those practices that landed some companies in hot water.

As I spoke to readers of my first book and continued to work with those in compliance, it became clear that there was a need for communicating these compliance best practices and success stories beyond the small groups within the industry. I have met people focused on building state-of-the-art compliance programs whose experiences and expertise need to be shared. Great companies have developed excellent compliance programs that have protected their employees, shareholders, and reputations over the years. Some companies suffered accounting scandals and rose from the ashes of prosecution, humiliation, and loss of reputation to be even stronger organizations today.

This book applies the United States Department of Justice and United States Sentencing Commission's Organizational Guidelines definition of an effective compliance program and its interrelated elements. It will provide chief executives, managers, board members, employees, students, and others with what they need to know about creating and maintaining robust compliance programs. I will discuss the concepts of compliance as well as the many compliance requirements for corporations and other businesses. You will find interviews with ethics and compliance officers who provide their insight and knowledge. Also included are case studies and best practices from "best in breed" companies and those emerging from compliance failures. The companies that have had fraud issues and have now instituted strong programs to mitigate future issues are great examples from which to learn.

The insights and strategies of corporate executives and other thought leaders in compliance are included in the book. There are examples from

United States-based organizations as well as from companies elsewhere in the world. Incorporated into the book are Compliance Insights detailing case studies, best practices, sample programs, survey findings, as well as commentary from experts in the field on a particular aspect, topic, or best practice of compliance. Although this book is intended to be a comprehensive overview of compliance, it could not possibly cover every possible aspect of this large and complex field. However, it is my intent to cover the underlying principles of effective compliance.

The major compliance failures of recent years resulted in significant changes to corporate cultures. Suddenly, integrity and accountability are key elements for every organization. These elements have always been there, but now they are moving to the forefront. People everywhere are talking about the importance of integrity. In fact, the word integrity was the Merriam-Webster Online Dictionary Word of the Year in 2005, reinforcing the greater focus on integrity and ethics.

Yet in 2006, Merriam-Webster named "truthiness" as its Word of the Year. If you haven't heard this word before, you are not a viewer of the mock news show *The Colbert Report* on the Comedy Central cable network. Stephen Colbert, the host of the show, introduced this word to his audience in October 2005. It is defined as "the quality of preferring concepts or facts one wishes to be true, rather than concepts or facts known to be true."[1] Truthiness may be the bending and stretching of the truth to suit one's personal motives but it has no place in compliance. It's the same as the smiling, confident CEO fervently believing in his innocence while standing in the courtroom as the grim-looking jury returns with their verdict after deliberating through mountains of overwhelmingly incriminating evidence. I trust that the move from integrity to truthiness as Word of the Year is not a sign that we have forgotten the past.

It is my hope that after reading this book, you will have a greater understanding of not only how to build and maintain a truly world-class compliance program but also the importance of creating that very special and lasting culture of compliance.

---

[1] American Dialect Society, http://www.americandialect.org/index.php/amerdial/truthiness_voted_2005_word_of_the_year/.

Acknowledgments

The more I get immersed in the literary process, the more I have come to realize how much I rely on the generous assistance and wise counsel of others. Writing a book is an arduous task and I could not have completed this one without the help of the many people I acknowledge here.

First and foremost, I thank my son, Daniel Biegelman, who is a contributing author and provided extraordinary assistance. Daniel was involved in every aspect of this book from the initial brainstorming, to research and writing, to editing and proofing. As a recent law school graduate, he took time from his budding legal career to assist me. His countless hours and tireless dedication helped make this book a reality.

A special note of thanks to my executive editor, Timothy Burgard, who first suggested the idea of writing about corporate compliance and as with my previous book, guided me through the writing and publishing process. Tim has continuously supported my literary adventures and has given me the unique opportunity to express my thoughts and experiences in writing. I am again indebted to him.

My sincere thanks to all those who provided ideas, content, interviews, and assistance: Pedro Fabiano, Thomas Feeney, Scott Moritz, George Stamboulidis, Joseph Murphy, CT Tomlin, Dick Carozza, John Gill, Walt Pavlo, Jan Shanahan, David Cafferty, Dr. Haluk Gursel, Craig Greene, and David McCarthy.

A special thanks to Pat Gnazzo, John McDermott, and Jennifer Hallahan from CA, Inc.; Dr. John Copeland and Holly Byars from the Soderquist Center; Simon Zarifeh and Michael Howard from Airservices Australia; and Megan Barry and Stephanie Jenkins of Premier, Inc., who graciously gave me access to their world-class compliance programs so I could profile them in this book. Steven Lauer, Corporate Counsel of Global Compliance, introduced me to the exceptional Premier, Inc. program and provided much of the research, content, and writing for that chapter. For that, I am especially grateful.

Marc Sherman, Laura Connor, and David Meilstrup of Huron Consulting Group wrote the excellent chapter on anti-money laundering compliance especially for this book. They took time from their busy work schedules to contribute their deep knowledge and experiences and I am deeply appreciative for their contributions.

I want to thank Rick Cruz, Caren Gordon, Ronnie Kann, and the Corporate Executive Board for providing best practices and other content. I also want to recognize Caren and Ronnie for writing the foreword for this book.

There are also two special people I want to thank but whose names cannot be revealed. They provided me great insight into the compliance failures at their organizations.

When I wanted someone to read the completed manuscript and give me honest feedback, I immediately turned to my old and wise friend, DeWayn Marzagalli. DeWayn, a former federal agent extraordinaire, provided the constructive and thoughtful comments I needed.

Although this work is solely ours and does not reflect the views or opinion of Microsoft Corporation, I would like to thank my company for allowing me to write this book. A special thank you to Alain Peracca at Microsoft who leads by example with integrity and accountability, and strongly supports a culture of compliance.

And, last but not least, my gratitude to my wife Lynn, who was indispensable as she spent many hours reviewing the manuscript and providing insightful feedback. Her patience as I spent all my free time engrossed in the book is exceptional.

About the Author

Martin T. Biegelman, CFE, is Director of Financial Integrity for Microsoft Corporation in Redmond, WA. In 2002, he joined Microsoft to create and lead a worldwide fraud detection, investigation, and prevention program based within internal audit. In addition to focusing on preventing financial fraud and abuse, his group promotes financial integrity, fiscal responsibility, and compliance in a COSO framework of improved business ethics, effective internal controls and greater corporate governance. He works closely with Microsoft's executive leadership, the Office of Legal Compliance, Internal Audit, and others in protecting Microsoft from financial and reputational risk.

He has more than 30 years of experience in fraud detection and prevention. Prior to joining Microsoft, he was a Director of Litigation and Investigative Services in the Fraud Investigation Practice at BDO Seidman, LLP, an international accounting and consulting firm. He is also a former federal law enforcement professional, having served as a United States Postal Inspector in a variety of investigative and management assignments. As a federal agent, he was a subject matter expert in fraud detection and prevention. He retired as the Inspector in Charge of the Phoenix, Arizona Field Office of the Postal Inspection Service.

Mr. Biegelman is a Certified Fraud Examiner as well as an adjunct faculty member, Regent Emeritus, and Fellow of the Association of Certified Fraud Examiners (ACFE). He serves on the Board of Directors of the ACFE Foundation, the Board of Advisors for the Economic Crime Institute at Utica College, and the Accounting Advisory Board for the Department of Accounting and Law in the School of Business at the University at Albany, State University of New York. He is also a member of ASIS International and served on its Investigations Council.

He is a nationally recognized speaker and instructor on white collar crime, corruption, security, fraud prevention, and corporate compliance. He has written numerous articles on many fraud related subjects including corporate crime, identity theft, Internet fraud, check fraud, fraud prevention, corporate investigations, and the Sarbanes-Oxley Act. Mr. Biegelman is the co-author of *Executive Roadmap to Fraud Prevention and Internal Control:*

Creating a Culture of Compliance. He is currently working on a book about the evils of identity theft. He is also a contributing author to *Fraud Casebook: Lessons from the Bad Side of Business.*

Mr. Biegelman has a Bachelor of Science degree from Cornell University and a Master's in Public Administration from Golden Gate University.

CHAPTER 1

Why Ethics and Compliance Will Always Matter

"There is no such thing as business ethics. There is only one kind—you have to adhere to the highest standards."
Marvin Bower, former managing partner
of McKinsey & Company

Imagine this nightmare scenario: A publicly traded company whose domineering leadership rules by fear. Dissenting opinion in any form is met with immediate termination of employment. A culture where written policies and procedures are few and far between and internal controls are shunned. Training is sporadic and lacking. Eventually, this company's senior-most executives conspire to prematurely and fraudulently recognize revenue to meet or exceed Wall Street's expectations. They conduct this massive fraud year after year. The board is totally in the dark and accepts management's explanations and assurances without independent verification. When their accounting practices finally are scrutinized and the government starts an inquiry, these executives attempt a cover-up by fabricating a story, obstructing the investigation, and suborning perjury by instructing other employees to lie to the government and outside counsel. Ultimately, eight of the company's senior executives including the CEO, CFO, and General Counsel, plead guilty to securities fraud and/or obstruction of justice charges. Shareholders lose over $10 billion due to the massive accounting fraud. Employees are left shocked and demoralized that their leaders have lied and defrauded their company. Investors are also horrified at seeing their investments diminish and that no one in the company did anything to stop it. Add to this explosive mixture the fact that the company had no compliance program. That's right, no compliance program. Think this couldn't happen? Think again because it did.

This all occurred at Computer Associates, now called CA, Inc. These blatant transgressions happened because an effective ethics and compliance program was not in place. Compliance involves many different elements; knowing and following all the relevant laws, rules, and policies is but one part of the mix. An effective compliance program would have made a difference at CA. A strong compliance program is absolutely necessary to protect an organization both internally and externally.

Compliance means following the law and more. It's making sure organizations adhere to all applicable legal requirements. It is a detailed and complex process. For any particular situation one must be aware of all potentially applicable laws and regulations—federal, state, local, as well as internal company-instituted rules. A company is obligated to be aware of and understand these rules and laws. That in itself can be an onerous process as even experienced and sophisticated lawyers sometimes have a difficult time deciphering the cryptic "legalese" that passes for statutory language. This compliance obligation is important as everyone in authority is charged with knowledge of the law. Ignorance of the law is no excuse. A person cannot escape a criminal charge or civil liability by claiming that he or she did not know the law was being broken. This is the role of compliance, to make sure people know the rules beforehand and help to ensure that they continuously follow them.

Knowledge and understanding of the law is the first step. Businesses also have to know to what and where it applies. Furthermore, once one has this information, one must implement it in an effective compliance program. But what does effective mean? A company must carefully craft a program, hire experienced compliance professionals, issue detailed policies and guidance, institute training, and promote all other aspects of the program to ensure the knowledge is spread to all who need it. This process must be continuous. The compliance program is the engine of compliance, putting all of this into effect.

Knowing the law and following it is only one side of compliance. Compliance goes much deeper than that, true compliance anyway. Simply following the law so that one doesn't get into trouble is not full compliance. State-of-the-art compliance involves a successful blending of compliance—following rules, regulations, and laws—with ethics—developing and sustaining a culture based on values, integrity, and accountability, and always doing the right things. True compliance ensures consistency of actions to eliminate, or at least lessen, opportunities for harm from criminal conduct or other compliance failures. It means going beyond the minimum requirements. More importantly, it involves the ongoing commitment from senior leaders in the organization to promote ethical conduct and compliance with the law. Leading by example and establishing the tone at the top set the stage for every other element of compliance.

The problem that can occur is when people use compliance as an excuse; those who profess to believe in it but use a compliance program to mask their own negligence or even wrongdoing. It may be said that this is even more dangerous than having no compliance program at all. That is because it gives shareholders, employees, vendors, and the public the false belief that the company cares about following the law when in fact, all it wants is to deceive others into believing so. Let us not forget that Enron had a 65-page code of conduct, but in the end, it was nothing more than empty words.

Enacting a compliance program and instituting training programs but not supporting them through lack of funding, lack of skilled personnel, or by management undercutting them in various ways, is also dangerous and counterproductive. Real compliance means that one believes in what one is doing day in and day out. It is not merely lip service; it's putting your money where your mouth is. This is the two-tiered approach to compliance — one's actions and one's mindset. An organization cannot have effective compliance without both of them. One alone will not work. This is tied into the idea of setting a positive tone at the top. If management believes in compliance and reinforces it by their actions, over and over again, then people below will follow their lead.

ETHICS IS JOB ONE

Executives are constantly confronted with the realities of business compliance. They must ensure compliance with their internal rules and policies. Those from public companies must follow the requirements of the Sarbanes-Oxley Act and other reporting enhancements. All organizations must follow federal, state, and local laws and all must comply with the United States' Federal Sentencing Guidelines, which mandate the creation of compliance programs. Moreover, a raft of other laws must be complied with, from anti-bribery rules to free trade provisions. Yet, chief among these requirements is the idea of ethics, the concept that lies at the heart of every corporate governance requirement.

Ethics include integrity and proper business conduct; it refers to standards and values by which an individual or organization behaves and interacts with others.[1] The famed Greek philosopher Aristotle in his *Nicomachean Ethics* argued that "moral behavior is acquired by habituation" and that without question, "moral behavior is good."[2] It is no different today. Ethics and compliance are clearly on the minds of executives, as well as investors, the public, and the government. Ethics has become a hot button topic, thanks to the many corporate scandals of the past years. This is hardly news to anyone. Despite the increased awareness given to ethics and compliance programs, the problem has not been solved. For instance, the Hewlett-Packard (HP) spying and pretexting scandal involved key executives and illustrates that there is more to successful compliance than just a code of conduct. HP had a comprehensive Standards of Business Conduct (including, slightly ironically now, several pages on how to handle sensitive information), yet it still was engulfed by negative front-page headlines and a shakeup among its leadership. Even great corporations like HP can, at times, face compliance failures. Merely having a program in and of itself is not the solution to protecting a company and keeping it in good graces with shareholders and the government. A truly successful compliance program goes far deeper.

The push toward compliance, especially since the enactment of the Sarbanes-Oxley Act and the reaction to the scandal culture of the Enron era, could almost be described as an "ethics fad." Sarbanes-Oxley strengthened corporate accountability and governance of public companies through rules covering conflicts of interests, financial disclosures, board oversight, and certification of financial statements.[3] The Act's passage left companies hurrying to comply. All of a sudden, every company had to have an ethics code; if there wasn't one there was scrambling to get one, or else be left behind. This rush merged with heightened concerns stemming from the penalties imposed on companies for ethical breaches. From the lighter treatment afforded to companies who came clean and "restated" their earnings, as compared to those formally investigated and charged by the government, companies got the message that it was in their best interest to cooperate and that having a compliance program would be something that would lessen potential penalties should the company commit further misdeeds.

Companies that the government caught red-handed had to pay very stiff financial and reputational penalties, not to mention the personal impact on those executives prosecuted and sent to prison. This sent companies searching for ways to avoid this disastrous outcome. At the same time, ethics enjoyed a renewed focus throughout the corporate world, first as companies struggled to understand the new requirements placed on them by the passage of Sarbanes-Oxley, and then rushed to embrace ethical conduct for chief executives and others. The ethics fever swept every industry and that was a good thing, a very good thing. While this practice makes compliance easier, there is still much to do as compliance lapses and criminal conduct persist. The Securities and Exchange Commission (SEC) has continued its strong enforcement program over the last few years. The results of SEC enforcement activity in Fiscal Years 2005–2006 in Compliance Insight 1.1 illustrate that we still have a long way to go for complete compliance.

COMPLIANCE INSIGHT 1.1: SUMMARY OF SECURITIES AND EXCHANGE COMMISSION ENFORCEMENT ACTIVITY, FY2005–FY2006, COMPLIANCE AND ETHICS LEADERSHIP COUNCIL RESEARCH, 2007

574 enforcement actions filed in 2006

$3.3 billion total in disgorgement and penalties ordered against securities law violators in 2006

$28.5 million average settlement in 2005, an increase from $26.4 million in 2004

$7.5 million median settlement in 2005, a 19% increase from $6.3 million in 2004

657 amended filings in 2005 for financial restatements of public companies due to accounting errors, a 58% increase from 2004

300 officers and directors barred in the last three years due to allegations of individual malfeasance

1,228 CEO departures from U.S. companies in 2005, an increase of 102% from 2004

129 CEO changeovers in the Fortune 1000 in 2005, an increase of 32% from 2004

Reprinted with permission from the Corporate Executive Board, Washington, DC © 2007 based on information from the United States Securities and Exchange Commission; Cornerstone Research; Challenger, Gray & Christmas; Burson-Marsteller; and United States General Accounting Office.

Ethics and ethical behavior are not things that can merely be created, or attained solely through corporate expenditure. They require a deeper commitment, one that can only be achieved through time, effort, and yes, expenditure. Though it is cliché, quality matters here far more than quantity. In many senses, a little goes a long way. Building a world-class compliance program requires smart decisions in building it, maintaining it, and sustaining it; by doing so, a company will be able to achieve truly effective compliance over the long term.

THE NYPD AND AN ETHICAL CULTURE

A commitment to ethical conduct cannot be accomplished by simply initiating a program and then checking the box that the process is complete.

Building a culture of compliance takes time. Integrity and character bring out the best in people and are critical components in ethics and compliance. Yet, human beings are not perfect creatures and tend to falter from time to time. The importance of ethical conduct needs to be nurtured, reinforced, and repeated over and over again lest people forget and stray from the course. There is no better example of this continuous need for attention to ethical conduct than the various police corruption scandals that have impacted the New York City Police Department (NYPD) over the past 100 years. Even legendary institutions can face the firestorm created when law enforcement officers forget their oaths and turn to crime and corruption. Compliance Insight 1.2 details the major corruption scandals that the New York City Police Department has faced over the years.

The feeling of déjà vu that the NYPD faced was due to not learning from the past. The NYPD of the 21st century has made great strides in understanding that ethical lapses can seriously impact a long-standing reputation. In building their compliance program, the NYPD starts with police recruits as soon as they enter the police academy. Look at what is presented to recruits in their *Police Student's Guide: Introduction to the NYPD*:

> *Our history is a source of great pride to us, and we have very little tolerance for officers who do not treat our hard won reputation with the respect it deserves.... When things go right in this Department—when we succeed in reducing crime; when we make spectacular arrests; when we make dramatic rescues—our actions are described in news reports throughout the country and across the world, and our officers are treated like heroes. But, when things go wrong—when officers are caught in scandal, or when they make some tragic mistakes—the same reporters and leaders who are quick to praise us are quick to condemn us. When this happens, the public often does not recognize that the problem may be limited to one or only a few officers. Instead, in the eyes of many people, we all become suspect, and the mistakes and sins of a few are generalized to all of us. This breeds distrust among the public, and makes it tougher for all of us to do the job the way we should.... Make certain that you carry yourself in a manner that brings only respect to yourself and to your brothers and sisters in this Department.[4]*

Warren Buffett, the billionaire investor and CEO of Berkshire Hathaway, Inc., has said "It takes 20 years to build a reputation and five minutes to ruin it. If you think about that, you'll do things differently." The NYPD understands this and so must all organizations. Yet, we often fail to learn

COMPLIANCE INSIGHT 1.2: A BRIEF HISTORY OF NYPD POLICE CORRUPTION

The New York City Police Department is considered by many to be the premier police department in the world. Yet, even the best sometimes falter. Police corruption can infect even the most professional of law enforcement organizations. Consider these very public police corruption investigations of the New York City Police Department over the last 100 years:

- **Lexow Committee (1894):** *Systematic police extortion and pay-offs from gambling operations*
- **Curran Committee (1913):** *Systematic monthly police extortion of gambling and brothel operations*
- **Seabury Commission (1932):** *Police Department involvement in extortions from speakeasies, bootleggers, and gamblers*
- **Helfand Investigation (1955):** *Large-scale protection by police of a gambling syndicate*
- **Knapp Commission (1972):** *Corrupt police officers were either "grass-eaters" or "meat-eaters"*[a]
- **Mollen Commission (1994):** *Shakedowns and protection by corrupt officers but also trafficking in cocaine and other drugs*

Why include an historical overview of police corruption in a book on compliance? To remind us that corruption, criminality, and non-compliance are always present. It often takes a major and very public incident for us to take notice and do something. Approximately every twenty years for the last century, corrupt police activities reached such a peak that investigating bodies were commissioned to conduct public inquiries to determine the corrupt acts and recommend solutions to the scandals. There are important lessons for us here. Rather than wait for the public scandal that does so much reputational damage for us to take remedial action, we must continuously apply state-of-the-art compliance standards to ensure that history does not repeat itself, as was the case with the New York City Police Department.

---

[a]The Knapp Commission investigation of police corruption in the New York City Police Department found two categories of corrupt officers. They were either "grass-eaters" or "meat-eaters." Grass-eaters were the overwhelming

majority who generally took small payoffs from business owners, gamblers, and others to look the other way on infractions. Grass-eaters usually did not solicit these payoffs but did not refuse them either. Meat-eaters were a small percentage of corrupt officers but were constantly on the prowl for large-scale financial scores involving narcotics, gambling operations, and other serious offenses. For more information, refer to the Commission to Investigate Allegations of Police Corruption and the City's Anti-Corruption Procedures, *The Knapp Commission Report on Police Corruption* (New York: George Braziller, 1973), 65.

from the past. The disclosure of stock option backdating scandals in 2006 at dozens of companies, large and small, in the United States brought back distressing memories of the accounting scandals of just a few short years ago. How could so many smart people forget the lessons of Enron, WorldCom, Adelphia, and others? The sheer number of companies involved is striking. Much of the misconduct took place a number of years ago and was only recently disclosed. Still, the participants were chief executives and other high level employees who should have known better. More importantly, their compliance programs did not work. A further discussion of the backdating of stock options can be found in Chapter 2.

WHAT IS COMPLIANCE?

Compliance is a state of being in accordance with established guidelines, specifications, or legislation.[5] The Compliance and Ethics Leadership Council defines compliance as "a company's or an individual's observance of relevant laws, regulations, and corporate policies.... Companies must have various programs, policies, and controls in place in order to be defined as being 'compliant' with certain laws, rules, regulations, or policies."[6] The United States Department of Justice (DOJ) has strongly reinforced the importance of effective compliance programs. The DOJ defines compliance programs as follows:

> *Compliance programs are established by corporate management to prevent and to detect misconduct and to ensure that corporate activities are conducted in accordance with all applicable criminal and civil laws, regulations, and rules. The Department encourages such corporate self-policing, including voluntary disclosures to the government of any problems that a corporation discovers on its own. However, the existence of a compliance program is not sufficient, in and of itself, to justify not charging a corporation for*

criminal conduct undertaken by its officers, directors, employees, or agents. Indeed, the commission of such crimes in the face of a compliance program may suggest that the corporate management is not adequately enforcing its program. In addition, the nature of some crimes, e.g., antitrust violations, may be such that national law enforcement policies mandate prosecutions of corporations notwithstanding the existence of a compliance program.[7]

The key to effectiveness is whether the program is adequately designed to ensure compliance. The United States' Federal Sentencing Guidelines for Organizations (FSGO) state that "to have an effective compliance and ethics program, an organization shall exercise due diligence to prevent and detect criminal conduct; and otherwise promote an organizational culture that encourages ethical conduct and a commitment to compliance with the law."[8] The constantly evolving compliance landscape requires executives and managers to constantly ensure that their programs are "best in breed" to fully protect organizations.

Organizations that run afoul of the law and commit crimes such as fraud, face severe penalties from the courts. Under the FSGO, organizations found guilty can face additional penalties based on certain aggravating factors calculated by a "culpability score." As stated in the FSGO, the factors contributing to increased penalties and fines include whether:

- Senior executives within the organization "participated in, condoned, or [were] willfully ignorant of the offense;"
- "[T]olerance of the offense by substantial authority personnel was pervasive throughout the organization;"
- There was prior history of a similar offense in the company's past; and/or
- The organization obstructed justice by impeding the investigation or prosecution.[9]

The FSGO also provide a significant "carrot" or benefit in that there are mitigating factors that can significantly lessen the penalties for criminal convictions. The questions that will determine if these factors are to be considered include:

- If the subject "organization had in place at the time of the offense an effective compliance and ethics program;"
- If the organization promptly "reported the offense to appropriate government authorities" once they became aware of its existence;
- If the organization "fully cooperated in the investigation;" and

- If the organization "clearly demonstrated recognition and affirmative acceptance of responsibility for its criminal conduct."[10]

While quality matters more than quantity, a solid compliance program needs a proper balance between the two. An under-funded and unsupported program is doomed to fail. Without sufficient support by the company and the management, a program cannot succeed in its objectives of changing and influencing employee behavior. Compliance requires direct input by company leadership, and the key support of a qualified compliance officer running a reliable compliance department, accessible to the rank and file to answer their questions and provide them with appropriate direction. However, spending too much money (without proper guidance on how to spend and direct funds) can lead to incredible inefficiency, and be just as ineffective as not spending.

The "Icarus Effect"

Professor David A. Skeel of the University of Pennsylvania Law School proposes an interesting theory in evaluating corporate scandals. He describes the "Icarus Effect," three factors that combine to create each of America's great corporate scandals. Icarus, in Greek mythology, was given wings made of wax and feathers by his father, the inventor Daedalus. Daedalus warned Icarus not to fly too close to the sun, as the wings would melt and Icarus would plummet to his death.[11] Sadly, seduced by his newfound power, Icarus disregarded his father's warning and suffered the deadly consequences.

Skeel identifies three "Icaran" factors: risk-taking, competition, and manipulation of the corporate form. Risk-taking is perhaps inherent in the corporate structure. The market rewards those who take successful risks in developing new products and technologies. Risk-taking often leads to innovation. Moreover, the types of people who rise to the highest level of corporate America tend to be bold, confident, and willing to take risks. After all, these are the types of traits that allow one to climb the corporate ladder. A would-be executive is unlikely to make it far up the corporate ladder without taking some risks. Risk-taking is not a bad thing. Corporate governance rules expressly allow for some measure of risk taking; the business judgment rule, for instance, protects rational business decisions, even if a judge or jury thinks them too risky or would have chosen a different course of action.

Executive compensation also encourages risk-taking. The majority of executive compensation is in the form of stock options. These options reward risk, since they are "all upside and no downside: they promise a big payoff if the company's stock price goes up, but there's no cost to the CEO if she gambles with the company's business and the stock price plummets."[12] Even though risk-taking has some distinct and crucial benefits, if it gets out of hand it can doom a company. Any level of risk-taking must be tempered with reasoned and rational thought.

Competition can reinforce managers' incentives to take risks. The marketplace is a tough environment with many different entities all competing for the same dollar. Increasing market pressure to achieve a certain level of financial success or more commonly to return to past levels of success often pushes management to make risky decisions in hopes of appeasing investors and Wall Street. Unfortunately, many times these competitive-driven risks turn out to be short-sighted and ill-advised.

Manipulation of the corporate form is the final factor. "The ability to tap huge amounts of capital in enterprises that are set up as corporations, together with the large number of people whose livelihoods depend in one way or another on the business, means that an Icaran executive who takes excessive or fraudulent risks may jeopardize the financial lives of thousands of employees, investors, and suppliers of the business."[13]

Individually, all of these factors are elements of a typical market, and in fact all can be used positively. Risk-taking and competition allow for the creation of better products, and the corporate form allows for distinct benefits, such as the ability to raise large amounts of capital and limited liability, and gives people an incentive to take risks and create a new and successful product or service. However, when these factors operate unrestrained, in conjunction with each other, they can create disastrous scandals. These Icaran factors will be on full display in Chapter 3 that details a brief history of corporate scandals and those responsible.

Compliance Program Individuality

Ideally a compliance program should be both industry-specific and unique; it should be tailored to fit the requirements of the individual company, its needs, and the overall compliance requirements of its particular industry, but should also reflect the compliance requirements imposed on all corporations and the laws that they must all follow. Each organization must ensure that their compliance programs are getting the individualized attention they need. If a code of conduct is nothing more than a cookie cutter guidebook, it is unlikely to truly foster a lasting change in the corporate compliance culture. A company may spend far more time on the appearance than the content of these codes.

With slick graphics, photos, and inspirational quotes, they may look like little more than the advertising material given out to potential customers. In fact, when perusing through the manuals given out at various companies, they all start to blend together. Many seem to come from the same exact template, with similar language. These are, essentially, nothing more than boilerplate codes of conduct. One even starts to see identical quotes appearing time and time again. What this shows are the misplaced priorities by the companies who issue them.

First, as noted above, it reflects a preference of style over substance, on the appearance over the content. Second, it shows the lack of attention paid to the full importance of a compliance program. Setting up a cookie cutter program means that the company scrambled to put something in place as soon as possible, such that it will not be anywhere as effective as it could be or the company hopes it to be, or that the company puts a low priority on having a truly effective compliance program. For these companies, the appearance of a good program is more important than actually creating a culture of compliance. It also shows that the company has not put in the effort needed to customize the compliance program to the individual needs of the company and its unique culture.

Most importantly, the focus on image and the lack of individuality ignores the great benefits a company can reap by putting a good program into place. Among other benefits, a strong compliance program can create better employee productivity and morale, higher profits, and a stronger reputation among consumers and investors. It can catch problems before they reach the level where they can hurt the company and its stock price as well as absorb the valuable time of employees who should be working to benefit the company, not to clean up its internal mess. With a strong program, an organization can take advantage of lessened sentences under the Federal Sentencing Guidelines for Organizations, as well as having a beneficial position when dealing with prosecutors should problems arise. It also will be more able to portray a wrongdoer as a rogue employee, rather than as a symptom of an endemic and widespread problem within the company.

Returning to the issue of slickly produced codes of conduct, it should be recognized that allowances must be made to get the employees' attention. It is an open question as to how many of the rank and file employees actually take the time to read the manuals they are given, much less internalize and fully understand them. This gap can be filled by having solid training programs to engage the employees and to make sure they know what they need to know and conversely, to make sure that they are not overwhelmed with information that is above their level and is best handled by superiors.

Additionally, good management oversight sets a good example for them to follow and can make sure that employees are acting in the proper manner. Having experienced compliance officers available to answer more specialized questions is helpful because there is no way that every contingency is addressed in the distributed materials.

BUILDING THE BUSINESS CASE FOR ETHICS

Running an ethical company that places a high value on compliance is not just simply a good idea. It also makes good business sense. One hears all about the importance of business ethics, the damage that can be caused by scandals, and the legal benefits and requirements, as outlined in places such as the Sentencing Guidelines. But less is heard about how an ethical business with strong corporate governance will outperform companies that don't focus on ethics.

Moreover, executives can damage their business and its future if they do not properly value ethics. "Too many corporate executives regard an ethics program as an expense that adds nothing to a company's bottom line. Even more disturbing, some executives fear that an emphasis on business ethics could put their company at a competitive disadvantage. They are unconvinced that ethics and profits are reconcilable."[14] Of course, this is not the case and ethics can even provide a company with an edge in a fiercely competitive global economy, as a reputation for ethical behavior can distinguish it from rivals. "Enlightened business leaders, however, know that building an ethical business culture is a powerful means of maximizing shareholder value and increasing business profits."[15] In the end, ethics increases the bottom line. The strong link between corporate management's public commitment to ethics and the corporation's financial performance has been borne out by numerous studies.[16]

According to Professor Curtis C. Verschoor of DePaul University, "well-managed companies that take their ethical, social, and environmental responsibilities seriously... have stronger long-term financial performance than the remaining companies in the S&P 500 Index."[17] A 2004 study, building on prior research done by Verschoor and others, demonstrates the benefits that are associated with superior governance attributes. The study analyzed companies in the Standard & Poor's 500 by measuring Market Value Added (MVA), which is the value of a company above and beyond what had been contributed by investors, i.e., the company's financial growth. Companies classified as having superior corporate governance substantially outperformed their less ethically focused competitors, to the tune of an average of $9.4 billion in 2004.[18] "This study provides powerful new evidence supporting the belief of many investors that firms having attributes of strong corporate governance... actually deliver superior financial returns to their shareowners. Corporate management and boards of directors should also

COMPLIANCE INSIGHT 1.3: BUILDING THE BUSINESS CASE FOR A COMPLIANCE AND ETHICS PROGRAM, COMPLIANCE AND ETHICS LEADERSHIP COUNCIL RESEARCH, 2005

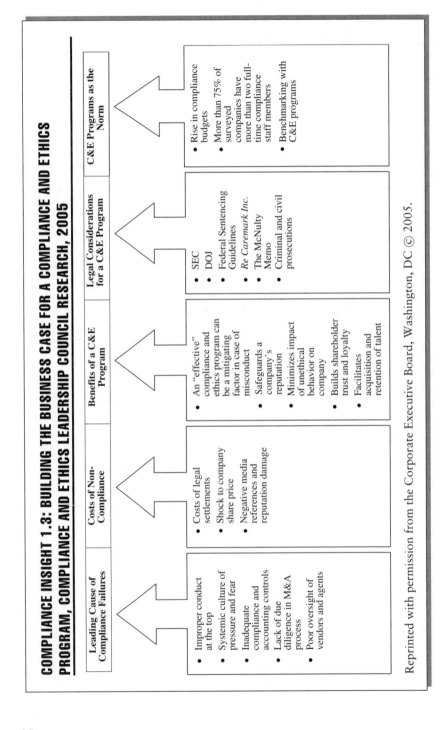

Leading Cause of Compliance Failures	Costs of Non-Compliance	Benefits of a C&E Program	Legal Considerations for a C&E Program	C&E Programs as the Norm
• Improper conduct at the top • Systemic culture of pressure and fear • Inadequate compliance and accounting controls • Lack of due diligence in M&A process • Poor oversight of vendors and agents	• Costs of legal settlements • Shock to company share price • Negative media references and reputation damage	• An "effective" compliance and ethics program can be a mitigating factor in case of misconduct • Safeguards a company's reputation • Minimizes impact of unethical behavior on company • Builds shareholder trust and loyalty • Facilitates acquisition and retention of talent	• SEC • DOJ • Federal Sentencing Guidelines • *Re Caremark Inc.* • The McNulty Memo • Criminal and civil prosecutions	• Rise in compliance budgets • More than 75% of surveyed companies have more than two full-time compliance staff members • Benchmarking with C&E programs

Reprinted with permission from the Corporate Executive Board, Washington, DC © 2005.

recognize the value the market is placing on attributes of good corporate governance, especially a well-managed program of ethics and compliance."[19] Compliance Insight 1.3 reinforces the importance of building a business case for an appropriate compliance and ethics program.

Another study, by the Aspen Institute and management consulting firm Booz Allen Hamilton, similarly found a financial benefit from strong corporate values. "Public companies that report superior financial results also report greater success in linking values to operations in areas that foster growth, such as initiative and innovativeness."[20] Again, the study found a strong correlation between strong financial performance and a focus on ethics and core values. "Among financial leaders—public companies that outperform their industry averages—98% include ethical behavior/integrity in their values statements, compared with 88% for other public companies. Far more of these financial leaders include commitment to employees, honesty/openness, and drive to succeed."[21] These same financial leaders also report that their practices are very effective in promoting initiative, adaptability, and innovativeness and entrepreneurship, at twice the rate of other public companies.[22]

Ethics are also beneficial in another business area, hiring and retaining top quality employees. Unethical behavior not only impacts a company's bottom line, it also impacts its workforce. It affects current employees as well as the company's ability to attract qualified new ones. A study by the consulting firm LRN "provides new evidence that links a company's ability to foster an ethical corporate culture with an increased ability to attract, retain and ensure productivity among U.S. employees."[23] Among the study's findings:

- 94% of employees say it is critical that they work for an ethical company.
- More than one-third of respondents reported leaving a job for ethical reasons.
- 56% say their employer embraces ethics and corporate values in everything it does.
- 30% say their company merely toes the line by following the law and company policies.
- 9% say they work at a company where they do what they are told, are not encouraged to ask questions about what is right or wrong, or they often see management and peers acting in questionable ways.[24]

While most organizations value ethics, strangely, some do not as evidenced by the many corporate frauds we have witnessed over these last few years. Employees are very sensitive to this, are acutely aware of their organization's culture, and pay attention to the tone set from the top and around them. Unethical behavior has a strongly deleterious effect on employee morale and distracts employees from the company's business at hand. One in four workers reported seeing unethical or even illegal behavior where they work; of those who saw unethical behavior, 89% said it affected them.[25]

An ethical reputation also pays dividends in hiring. Of 800 MBA graduates surveyed, 97% were willing to be paid less to work for an organization with a better reputation for corporate social responsibility and ethics. This survey provides even more evidence that good corporate citizenship helps to attract superior management talent.[26]

COMPLIANCE OBSTACLES

I met a person who works at a well-known technology firm. She and I started discussing compliance. She commented that with all the advances in technology today, there had to be a way to develop software tools to automate and ensure compliance. She felt that technology is the key to solving compliance concerns. I remarked that that was a noble goal, and while the power of technology and software is immense, ultimately technology and tools are no substitute for the human factor. It always comes down to people. One cannot automate integrity and honesty. Either people have it or they do not. Compliance Insight 1.4 is a sad example of what can happen when a company is not committed to building and maintaining a compliance program.

True corporate responsibility requires all companies, public or private, large or small, foreign or domestic, to have effective compliance programs. An organization can have 100% of its employees complete code of conduct training but that will not ensure that everyone will comply with the code. An organization can have a hotline in place but that will not guarantee that an employee will call to report an allegation of fraud that he or she discovers. Compliance must be embedded into the fabric of an organization so that it continues no matter who the CEO is. As Thomas Friedman of the *New York Times* wrote in one of his columns, "The greatest restraint on human behavior is not a police officer or a fence—it's a community and a culture."[27]

KEN LAY ON ETHICAL CONDUCT

On April 6, 1999, The Center for Business Ethics at the University of St. Thomas in Houston, Texas sponsored a conference entitled *Corporate*

COMPLIANCE INSIGHT 1.4: OBSTACLES ENCOUNTERED IN IMPLEMENTING A COMPLIANCE PROGRAM

It's fair to say that building an effective compliance program is critical to any organization today. There must be support from the highest levels of leadership as well as an ongoing and honest commitment to successful implementation. One of the worst approaches is to have a compliance program as simply "window-dressing" with no real intent to actually follow through on compliance requirements. The following is an example of an actual company that did just that. Some details have been changed so as not to identify this company or the source of this information.

In 2005, the company was a privately-held, service-oriented entity with over 50,000 employees, $3 billion in annual sales, and several hundred million dollars in debt. Anticipating going public with an initial public offering and the resulting Sarbanes-Oxley reporting requirements, a decision was made to create a compliance department with reporting to the General Counsel. Several new hires were authorized: a Chief Compliance Officer, a Manager of Contract Compliance, a Manager of Licensing, a Regulatory Specialist, and a Quality Assurance Specialist.

The compliance department was initially assigned the responsibility for review and oversight of the company's licensing and regulatory affairs, contract compliance, whistleblower hotline monitoring and oversight, administration of corporate policies and procedures, internal corporate investigations, quality assurance reviews, and field compliance reviews. Initial plans also included a small staff that would be assigned the responsibility to conduct internal audits and internal corporate investigations.

Almost at the onset, it became clear the Compliance Department was simply "window dressing." Little, if any, corporate support was provided toward achievement of the Compliance Department's initial goals. The company's strategic plan included aggressive pursuit and acquisition of a number of competitors, which required continued in-house due-diligence procedures, corporate re-formation activities, and re-licensing and re-branding of a new business entity, all of which were tasked to the Compliance Department. Several months after the department was formed, the General Counsel was terminated for no apparent reason, leaving this important position vacant for over seven months. This left the department without vital support at the highest executive level.

To make matters worse, the Chief Executive Officer was not involved in the day-to-day operations of the company and was focused primarily on new acquisitions. It was widely known that the Chief Financial Officer did not support the audit functions originally envisioned for assignment to the Compliance Department. As a result, the CFO provided neither financial nor other support vital for the success of the new entity. The CFO was indifferent to the compliance operation and felt no need to maintain an open line of communication with any operation other than those who directly reported to him.

In early 2006, the company reported a sizable loss. Shortly after the hiring of a new General Counsel, the Manager of Contract Compliance position was eliminated and the responsibilities of the position were reassigned to the Regulatory Affairs Specialist. This created a significant void in original plans to monitor and audit any of the approximately 4,300 contracts in effect with clients, which was an important component of the original compliance program. Using the money saved from this position, the CFO reclassified a number of financial management positions and created several new titles and moved the positions to his staff. Among the new titles the CFO created was a Chief Auditing Executive, which was done without the knowledge of the General Counsel or Compliance staff.

Due to the poor financial earnings of the company, the auditor/investigator positions were never filled and the Chief Compliance Officer (CCO) served as the sole corporate investigator and internal auditor in addition to his other duties. The CCO monitored, audited, initiated, and conducted investigations based upon allegations received through the whistleblower hotline. Generally, following receipt and investigation of a hotline issue, an investigative report would be prepared and issued to corporate management.

A number of investigations focused upon the allegations of "ghost" employees within the company. If internal control deficiencies were identified incident to an investigation, including the "ghost" investigations, a separate audit report containing detailed findings and recommendations for corrective action would be issued to the CFO. The CFO generally ignored these recommendations and considered these issues to be immaterial and not indicative of corporate-wide problems. The Corporate Controller, whose experience was quite limited, had a similar perception that there was little, if any, fraud inherent in his operation.

There was no interaction with the external auditors regarding compliance or fraud related issues. The auditors were shielded by the CFO from making any contact with Compliance Department personnel. Similarly there were no interactions with the Corporate Audit Committee, who generally met only with the CEO, CFO, and Corporate Counsel. Some of the primary concerns of the Audit Committee from a compliance perspective included their unusual interest in providing state-by-state breakdowns in employee relations issues, with little interest in the detection and prevention of internal corporate fraud. Why the external auditors didn't do more or exhibit professional skepticism is unknown.

The CCO clearly felt there was a lack of support at the highest levels of management. In frustration, the CCO left the company and took a position with another organization. Following his departure, there was little support demonstrated by senior executives to hire a replacement CCO. The tone at the top consisted of deaf indifference to the support of a robust compliance program. The program was permitted to fail, based upon the combined reckless indifference of senior executives, the board of directors, and audit committee.

Unfortunately for this company, its lack of commitment to compliance led to serious harm. The company had to restate several years of earnings because of improper accounting. This was allowed to happen because the compliance function languished without sufficient leadership or internal company support. In a true sign of this company's lack of ethical commitment, no senior executives have been fired or reprimanded, and the compliance office has all but been dismantled. This is a sure-fire recipe for disaster.

Governance: Ethics Across the Board. The conference brochure at the time stated the conference "will explore the changing nature and growing importance of corporate governance."[28] The late Ken Lay, who was Chairman and CEO of Enron at the time, was a conference speaker. The subject of his presentation oddly enough was "What a CEO Expects from the Board." In his own words, Lay spells out in theory what an ethical CEO should expect from a board and what an ethical board should deliver. Lay said the following:

> *Like any successful company, we must have directors who start with what is right, who do not have hidden agendas, and who strive to make judgments about what is best for the company, and not about what is best for themselves or some other constituency.... The responsibility of our board—a responsibility which I expect them to fulfill—is to ensure legal and ethical conduct by the company and by everyone in the company.... What a CEO really expects from a board is good advice and counsel, both of which will make the company stronger and more successful; support for those investments and decisions that serve the interests of the company and its stakeholders; and warnings in those cases in which investments and decisions are not beneficial to the company and its stakeholders. And let me conclude by acknowledging that it is not an easy task to get all of this just right.*[29]

Whether he actually meant what he said at the time or it was just empty rhetoric, we will never know. What we do know is that nothing of what he said in 1999 was of any help to the investors and employees of Enron who ultimately suffered a severe financial and emotional toll as the company imploded. Compliance Insight 1.5 details some of the obstacles faced when embedding a compliance program within an organization.

THE WARNING SIGNS OF COMPLIANCE FAILURES

Marianne Jennings is a professor in the W.P. Carey School of Business at Arizona State University and an expert on business ethics. She is a well-known speaker and prolific author on the subject. Her latest book is entitled *The Seven Signs of Ethical Collapse* in which she identifies the seven indicators of ethical collapse. While these signs are not a guarantee of an ethical collapse, they definitely can be used as potential harbingers of ethical challenges. These seven signs are: (1) the pressure to maintain the business numbers; (2) a culture of fear and silence; (3) a "bigger than life" CEO and awe-struck direct reports that won't go against their leader; (4) a weak board of directors; (5) a practice of conflicts of interest; (6) a belief that the organization is above the law; and (7) that "goodness in some areas" such as corporate giving "atones for evil in others."[30] An excellent best practice is to always consider red flags such as these in analyzing a compliance program's level of potential risk.

COMPLIANCE INSIGHT 1.5: KEY OBSTACLES TO EMBEDDING COMPLIANCE IN THE BUSINESS, COMPLIANCE AND ETHICS LEADERSHIP COUNCIL RESEARCH, 2005

Goal

The compliance function seeks to build a culture of compliance and ethical conduct.

Critical Failure Paths

Goals and incentives are consistent with ethical conduct and compliant activity.

Employees understand the importance and real consequences of noncompliance.

Employees undergo relevant training that reinforces ethical behavior.

Outcome

Employees strive to ensure compliance and ethical behavior and preempt compliance violations.

Insufficient or Misaligned Compliance Performance Incentives

- Pressure to meet financial goals causes business units to neglect compliance
- Lack of compliance or ethics related performance objectives

"To really build a culture of compliance, we have realized that we have to include compliance in employee scorecards. Only when compliance is included in performance reviews and compensation can we move it from the mission statement to daily decision making."

Chief Compliance Officer
Insurance Company

Lack of Emphasis on the Consequences of Noncompliance

- Compliance messages easily dismissed by employees due to overconfidence in company's dedication to ethics and belief of "that doesn't happen here."
- Companies fail to provide real examples of noncompliance or their consequences

"It's hard for employees to understand if you don't show noncompliance is happening in your organization. Recounting stories about misconduct at Enron and WorldCom is well and good, but employees can always distance themselves from those events. We need to bring it home and show them that it can happen here."

VP, Ethics and Compliance
Chemicals Company

Generic Training Does Not Influence Employee Behavior

- Enterprise-standard approach to training does not cater to individual needs and preexisting knowledge
- Generalized training results in wasted effort in terms of time and resources dedicated

"We have to train 40,000 employees in 25 countries on compliance—one of the main challenges in rolling out a training program is knowing which individual should receive specific training about which areas."

SVP, Compliance
Energy Company

Reprinted with permission from the Corporate Executive Board, Washington, DC © 2005.

21

NOTES

1. "Preempting Compliance Failures: Identifying Leading Indicators of Misconduct," *Compliance and Ethics Leadership Council*, April 26, 2007.
2. Aristotle, *Nicomachean Ethics*, translated by Martin Ostwald, (Englewood Cliffs, NJ: Prentice Hall, 1962), xix.
3. Martin T. Biegelman and Joel T. Bartow, *Executive Roadmap to Fraud Prevention and Internal Control: Creating a Culture of Compliance*, (Hoboken, NJ: John Wiley & Sons, 2006), 64.
4. New York City Police Department, *Police Student's Guide: Introduction to the NYPD*, July 2005, 4–5, home2.nyc.gov/html/nypd/html/dc_training/pdf/2005%20Police%20Students%20Guide/1st%20Trimester/01-Intro%20to%20the%20NYPD.pdf.
5. Definition of compliance found at PEMCO Corporation Corporate Services library site, www.pemcocorp.com/library/glossary.htm.
6. "Preempting Compliance Failures."
7. Paul J. McNulty, "Principles of Federal Prosecution of Business Organizations," Department of Justice, December 2006, www.usdoj.gov/dag/speech/2006/mcnulty_memo.pdf.
8. *Federal Sentencing Guidelines*, Chapter 8, Part B, Effective Compliance and Ethics Programs, www.ussc.gov/2005guid/8b2_1.htm.
9. *Federal Sentencing Guidelines*, Chapter 8, Part C, Fines, www.ussc.gov/2005guid/8c2_5.htm.
10. Ibid.
11. Though it is not as commonly remembered, in some versions of the tale Daedalus is also warned not to fly too low, so as to avoid the sea's powerful waves. As Skeel puts it, "as with executive risk-taking, this account suggests, there are dangers in both directions [taking too much risk or completely avoiding it]." David A. Skeel, "Icarus and American Corporate Regulation," *The Business Lawyer*, November 2005, 157, n. 10.
12. Ibid., 157.
13. Ibid.
14. Dr. John D. Copeland, "Business Ethics: Three Critical Truths," 6, www.soderquist.org/resources/pdf/Copeland_ThreeTruths-publication.pdf.
15. Ibid.
16. Ibid., 9.
17. Curtis C. Verschoor, "Does Superior Governance Still Lead to Better Financial Performance?," *Strategic Finance*, October 1, 2004, 13.

18. Ibid. Roughly 150–160 of the S&P were deemed to have "superior governance" in the years 2000–2004. The 9.4 billion number means, that in 2004, the MVA for a company with superior governance was 9.4 billion higher than a company that did not. In 2000, in the midst of the stock market bubble, the additional MVA was 28.6 billion while in the doldrums of 2003 it was $5.8 billion. These numbers indicated that no matter the health of the stock market, superior governance is always valued, and is valued even more in a rising market, as 2004 was. Further research showed that the numbers were not skewed by the largest companies, as even middle-sized companies returned substantially more value to shareholders.

19. Ibid.

20. "New Study Finds Link Between Financial Success and Focus on Corporate Values," Booz Allen Hamilton, February 3, 2005, www.boozallen .com/publications/article/659548.

21. Ibid.

22. Ibid.

23. "New Research Indicates Ethical Corporate Cultures Impact the Ability to Attract, Retain, and Ensure Productivity Among U.S. Workers," LRN, August 3, 2006, www.lrn.com/about_lrn/media_room/press_ releases/263. LRN specializes in legal, compliance, ethics, and governance solutions.

24. Ibid.

25. Ibid.

26. Verschoor, "Superior Governance," 13.

27. Thomas Friedman, "Calling All Democrats," *New York Times*, February 10, 2005.

28. The Center for Business Ethics at the University of St. Thomas, Houston, Texas, at their conference overview site, www.stthom.edu/academics/ centers/cbes/CorporateGovernanceEthicsAcrosstheBoard.html.

29. Kenneth L. Lay, "What a CEO Expects from the Board," presentation at the Corporate Governance: Ethics Across the Board Conference, Houston, TX, April 6, 1999, www.stthom.edu/academics/centers/cbes/ kenneth_lay.html.

30. Marianne M. Jennings, *The Seven Signs of Ethical Collapse: How to Spot Moral Meltdowns in Companies ... Before It's Too Late*, (New York, NY: St. Martin's Press, 2006).

CHAPTER 2

Tone at the Top and Throughout

"If ethics are poor at the top, that behavior is copied down through the organization."
Robert Noyce, inventor of the silicon chip

T he road to compliance starts at the top. An organization's entire culture is largely guided by senior management. The leadership sets the tone for the rest of the organization, and the culture reflects their actions, whether positive or negative. This is the often-mentioned "tone at the top." Employees pay careful attention, whether consciously or not, to their leaders and their actions. They can tell when a CEO truly supports the mission of the company or if the words are merely empty rhetoric. They hear what he or she says, and more importantly, see what he or she does. Employees look around their offices and understand their culture, even though it is not something that can readily be explained or easily put into words. Employees know if small transgressions are overlooked so long as financial goals are met, or if management is weak on ethics. Lax attitudes about ethics will prevent an organization from being able to achieve a culture of compliance.

A compliance program cannot operate with full efficiency and effectiveness in an environment that is not conducive to strong ethics. A negative ethical corporate culture is anathema to compliance. Of course, it should be noted that the objectives of running an ethical company that fully meets its compliance requirements, and running a successful and profitable company are hardly antithetical to each other. In fact, as was explained in the previous chapter, they can go hand in hand. For example, think of how beneficial it could be if a chief executive always includes comments on integrity, ethics, and compliance in every presentation he gives to employees. It's that constant reinforcement by an executive officer that demonstrates to all employees the utmost importance of honesty and accountability at all levels of an organization.

Tone at the top can be defined as the example set by upper levels of management, especially the CEO and the organization's most senior people, by words and especially by actions, for the rest of the company. Actions resonate more than words. Nothing can be more damaging to setting a proper tone than management who says one thing but does another. This tone must also filter down throughout the management chain. Employees need to see that their immediate supervisors, as well as the company's senior executives, are behaving ethically and doing the right thing.

While tone coming from the top of an organization is important, it is also just as critical in the ranks of junior executives and managers. Managers and other supervisors are involved day to day with employees. Their interaction with their direct reports and others reinforce policies and the code of conduct. They are role models and lead by example. More often than not, if employees want to raise a compliance concern or ask a question, they should first ask their managers. It can be said that tone in the middle furthers and enhances tone at the top. In addition, these middle managers may climb the corporate ladder and hopefully bring the good values with them.

INTEGRITY AT THE TOP

So much of leadership comes from one's integrity. Every other quality builds upon integrity. Either someone has it or doesn't. It can't be learned overnight or obtained from a training class. Integrity is at the very core of compliance. Not too long ago, I read a moving quote that summed up the importance of integrity. It was written, not by a CEO or compliance expert, but by a man with spirit, perseverance, and integrity. Bob Croft was a noted fraud investigator in both the public and private sectors. Bob was always a person of learning and, while working full-time, was pursuing a Master's degree in Economic Crime Management from Utica College in New York. Shortly after starting the program, he was diagnosed with Amyotrophic Lateral Sclerosis (ALS). That didn't stop Bob. Although the disease ravaged his body, his spirit remained strong and he graduated in May 2001. Unfortunately, Bob succumbed to ALS in April 2003. In a paper he wrote for his Masters program entitled "The Manager in a Global Environment," Bob said:

> *My core principles that have been central to my life have remained the same since my childhood, in spite of the many challenges that presently confront me. Namely, trust in God, be yourself, believe in*

yourself, do unto others, and cherish your integrity. In my opinion,
in the end—when it is all said and done, and you're looking at the
end of your life . . . the only thing you really have left to take with
you is your integrity, and not much more.

Bob Croft understood the value of integrity and how very important it is in all aspects of life.

Compliance, like integrity, is not something that can be easily achieved. It requires effort and commitment. A negative ethical culture, such as one where ethics is viewed as a hindrance to the business, indicates that management is not dedicated to making this commitment. In a culture such as this, the compliance program is merely window-dressing. It has been put into place to satisfy the barest minimums of the law and to make it appear to outsiders, such as investors or the government, that the organization works to achieve compliance, even though that is not really the case.

A compliance officer at a public company told me a sobering story. He was specifically hired in his role as Chief Compliance Officer because the company had significant ethical lapses and needed to rebuild their compliance program. The company publicly stated that it was bringing in an experienced compliance professional for this purpose. They pledged to do everything they could to ensure that the business conduct violations that had occurred would never recur. Unfortunately, the public comments were just a facade. The Chief Compliance Officer was never a part of senior leadership, was kept in the dark by executive management, and had no authority to make any real changes to the compliance program. As a result, an effective compliance program was never created, according to my source. In addition, it was learned that the company was to be sold and there needed to be a semblance of a compliance program in place to enable the sale. The compliance professional ultimately left the company.

Tone at the top is not easily measured. It is regarded by many as one of the scores of things that "you know it when you see it." However, there are ways to ensure that an organization has an appropriate tone at the top. Creating a well-thought out and easily understandable code of conduct is a good start. Then communicating it to all employees and reinforcing it by having each senior executive and director embody the code is next. "The first and critical step in making a code workable is for the senior management team and board of directors to exhibit the values embodied in the code, effectively establishing the tone at the top. Organizations whose management and board espouse a culture of integrity, high ethical standards, and compliance help to create a well-governed company, with a strong and positive tone at the top."[1] Compliance Insight 2.1 is a story of tone at the top and how it fosters being a good corporate citizen.

COMPLIANCE INSIGHT 2.1: REDFLEX TRAFFIC SYSTEMS AND DOING THE RIGHT THING

Compliance is more than just following laws, regulations, and policy. It is often about doing the right thing when faced with compliance challenges. A case in point is Redflex Traffic Systems (Redflex), based in Scottsdale, Arizona. Redflex manufactures photo-enhancement cameras to catch red-light runners and speeders.

As stated on their corporate Web site, Redflex "provides innovative safety solutions to local and state government in the USA and abroad. Redflex partners with public safety officials in law enforcement, transportation, and engineering to reduce traffic crashes and eliminate the resulting injuries, fatalities, and loss of property." Redflex is the largest supplier and operator of photo enforcement in the United States. The market for Redflex's cameras is growing globally in cities and municipalities. Redflex is a division of Redflex Holdings Limited which is a publicly traded company listed on the Australian Stock Exchange.

In early 2006, Redflex salespeople met with representatives of the St. Peters, Missouri city government to secure a contract to install digital red light and speeding enforcement systems in the city. As a result, in May 2006, "a bill was introduced to authorize the city administration to negotiate for a traffic enforcement system with Redflex."[a] The bill was passed by the St. Peters' Board of Aldermen on June 8, 2006.

Shortly thereafter, the Mayor of St. Peters, Shawn Brown, contacted a Redflex representative and "threatened to veto the bill unless they paid him a bribe."[b] In an example of hubris over common sense, Brown ordered the bribe be paid via a check made payable to him, and to be delivered to his home. Demonstrating that there is no bribe amount too small, Brown demanded $2,750 but that seemed to be fine with him.

Immediately upon receiving notice of the extortion attempt, Redflex contacted law enforcement to report the incident. The Federal Bureau of Investigation (FBI) in St. Louis, Missouri quickly opened an investigation and Redflex offered their full cooperation with the government. The FBI told Redflex to go through with the bribe payment to catch Brown in the act. The $2,750 check was delivered to Brown who then cashed it at a local bank in St. Peters. All the while, the FBI was covertly watching.[c]

On August 17, 2006, Brown was indicted on federal bribery charges. Specifically, Brown was charged with "threatening to veto an ordinance authorizing the city to purchase digital red light and speeding enforcement systems unless the company paid him a bribe."[d] The FBI Special Agent in Charge in St. Louis said that Redflex "provided the information that resulted in the initiation of the case and eventually the indictment."[e] The FBI also sent a letter to Redflex thanking them for being a good corporate citizen and stating, "Without honest, courageous firms like Redflex and its employees, the work of law enforcement would be much more difficult."[f] On August 21, 2006, Redflex posted a press release on its Web site detailing the investigation and their assistance to the FBI.

Due to the overwhelming evidence, Brown pleaded guilty on October 20, 2006 to the federal bribery charges. On January 29, 2007, Brown was sentenced to 18 months in prison, followed by two years of supervised release.[g]

Redflex could easily have just said no to Brown's bribe demand and never reported the incident. They may have lost the contract but it is also possible that Brown was just bluffing and would not have actually gone through with his threat. Instead, Redflex showed their culture of compliance and did the right thing resulting in the prosecution, conviction, and removal from office of a corrupt public official.

---

[a]Press Release issued by the United State's Attorney's Office for the Eastern District of Missouri, January 29, 2007, announcing the sentencing of defendant Shawn Brown, www.usdoj.gov/usao/moe/press%20releases/archived%20press%20releases/2007_press_releases/january/brown_shawn.html.
[b]Ibid.
[c]Michael Ferraresi, "Red-light Firm Aids FBI Bust," *Arizona Republic*, August 19, 2006, A1.
[d]Press Release issued by the United State's Attorney's Office for the Eastern District of Missouri, January 29, 2007, announcing the sentencing of defendant Shawn Brown, www.usdoj.gov/usao/moe/press%20releases/archived%20press%20releases/2007_press_releases/january/brown_shawn.html.
[e]Michael Ferraresi, "Red-light Firm Aids FBI Bust," *Arizona Republic*, August 19, 2006, A1.
[f]Ibid.
[g]Press Release issued by the United State's Attorney's Office for the Eastern District of Missouri, January 29, 2007, announcing the sentencing of defendant Shawn Brown, www.usdoj.gov/usao/moe/press%20releases/archived%20press%20releases/2007_press_releases/january/brown_shawn.html.

In the end though, tone always comes back to management. It is their influence that sets the tone and drives the culture. Management decides the rules, and thus the culture springs up around these rules, based on what is permissible and what is not. For compliance to flourish, there must be *meaningful accountability*. To have meaningful accountability, people must take responsibility for their actions, and their actions must have consequences. It is not enough to catch someone who has violated a law or an internal company rule. They must be disciplined appropriately, with the punishment fitting the action. Also, management must take responsibility for its actions, rather than simply pointing the finger at others. Again, it cannot be empty rhetoric, of the "I'm sorry ... but I'm really only sorry that I got caught" variety.

Alan Greenspan, former Chairman of the Federal Reserve, said "If the CEO chooses, he or she can by example and through oversight induce corporate colleagues and outside auditors to behave ethically.... Rules exist to govern behavior, but rules cannot substitute for character. In the years going forward, it will be your reputation—for integrity, judgment, and other qualities of character—that will determine your success in life and business."[2] The late management guru Peter Drucker reinforced the important concept of integrity and leadership when he said, "The proof of sincerity and seriousness of a management is uncompromising emphasis on integrity of character."[3] Compliance Insight 2.2 is another story of tone at the top where compliance wins out over competition.

IT'S BETTER TO BE LUCKY THAN GOOD

Sometimes it's better to be lucky than good, especially if one happens to be a CEO receiving stock options. In fact, this term has taken on new meaning as a result of an academic study conducted by professors from Harvard and Cornell Universities, and INSEAD, the French business school. This study was released amid a backdating options scandal engulfing numerous companies. Dozens upon dozens of companies have been implicated in the scandal that involved the falsification of the date of exercise of a stock option, so as to give the recipient the maximum benefit by allowing the improper purchase of stock at the lowest possible price. This amounts to nothing more than simple theft. This fraud, according to one study, has cost investors over $100 billion.[4] While executives may have argued that their exercise of stock options happening to fall on the date of the lowest price was nothing more than "luck," this new study shows otherwise.

In the "Lucky CEOs" study, the researchers studied the relationship between corporate governance and what they describe as "opportunistic

COMPLIANCE INSIGHT 2.2: A TRUCE IN THE COLA WARS TO PROTECT TRADE SECRETS

The century-old rivalry and intense business competition between Coca-Cola and PepsiCo are nothing short of legendary. Both soft drinks were invented and first marketed in the late 1800s and continue to this day as the world's most popular sodas. Their unique tastes and impact on people and culture are the keys to their success. Few trade secrets are better protected than the soft drink formulas of these two companies. In this age of industrial espionage and theft of intellectual property, as well as the demand for continually improving profits, there is always the temptation to use whatever means are available to obtain a competitive advantage over business rivals. Yet, integrity, corporate culture, and a commitment to compliance are even stronger motivators to do what is right when faced with an integrity challenge. This was the case with PepsiCo who proved that compliance wins out over competition.

On May 19, 2006, PepsiCo contacted Coca-Cola in Atlanta, Georgia and provided them with a letter that they received at their corporate headquarters in Purchase, New York. The letter was from a person who claimed he was a high-level Coca-Cola employee and had access to "very detailed and confidential information" about a new Coke product. PepsiCo did not hesitate to do what was right.[a] PepsiCo immediately informed Coca-Cola about this theft of trade secrets. Coca-Cola quickly contacted the Federal Bureau of Investigation (FBI) in Atlanta who began an investigation. An undercover FBI agent began communicating with the intermediary who ultimately wanted more than $1.5 million to hand over samples of new Coke products and related highly secret documents.

The FBI, through various investigative techniques, learned that PepsiCo had been contacted by an intermediary of an executive assistant at Coca-Cola who had access to the trade secrets detailed in the letter to PepsiCo. The FBI, working with Coca-Cola corporate security, were able to obtain video surveillance of the Coca-Cola employee removing restricted documents from the office and handling a sample of the new product offered to PepsiCo. The FBI also identified a third member of the conspiracy who was not a Coca-Cola employee. At a meeting with the undercover FBI agent, the stolen items were exchanged for cash. In short order, all three subjects were arrested on July 5, 2006 and charged with conspiracy to steal trade secrets.

In a letter to all employees on July 5, 2006, and posted on its Web site, Coca-Cola Chairman and CEO Neville Isdell provided details of the trade secret leak and the arrests of the Coca-Cola employee and the other two defendants. Isdell said:

> *Sadly, today's arrests include an individual within our Company. While this breach of trust is difficult for all of us to accept, it underscores the responsibility we each have to be vigilant in protecting our trade secrets. Information is the lifeblood of the Company. As the health of our enterprise continues to strengthen and the breadth of our innovation pipeline continues to grow, our leaders and our competitive data carry increasing interest to those outside our business. Accordingly, I have directed a thorough review of our information protection policies, procedures, and practices to ensure that we continue to rigorously safeguard our intellectual capital.[b]*

Isdell went on to add, "I would also like to express our sincere appreciation to PepsiCo for alerting us to this attack."[c] A PepsiCo spokesperson further stated, "We did what any responsible company would do. Competition can be fierce, but it must also be fair and legal."[d] PepsiCo's Worldwide Code of Conduct states, "In all of its business dealing with suppliers, customers, and *competitors*, PepsiCo will: Compete vigorously and with integrity.... Avoid any unfair or deceptive practice.... And in everything we do, we strive to act with honesty, fairness, and integrity (emphasis added)."[e]

The former Coca-Cola employee was indicted and subsequently went to trial. Her two associates pleaded guilty and testified against her. The evidence was overwhelming and she was convicted after jury trial on February 2, 2007 of conspiring to steal Coca-Cola trade secrets. On May 23, 2007, the defendant was sentenced to eight years in prison. The federal judge on the case departed from the sentencing guidelines to give a longer prison sentence due to the defendant's lying on the stand during the trial and obstruction of justice.

Both PepsiCo and Coca-Cola did the right things and followed corporate compliance. PepsiCo followed their Code of Conduct and quickly reported the offer of trade secrets to Coca-Cola. Coca-Cola responded by contacting law enforcement and assisting in the subsequent investigation and convictions. After the arrests, Coca-Cola advised all its employees of the investigation and the involvement of

one of their employees. Coca-Cola further advised that it was reviewing its protection of trade secrets to further safeguard their intellectual
capital. Compliance does work.

---

[a]"Two Defendants Plead Guilty in Coca-Cola Trade Secrets Case," Department of Justice Press Release, United States Attorney's Office, Northern
District of Georgia, October 23, 2006, www.usdoj.gov/usao/gan/press/2006/
10-23-06.pdf.
[b]Memo from Neville Isdell, Coca-Cola Chairman and CEO, to all employees
worldwide, and posted at the Coca-Cola Web site, July 5, 2006, www.thecoca-
colacompany.com/presscenter/viewpoints_trade_secrets_investigation.html.
[c]Ibid.
[d]Betsy McKay, "Coke Employee Faces Charges in Plot to Sell Secrets," *Wall
Street Journal*, July 6, 2006, B6.
[e]PepsiCo Worldwide Code of Conduct, www.pepsico.com/PEP_Investors/
CorporateGovernance/CodeofConduct/english/pg1.shtml.

option grant manipulation" for option grants made over a nine-year period
in the United States.[5] They found the incidence of what they called "lucky
grants" to executives to be more likely due to manipulation than actual
luck. The researchers defined a lucky grant as "grants given at the lowest
price of the month." These lucky grants were more likely to occur when
the company did not have a majority of independent directors on the board
and/or the CEO had a long tenure at the company. During the period of the
study from 1996 to 2005, the authors estimated that 1,150 lucky grants were
the result of manipulation and that 12% of organizations studied provided
one or more lucky grants to executives.[6] No companies or executives were
named in the study.

Some of the other revealing findings of the study included:

- The higher the potential payoff, the "luckier" the grant.
- "Luck was persistent: A CEO's chance of getting a lucky grant increases
  when a preceding grant was lucky as well."
- Grant manipulation was prevalent across all types of industries and not
  just in new economy firms.
- There was no evidence that gains from manipulated option grants served
  as a substitute for compensation paid through other sources. It only
  served to increase CEOs total compensation.
- The average gain for CEOs from grants backdated to the month's lowest
  price exceeded 20% of the reported value of the grant. This resulted in

an increase to the CEO's total reported compensation for the year by more than 10%.

- "About 1,000 (43%) of the lucky grants were 'super-lucky,' having been given at the lowest price not only of the month but also of the quarter, and we estimate that about 62% of them were manipulated."
- There were certain pools of grants with an especially high probability of manipulation. In one pool of 600 grants, 88% are estimated to be manipulated.[7]

The professors also conducted a companion study on stock options received by outside directors. This study was entitled "Lucky Directors" and studied 29,000 grants awarded to outside directors at 6,577 public firms between 1996 and 2005. The study found that "9% of director grants were lucky events falling on days with a stock price equal to a monthly low.... about 800 lucky grant events owed their status to opportunistic timing, and that about 460 firms and 1,400 outside directors were associated with grant events produced by such timing."[8] The study also found that there was a correlation between a director's luck and that of an executive's luck in the awarding of lucky grants. Thus, when executives at a company did well in receiving the lowest options price of the month, so did the directors. The study also found that these lucky grants to directors were more likely to occur when the company "had more entrenching provisions protecting insiders from the risk of removal, and when the board did not have a majority of independent directors."[9]

An Absence of Tone at the Top

Absence of tone at the top in the cases of these lucky CEOs and directors is obvious. In the case of directors, they are gatekeepers. The Lucky Directors' study "suggests that outside, or independent, directors—who are supposed to play a special role safeguarding against cozy board relationships with management—may have been co-opted in options backdating."[10] In my 2006 book, *Executive Roadmap to Fraud Prevention and Internal Control: Creating a Culture of Compliance*, we devoted a section to the important role of gatekeepers. Gatekeepers are the auditors, lawyers, analysts, and also directors who are responsible for monitoring and oversight of others in protecting the integrity of the financial markets. "They are the people in important positions to whom the investing public, the government, and others, look for truth and honesty in financial reporting. They must be beyond reproach and accountable for their actions."[11]

There is some good news. These two studies add to the public's knowledge, along with the widespread publicity surrounding the many government and internal investigations conducted for backdating and manipulating stock option grants. With so many companies implicated and with so many executives and directors removed from their positions, there is hope that this misconduct will never again happen to this degree. A lawyer in a corporate governance practice called this behavior of the lucky directors "appalling" and added "Directors are fiduciaries for all stockholders; to act in their own self-interest is a breach of loyalty. It's the cardinal sin."[12] Nothing speaks louder to tone at the top than the actions of corporate executives and directors, especially when safeguarding the interests of investors and employees. Compliance Insight 2.3 is a listing of some of the many companies named in the probes of backdating stock options.

COMMUNICATING VALUES

Beyond anecdotal evidence, surveys have shown the importance of tone at the top in the workplace. Employees really do follow the lead given by the top, and it does resonate throughout. Moreover, an organization's culture has a strong role in guiding the actions of those within. Top companies have deeply ingrained core values; these guiding principles "will... not be compromised for financial gain or short-term expediency."[13] These "core values need no rational or external justification. Nor do they sway with the trends and fads of the day, nor do they shift in response to changing market conditions."[14] These core values are the bedrock of a company; great values are directly linked to great success.

Of course, companies face challenges in aligning their values with their business strategy, so that executives can make appropriate decisions supporting and furthering these values. The most important way a company does this is through the behavior of the CEO. 85% of senior executives said in a recent survey that "their companies rely on explicit CEO support to reinforce values and 77% say it is one of the 'most effective' practices for reinforcing the company's ability to act on its values."[15] In comparison, "only 34% identified training as a 'most effective' practice, 32% cited internal communications, and 30% identified incentive compensation."[16] In view of this, the CEO is the best communicator of an organization's values to the executives and other employees. This is not to say that the other cited practices, such as training, internal communications and incentive compensation, should be abandoned. In fact, the opposite is true; while they are not as effective as the CEO in conveying an appropriate tone at the top, they do serve to reinforce the established values. Compliance Insight 2.4 provides a compliance consultant's point of view on tone at the top and other compliance issues.

COMPLIANCE INSIGHT 2.3: A SAMPLING OF COMPANIES NAMED IN PROBES OF BACKDATING STOCK OPTIONS

Affiliated Computer Services

American Tower

Apollo Group

Apple, Inc.

Applied Micro Circuits

Atmel

Barnes & Noble

Boston Communications Group

Broadcom

Brocade Communications Systems

Brooks Automation

Cablevision

Cirrus Logic

CNET Networks

Comverse Technology

Cyberonics

Foundry Networks

F5 Networks

HCC Insurance Holdings

Home Depot

Jabil Circuit

Juniper Networks

KB Home

KLA-Tencor

Linear Technology

Marvell Technology

McAfee, Inc.

Medarex

Mercury Interactive

Monster Worldwide

Openwave Systems

Power Integrations

Rambus

SafeNet

Sanmina-SCI

Sycamore Networks

Take-Two Interactive Software

Trident Microsystems

UnitedHealth

Verisign

Vitesse Semiconductor

Zoran

COMPLIANCE INSIGHT 2.4: A COMPLIANCE CONSULTANT'S POINT OF VIEW

Scott Moritz is an Executive Director with Daylight Forensic & Advisory, a global regulatory compliance and investigative consulting firm advising financial institutions, Fortune 500 companies, law firms, and government agencies on regulatory and investigative issues worldwide. He has over 20 years of complex investigative, forensic accounting, compliance, court-appointed monitoring, and law enforcement experience. Prior to joining Daylight, he was a director at a "Big Four" accounting firm, where he served as both Director of Corporate Intelligence and Leader of the Data Governance and Privacy Protection Team for the Forensic Practice. For nearly 10 years, Moritz served as an FBI Special Agent where he was nationally recognized for his expertise in money laundering and asset forfeiture investigations. Here Moritz provides a compliance consultant's point of view.

THE COMPLIANCE CONUNDRUM

Implementing the provisions of the Foreign Corrupt Practices Act, Office of Foreign Assets Control, USA PATRIOT Act, or the

Sarbanes-Oxley Act have proven to be extremely challenging for U.S. and foreign-owned corporations alike. The acts themselves are quite complex as are the organizations that must adhere to them. The greatest challenge to these corporations is that they require an enterprise-wide approach to effectively implement these compliance mandates.

Most complex entities are organized by functional areas of expertise, geography, or both. These types of organizational structures, arguably comprising the known universe of modern-day companies, often result in silos which make any enterprise-wide implementation of compliance protocols challenging because they require cross functional, cross-geographical coordination, and communication. In addition, most organizations don't communicate well internally. Further fueling this recipe for compliance disaster is organizational culture. At some level, every organization suffers from the fundamental cultural divide between compliance and business operations and sales.

Organizations are established to generate revenues and the operations and business development personnel are quite understandably focused on that objective. Compliance requirements are viewed by many, particularly by those in operations, sales, and frequently executive management, as "necessary evils" and an impediment to their ability to deliver on sales goals and quarterly earnings forecasts. This cultural divide, left unchecked, can lead to potentially catastrophic regulatory actions.

"Tone at the top," though a much-used term, remains vitally important to an organization's culture. If senior management does not provide meaningful support to major compliance initiatives by their words, actions, and budgetary allocations, the organization's compliance efforts are likely doomed to failure. The result can be potentially devastating fines, loss of public confidence, market capitalization, and legal liability.

But tone at top alone isn't always enough to implement a meaningful compliance program. Outside perspective is often required. This can be accomplished in one of two ways. The organization can either designate a company insider from another part of the company to project manage a compliance initiative or retain outside compliance experts. The reality is that most organizations tend to utilize outside experts out of concern that an internal diversion of resources can damage one part of the organization while trying to repair another. Regardless of who is leading a compliance initiative, the key elements needed for a successful project are objectivity, subject matter expertise, and empowerment.

OBJECTIVITY AND THE IMPORTANCE OF CROSS FUNCTIONAL COMMUNICATION

How often have we all heard the phrase "that's the way we've always done it?" How about "that's not part of my department's role." As a consultant, I have heard these utterances many times, often from members of senior management with wide-ranging compliance obligations. They just did not understand what their compliance responsibilities were, gave compliance short shrift, and did not know their compliance obligations affected the rest of the organization. In order for any compliance consulting project to be effective, the outside consultants have to gather and absorb a great deal of information about policies and procedures, whether these policies and procedures are appropriate, and whether they are being followed in practice.

In addition, the consultants must interview a significant cross section of people throughout their organization. These interviews allow the consultants to gauge employees' qualifications for their positions, their understanding of the company's compliance obligations as it relates to their positions, non-compliance implications, and how their business unit interacts with others both in terms of operations and compliance. These interviews are central to any compliance consulting project, as they allow the consultants to give an objective opinion as to how "effective" the organization's compliance program really is.

Because outside consultants or their internal equivalents are not involved in the business operations under review, they end up with a unique perspective on where the company is performing well, where there is room for improvement and, most importantly, they know where the compliance land mines are buried. Of course, finding these land mines is as important as making suggestions for immediate corrective actions. Equally important, the outside consultant facilitates communication across the organization, raising internal awareness of crucial compliance issues. Most often, the difference between high performing compliance organizations and those that perform poorly hinges on cross-functional coordination and communication.

SUBJECT MATTER EXPERTISE

In order to have credibility with regulators and/or prosecutors, a compliance remediation project must be led by one or more professionals with relevant subject matter expertise. Indeed, financial regulators often require banks that are operating under a regulatory order to seek their approval before selecting a vendor to implement some or all of the requirements set forth in the order. Although not all compliance remediation projects are subject to this level of regulatory approval, it is a recommended practice to hire only those outside parties or internal personnel that have the experience and subject matter expertise that is required.

EMPOWERMENT

I have led numerous training sessions for major financial institutions regarding anti-money laundering compliance. For each session, we request that our client have a member of senior management kick off the training emphasizing the importance of the training and the organization's commitment to improving their overall compliance. On more than one occasion, the head of the business unit started the session with words to the effect of "this really doesn't apply to us but we have an obligation to sit through this so we can say we've all been trained." By introducing me in this way, these executives undermined the training session and opened themselves up to embarrassment. Indeed, they left me no choice but to contradict them in front of their entire staff. Needless to say, their lack of "buy-in" was in stark contrast to what is considered best practices in corporate governance.

Another client training session set a very different tone for the students in the session. At the beginning of this session, the senior executive put compliance in perspective for the students. He said "every year, we have to reserve a certain amount of money for regulatory liability. This is money that is not available for other organization needs including bonus compensation. If we get this right [meaning compliance], we have to reserve less money every year leaving a lot more money available to pay year end bonuses." Of the two training sessions described here, which of the two do you suppose was a more attentive group?

While these stories are about training, they are really about empowerment. By undermining me before the first training session, that executive made it clear that he was not onboard and sent that same message to his direct reports. The other executive both adopted the appropriate "tone at the top" and provided the students/employees with an important incentive to learn the subject matter. The key message here is that the actions and words of senior management and the extent to which they support compliance initiatives are directly related to the success or failure of a compliance remediation project.

IMPLEMENTATION AND FOLLOW-UP

Once a compliance program has been developed or remediated, implementation is the next critical task at hand. Failure to implement remedial changes to the compliance program can be extremely damaging to the organization and can provide a roadmap for prosecutors and regulators as to where to look for substantive non-compliance. There needs to be an institutional commitment to implementing the compliance program fully and an appreciation for how damaging failing to do so can be.

Equally important is the need to institute a system to regularly monitor the organization's adherence to the compliance program. This monitoring can either be undertaken by the company's internal audit group or an outside compliance consultant. The monitoring should be performed at least once annually and should include testing across the entire spectrum of the compliance program. The results of the compliance audit should be communicated to senior management and any findings should be addressed in a timely fashion and re-tested during the next compliance audit.

To summarize, an effective compliance program should consider all of the legal and regulatory mandates applicable to the organization; it should be consistently communicated in a variety of ways across the organization; and it should have the backing of senior management and the buy-in of the employees and officers expected to implement it. And, of course, it should be monitored regularly to ensure that there is not any slippage that could result in regulatory or legal liability.

Regularly communicating everyone's individual compliance obligations and relating those obligations to their specific roles can go a long way toward bridging the cultural divide between operations and compliance, moving the company in the direction of being a high performing compliant organization, and, most importantly, protecting the company and its executives against legal liability and reputational harm.

HOW THE CEO CAN MAKE THE DIFFERENCE

Joseph E. Murphy is an acknowledged expert on corporate compliance. He has more than 30 years of experience in the full range of compliance issues including drafting code and policy documents, evaluating programs, conducting compliance audits, investigating allegations of misconduct, and training. He lectures and writes extensively on these topics. Murphy is currently of counsel to Compliance Systems Legal Group, cofounder and Senior Advisor to Integrity Interactive Corporation, and coeditor of *Ethikos*, a bi-monthly publication on corporate compliance and ethics.

Murphy understands the importance of tone at the top. He is constantly thinking of ways to put these words into practice in an organization. He has put together a thought-provoking list of ideas for corporate executives and leaders everywhere to consider when demonstrating one's tone at the top. Joe Murphy makes it clear that this is not an all-encompassing list but one that is a living document. It is a toolkit that should be constantly used and added to with new ideas and practices so that a true leader can "walk the talk." People emulate their leaders and nothing reinforces appropriate behavior and compliance like leading by example. As Mahatma Gandhi said, "You must be the change you want to see in the world." Here is Joe Murphy's list:

1. Have a used, dog-eared copy of the company's code of conduct on the top of your desk, and be seen using it.
2. Make sure the compliance and ethics officer has plenty of clout, including direct reporting to the board's audit committee, and is professional and subject to strong professional ethical standards.
3. At your senior executive meetings, go around the table and have each senior officer report on what he or she has done specifically to promote the compliance and ethics program in his/her business unit. Be sure the compliance and ethics officer is there to sort the wheat from the chaff in this discussion. As is true for the CEO, just mouthing the right words counts for little, if anything.
4. Insist that compliance and ethics be tied into the incentives and evaluations, including those for officers, in a meaningful way.

5. Be the model in your business decisions. Turn down a trip offer from a vendor; pass on to the company a gift you received; reject a business deal if you think the ethical risks are too high.
6. Be the model in the compliance program. Take the training first; do the safety walk-through; call the company helpline with a question; call and ask a field line manager about his/her role in the code of conduct roll-out and training. Attend a Society of Corporate Compliance and Ethics (SCCE) program.
7. Personally recognize outstanding compliance and ethics performance. Personally insist on the toughest discipline when one of the top brass breaks the rule or threatens retaliation.
8. Recruit a compliance and ethics officer from another company for your board's audit committee.
9. Get a truly independent outside review of your compliance and ethics program, with the results reported directly to the audit committee.
10. Ask your company's suppliers to embrace your commitment to compliance and ethics, and offer your company's help for them to do this.
11. Network with your peers in other companies on ways to promote compliance and ethics.[17]

Studies have shown that ethical behavior and honesty can be enhanced within organizations when their leaders consistently display such behavior. There is no doubt that directors and officers of corporations set the "tone at the top" for ethical behavior throughout their organization. Similarly, managers throughout the organization are just as important in reinforcing positive behavior and being great role models for their employees. Leading by example in a positive way will always be an effective way to ensure that tone at the top translates into a culture of compliance.

NOTES

1. Julie Walsh, "Setting the Tone at the Top," *Law Now*, February 1, 2005.
2. Remarks from Commencement Address by former Federal Reserve Board Chairman Alan Greenspan at the Wharton School, University of Pennsylvania, Philadelphia, PA, May 15, 2005, www.federalreserve.gov/boarddocs/speeches/2005/20050515/.
3. Peter F. Drucker, "Peter Drucker's Essential Tips for Managers in 2005," *Wall Street Journal* Executive Career Site, www.careerjournal.com/myc/management/20050106-drucker.html.

4. "Study: Backdating Has Cost $100 Billion," *Associated Press*, December 20, 2006, www.msnbc.msn.com/id/16302216.

5. Lucian Arye Bebchuk, Yaniv Grinstein and Urs C. Peyer, "Lucky CEOs," Harvard Law and Economics Discussion Paper No. 566, November 2006, http://ssrn.com/abstract=945392 and at www.issproxy .com/pdf/LuckyCEOs_Bebchuk-Grinstein-Peyer.pdf.

6. Ibid.

7. Ibid.

8. Lucian Arye Bebchuk, Yaniv Grinstein and Urs C. Peyer, "Lucky Directors," Harvard Law and Economics Discussion Paper No. 573, December 2006, http://ssrn.com/abstract=952239.

9. Ibid.

10. Steve Stecklow, "Study Cites Role Outside Directors Had With Options," *The Wall Street Journal*, December 18, 2006, A10.

11. Martin T. Biegelman and Joel T. Bartow, *Executive Roadmap to Fraud Prevention and Internal Control: Creating a Culture of Compliance*, (Hoboken, NJ: John Wiley & Sons, Inc, 2006), 97.

12. Kathy Kristof, "Doubt cast on stock options of directors," *Los Angeles Times Online*, December 18, 2006, www.latimes.com/business/la-fi-options18dec18,1,1938511.story?coll=la-headlines-business&ctrack =1&cset=true.

13. Dr. John D. Copeland, "Business Ethics: Three Critical Truths," 8, www.soderquist.org/resources/pdf/Copeland_ThreeTruths-publication .pdf, quoting James C. Collins and Jerry I. Porras, *Built to Last: Successful Habits of Visionary Companies*, (New York: HarperCollins, 1994), 73.

14. Dr. John D. Copeland, "Business Ethics: Three Critical Truths," 8, www.soderquist.org/resources/pdf/Copeland_ThreeTruths-publication .pdf, quoting James C. Collins and Jerry I. Porras, *Built to Last: Successful Habits of Visionary Companies*, (New York: HarperCollins, 1994), 75.

15. "New Study Finds Link Between Financial Success and Focus on Corporate Values," Booz Allen Hamilton, February 3, 2005, www.boozallen .com/publications/article/659548.

16. Ibid.

17. Joseph E. Murphy, "Compliance and Ethics: How Can the CEO Make the Difference," Society of Corporate Compliance and Ethics, www.corporatecompliance.org/resources/documents/HowCanCEO_ MakeDifference.pdf.

CHAPTER 3

The Growth and Evolution of Compliance

"Those who cannot remember the past are condemned to repeat it."

George Santayana

What is now known as corporate compliance is the result of many years of evolution and development. The laws covering businesses have grown over the years in size and scope just as the ways of dealing with these laws have grown more formal and complex. Regulation started slowly in the 19th century and picked up momentum in the ensuing years. This regulation began as a response to individual scandals, and sought to address the underlying causes of each of these scandals. By the 1960s, with increasing complexity in both the business and regulatory arenas, the foundations of modern compliance began to emerge. This trend continued into the 1970s and 1980s, until it reached a tipping point with the release of the Sentencing Guidelines for Organizations in 1991. Compliance programs existed well before these sentencing amendments, but the amendments gave these programs a major push into the mainstream of business. The entire compliance framework only developed further with the passage of the Sarbanes-Oxley Act and the increased importance and role of compliance officers in the 21st century.

A BRIEF HISTORY OF COMPLIANCE

In many ways, the history of American business parallels the history of scandal. This history could be accurately described as an ongoing tug of war between regulators who seek to reign in corporate excess and businesses that resist regulation in order to achieve greater flexibility and innovation.[1] Particularly, regulators step in during the wake of massive corporate scandals. As devastating as they have been, these "scandals also have a crucial silver lining; in each case, public outrage has forced lawmakers to step in. This pattern, as it turns out, lies at the heart of American corporate governance. For the past century, American corporate regulation has consisted of periodic, dramatic regulatory interventions by federal lawmakers after a major scandal, together with more nuanced ongoing regulation by the states."[2] In the aftermath of these scandals, the public outrage and calls for justice transform into broad support for tangible reform that would be otherwise impossible had the scandals not occurred.

It is important to remember that the history of corporate scandal did not begin with Enron and end with stock option backdating, and that Sarbanes-Oxley is not the be-all and end-all of government regulation. Big-time corporate scandals have existed as long as big business has existed. In the 1860s, Philadelphia banker Jay Cooke grew to fame and fortune by selling government bonds to raise money for the Union army. After the Civil War, he used similar techniques and extensive advertising to sell bonds to raise money for the Northern Pacific Railroad. However, he continued to throw money into the railroad even when almost everyone else thought it was too risky. He ignored the warning signs of rising inflation and widespread railroad building that far outstripped demand. The impact of this scandal was not so much in the way it happened, but in who it involved. Cooke's company "had been regarded as a pillar of financial stability."[3] To make an analogy to the present, this would be as if financial icons Bill Gates or Warren Buffett staked their personal reputation and their company's fortunes on an ultimately unsuccessful venture, ruining their companies in the process. The subsequent implosion of both Cooke's bank and the railroad led directly to the economic depression of the Panic of 1873. This scandal was significant as it did not affect just the rich but also people of far more moderate means who had invested in the bonds. Outrage came even from people who had no financial stake in the railroad.[4]

Though many people suffered in these collapses and lost a great deal of money, some benefit was derived from it by the corporate reforms enacted afterwards. The railroad collapse of 1873, and the details of blatant corruption, self-dealing, and bribery that emerged soon afterwards, led Congress and several states to enact statutes designed to better police corporations and to limit their influence over the political process. The existing laws of the 19th century were designed for small-scale concerns, not for the massive behemoths of the Industrial Age. Courts also worked to fashion a regulatory environment by shaping rules to prevent the self-dealing contracts railroad managers used to siphon off company money for their own benefit. The panic burned itself into the memory of the nation and eventually led to substantive regulation of the railroads with the Interstate Commerce Act of 1887 and federal regulation of monopolies with the Sherman Antitrust Act of 1890.[5] In this era, Congress enacted another far-reaching anti-fraud law, the Mail Fraud Statute. The Mail Fraud Statute was the first federal law to protect Americans from fraud and scams, enacted in 1872 after an epidemic of frauds targeted consumers and business owners. Today, a multitude of frauds, including corporate frauds, are prosecuted using the Mail Fraud Statute.

While states did pass laws to regulate corporations, they did little to affect the wave of mergers and unchecked corporate growth of the Industrial Age. "The states' abandonment of the fight against corporate combinations shifted the campaign against corporate monopoly from the states to Congress and federal regulators. Two decades later, a trust-busting campaign led by Teddy Roosevelt would firmly establish federal regulators as the principal guardians for competition in American industry."[6]

Teddy Roosevelt and Corporate Regulation

Teddy Roosevelt's interest in regulating corporations coincided with substantial public anxiety about the power, reach, and lack of accountability of America's giant corporations of the Gilded Age. That was an era of growing corporate power and influence in people's lives and in the government's business on a scale never before seen, as well as the rise of muckrakers who sought to expose the ills of society and the misdeeds of the monopolies and corporate robber barons. President Roosevelt recognized this and also saw that the states were either unable or unwilling to sufficiently regulate them. However, even though he recognized the dangers of corporate power, he did not seek to completely destroy it or even substantially weaken it, as he felt that strong business was central to America's growing economy and world power. Certainly he would not seek to weaken America's economic power at a time when his "Big Stick" diplomacy pushed American power into places like Latin America and the Philippines. Roosevelt wanted to balance corporate power and economic interests with public interests and the welfare of its citizens. The way to accomplish this was through centralized government regulation of business activities, particularly of corporate misdeeds.[7]

Roosevelt addressed these issues in his second State of the Union Address, given on December 2, 1902. This important speech set the tone for the century of federal corporate regulation that was to follow:

> *Our aim is not to do away with corporations; on the contrary, these big aggregations are an inevitable development of modern*

industrialism, and the effort to destroy them would be futile unless accomplished in ways that would work the utmost mischief to the entire body politic. We can do nothing of good in the way of regulating and supervising these corporations until we fix clearly in our minds that we are not attacking the corporations, but endeavoring to do away with any evil in them. We are not hostile to them; we are merely determined that they shall be so handled as to subserve the public good. We draw the line against misconduct, not against wealth. The capitalist who, alone or in conjunction with his fellows, performs some great industrial feat by which he wins money is a welldoer, not a wrongdoer, provided only he works in proper and legitimate lines. We wish to favor such a man when he does well. We wish to supervise and control his actions only to prevent him from doing ill. Publicity can do no harm to the honest corporation; and we need not be over tender about sparing the dishonest corporation.[8]

Unfortunately, the century that was to follow would be marked by the misdeeds of corporate wrongdoers.

In 1932, the collapse of Samuel Insull's electricity empire came during another economically perilous time, the Great Depression, and helped spur Franklin Delano Roosevelt to enact sweeping New Deal corporate reforms. Insull, a former associate of Thomas Edison and a Chicago energy magnate, built a massive business empire by relentlessly acquiring and eliminating rival energy companies and other businesses.[9] However, the empire's finances were nowhere as secure as they appeared. To disguise the business' precarious financial position, Insull created an elaborate holding company structure, similar to what Enron would do seventy years later. Insull hid his finances in a maze of parent companies and subsidiaries, some with substantial assets and some that were not worth the money on which their charter was printed on.[10] Predictably, this shaky foundation soon came crashing down and led some to describe it as one of the "biggest business failures in the history of the world."[11] In a particularly ironic bit of history, the accounting firm of Arthur Andersen rose to national prominence and gained a reputation of great integrity for its work in the investigation of Insull's firm and his subsequent prosecution.[12]

Insull, like Cooke before him, and like many fallen corporate executives to come, displayed incredible hubris and a feeling of invincibility that led him to skirt the law for his own ends. "With each of these scandals, as with our more recent collapses, the high-flying businessmen at the heart of the scandals were not alone. Cooke and Insull personified a breakdown in accountability that pervaded all of American corporate and financial life."[13]

FDR and a New Deal for Investors

Further regulations emerged from the wave of scandals in the late 1920s and early 1930s. Franklin Delano Roosevelt campaigned on a promise to clean up corporate America, following in the footsteps of his cousin Teddy, and made good on this promise as part of the New Deal. In fact, he specifically campaigned, both in the 1930 New York governor's race and in his first presidential campaign, against the "Insull monstrosity."[14] The broad array of sweeping reforms enacted then still provides the principal infrastructure of American corporate and market regulation today. Congress enacted the first securities laws in the early 1930s as a result of the stock market crash of 1929 and the resulting Great Depression. The Securities Acts of 1933 and 1934 established the Securities and Exchange Commission (SEC) and introduced extensive new disclosure requirements and antifraud provisions. The SEC's mission was to ensure fair markets and protect investors. The New Deal reformers also prohibited banks from engaging in both commercial and investment banking, and also restructured the utilities industry to prevent the kind of complicated holding company structures that Insull and others had used to mislead investors.[15]

By examining these scandals and the resulting legislation, a pattern emerges: "A shocking scandal galvanizes attention, neutralizing the influence that corporations have under ordinary circumstances; Congress quickly responds by enacting reforms that are demanded by ordinary Americans. It is these reforms that provide the federal regulatory infrastructure for the decades that follow."[16] It is this pattern that led directly to the creation of what is now thought of as compliance. Growing regulations, with increasing complexity required that companies find ways to ensure that they and their employees follow them.

The Development of Modern Compliance

Compliance has always been around, in some form or another, since the beginnings of organized commerce. Self-regulation of business stretches back to Middle Age merchant and craft guilds setting business standards for themselves.[17] Businesses have adopted their own codes of conduct, often in the wake of other companies' scandals. However, these types of self-imposed regulations are voluntary, informal, and relatively simple. As regulation grew in the middle of the 20th century, some companies had to find new ways to make sure they followed the law. They needed a more formal and structured way to deal with the complexity of modern regulation.

One school of thought is that modern compliance programs were first created after the electricity industry's antitrust scandal in the early 1960s. A widespread bid-rigging and price-fixing conspiracy involving electrical equipment manufacturers such as General Electric and Westinghouse resulted in dozens of individuals and corporations convicted of antitrust violations. The enormity of the case and related publicity of the first prison sentences handed down in the 70-year history of the Sherman Antitrust Act spurred the development of antitrust compliance codes of conduct and programs.[18] In this period, companies in the most heavily and complexly regulated industries began internal compliance efforts, particularly involving the above-mentioned antitrust issues. With further scandal, these compliance efforts would start to reach other industries.

It is often public outrage combined with governmental pressure that spurs business to adopt much-needed reforms. In 1977, Congress passed the Foreign Corrupt Practices Act (FCPA) that made it a crime to pay bribes to facilitate business in foreign countries. The FCPA was enacted after the Watergate investigation discovered that companies were paying bribes to foreign and domestic officials using funds maintained "off the books." The law makes it a crime for American companies, as well as individuals and organizations acting on their behalf, to bribe any foreign government official in return for assistance in obtaining, retaining, or directing business.[19]

The "bribery scandal, and the underlying corporate dysfunction it revealed, accelerated the widespread development of corporate ethical conduct codes."[20] Many companies did not have effective checks and balances in place to regulate their behavior and internal counsel was often unable or unwilling to give clear, pertinent legal advice. Management acted overzealously and took great risks, as short-term and personal concerns dominated corporate decision-making.[21] This coincided with greater public and scholarly attention on corporations' illegal and harmful acts, which led to further regulation.

The Outrageous $300 Hammer

In the early 1980s, the public was again shocked with news stories detailing questionable and highly inflated defense contracts. The United States military had purchased outrageously priced $300 hammers, $600 toilet seats, and other such items from defense contractors. Ultimately, billions of dollars of the defense budget were wasted. Then President Ronald Reagan established the Blue Ribbon Commission on Defense Management to investigate and make recommendations for improved compliance. The Packard Commission, as it was commonly called after its chairman, David Packard, of Hewlett-Packard fame, made numerous recommendations in its 1986 interim report to deter waste, fraud, and abuse in the procurement process. Among the findings were recommendations to "distribute copies of the code of ethics to all employees and new hires," and "make business conduct standards and typical business situations a regular part of the employees' experiences and performance evaluations."[22] It was also recommended that internal controls be implemented and monitored to ensure the codes and compliance. The compliance recommendations that the Packard Commission made for defense contractors were also applied to government agencies and other businesses.[23]

Unfortunately, fraud is a continuing plague and history often repeats itself. In August 2007, a South Carolina defense contractor pleaded guilty to defrauding the Pentagon of $20.5 million over a ten-year period. In one of the most egregious examples of a pervasive pattern of fraud and deceit, the contractor falsely billed $998,798 for two 19-cent washers.[24]

As a result of the findings of the Packard Commission, the Defense Industry Initiative (DII) on Business Ethics and Conduct was established in 1986 by 32 major defense contractors to improve compliance. As they state on their Web site, the DII is "pledged to adopt and implement a set of principles of business ethics and conduct that acknowledge and express their federal-procurement-related corporate responsibilities to the Department of Defense, as well as to the public, the Government, and to each other."[25] The DII has worked extensively throughout the defense industry for more than 20 years to design principles for achieving high standards of business conduct and ethics. Additional information on the DII can be found in Appendix C.

In 1987, the Report of the National Commission on Fraudulent Financial Reporting, also known as the Treadway Commission, "studied the financial reporting system in the United States to identify causal factors that lead to fraudulent financial reporting and steps to reduce its incidence."[26] The Commission's key recommendations fall into several categories including the tone at the top as set by senior management; the quality of internal accounting and audit functions; the roles of the board of directors and the audit committee; the independence of external auditors; the need for adequate resources; and enforcement enhancements.

During this period, there was a strong sense that corporations needed to be held accountable for their actions and that existing laws were not up to the task. This, of course, was an era encapsulated by the mantra from the movie *Wall Street* "greed is good, greed works" with hostile takeovers and insider trading fueling the perception that business was out of control. Even after years of regulation, critics complained that the business' behavior had not improved and if anything, had gotten less ethical. Conversely, other critics blamed the Reagan-era deregulation movement as the culprit for business woes.

This is not to say that all businesses in the 1980s ignored ethical concerns. Many companies followed the lead of the DII and the Treadway

Commission in developing compliance initiatives and made major strides. Companies began to tackle compliance issues head on, but unfortunately without significant guidance or oversight, many of these programs did not achieve their stated goals. As noted at the time, "[m]any companies and industries maintain[ed] their own internal compliance and inspection programs...Unfortunately, while they [were] capable of doing so, they [did] not self-regulate effectively."[27] Companies had compliance mechanisms in place; all they needed were appropriate incentives to make their programs effective.

Sentencing Guidelines for Organizational Crime

The ongoing development of corporate compliance programs now set the stage for 1991's United States Federal Sentencing Guidelines for Organizational Crime that held organizations accountable by applying "just punishment" for criminal actions and "deterrence" incentives to detect and prevent crime.[28] These Organizational Guidelines were a newer addition to the overall Sentencing Guidelines, as the original Guidelines did not address organizations. The United States Sentencing Commission (USSC) and many other commentators believed that due to the inherent characteristics of an organization, it needed to be treated differently than an average offender. The USSC recommended seven minimum requirements for an effective program to prevent and deter violations of law that encompassed self-reporting and acceptance of responsibility. The Sentencing Guidelines for Organizations gave companies a strong incentive to have an effective compliance program, either to receive a lessened sentence or mandated as part of probation.

The seven steps first recommended in 1991 and then significantly enhanced in 2004's Amendments to the Federal Sentencing Guidelines for Organizations (FSGO) strengthened corporate compliance and ethics programs of business organizations to mitigate punishment for criminal offenses.[29] There will be more discussion of the FSGO and effective compliance programs in Chapters 9 and 10. Appendix A contains a detailed summary of the Amendments to the FSGO as well as recommended action steps to achieve effective compliance.

Furthermore, the introduction of the FSGO helped to create an entirely new position, that of the Ethics and Compliance Officer.[30] These guidelines spurred the creation of new compliance programs or improvements to existing ones. Companies had both proper incentives and guidance in devising a formal structure to ensure compliance with the law, as they would suffer the consequences if they did not. This trend continued further with the Sarbanes-Oxley Act in 2002 and the aforementioned 2004 Amendments.

The corporate scandals that led to the creation of these two compliance enhancements, highlighted by the Enron and WorldCom failures, only serve to underscore the importance of understanding the history of these scandals and their consequences, so their mistakes will not be repeated.

CRACKING DOWN ON FRAUD

The government has strongly cracked down on corporate criminals. Thanks to public outrage at the multitude of scandals, and an apparent wave of misbehavior and malfeasance throughout corporate America, Congress and the Department of Justice have been given the ammunition to harshly deal with corporate crime. Jail sentences have gotten longer in the last few years. After the passage of Sarbanes-Oxley and the amendments to the FSGO, the average federal sentence faced by corporate executives has more than tripled.[31] A twenty-five year sentence for CEO Bernie Ebbers, as part of the massive WorldCom fraud, was found to be reasonable by an appeals court. The Court expressly stated that the twenty-five year sentence was not unreasonable in light of the new fraud sentencing guidelines authorized by Congress.[32]

Additionally, another court has found a nearly ten-year sentence for a fraud conviction reasonable, despite it being above the Sentencing Guidelines range for the offense. Even though a normal fraud conviction would not warrant that long a sentence, the court looked at the overall severity of the fraud, which involved over one hundred million dollars and an elaborate corruption scheme.[33] By considering the severity of the offense and the harm to those involved, as well as the threat to the public at large, courts can impose hefty sentences on those executives who violate the law. These high sentences show no signs of coming down any time soon, particularly now that all corporate leaders should be well aware of the government's anti-corporate crime campaign and the downfall of many of their criminally-minded peers. Ignorance is no excuse.

Oftentimes, when brought before a court of law to answer for their transgressions, corporate officials plead ignorance, with broad assertions of lack of criminal intent even in the face of repeated and unheeded factual red flags.[34] This ignorance flies in the face of common sense and a reality where corporate executives keep a close watch on their businesses. Moreover, pleading ignorance is not an effective defense. This type of defense will be effectively undercut by the use of a standard "ostrich" jury instruction. Essentially, the instruction tells the jury to determine the defendant's knowledge from all of the facts of the case and from their actions; knowledge may be inferred by a combination of suspicion and indifference to the truth. A person cannot avoid liability by deliberately averting their eyes and ignoring conduct they suspect to be improper.

Corporate leaders must be fully aware of the 2004 Federal Sentencing Guidelines for Organizations, which emphasize that an organization must both promote an organizational culture that encourages ethical conduct and exercises due diligence to prevent and detect criminal conduct. As corporate leaders' duties are well known and corporate crime is taken very seriously by prosecutors, they can expect stiff sentences, in an effort to create an atmosphere of general corporate crime deterrence and specific deterrence so that the defendants will never again engage in the behavior that got them into trouble in the first place.[35] Compliance Insight 3.1 is another sad story of the fall from grace of a corporate legend who forgot his teachings.

Given the high priority placed on prosecuting corporate crime by the Justice Department, it is important to understand the government's perspective when building a compliance program. Specifically, it is important to understand the consequences of compliance failure, as well as the ways an effective compliance program can, to some degree, mitigate potential damage. The Federal Sentencing Guidelines for Organizations specifically mention an effective compliance program as a factor that influences sentencing decisions. Additionally, an organization's compliance program and ethical culture also factor into charging decisions by the government and in negotiations between the opposing sides. The federal government has specifically laid out its policies and expectations in a series of memoranda. The words I wrote about the Thompson Memo in my previous book, *Executive Roadmap to Fraud Prevention and Internal Control*, still ring just as true when applied to the current McNulty Memo: "[B]y understanding how the government thinks about prosecuting businesses, organizations can implement robust compliance and fraud prevention programs to lessen their culpability... Every corporate executive and general counsel should be familiar with this government strategy memo. In fact, it should be read and reread by every CEO and CFO as a reminder of the consequences for a culture of noncompliance."[36]

THE McNULTY MEMORANDUM

In December 2006, the Justice Department issued the "McNulty Memo" outlining its revised principles of federal prosecutions of business organizations. This memo supplanted its predecessor, the famed "Thompson Memo." The 2003 Thompson Memo directly set forth goals of ensuring authentic cooperation with government investigations, rather than obfuscation and obstruction, and developing effective corporate governance procedures. By stressing the importance of cooperation and the euphemistically named "voluntary disclosures," the memo set the tone for corporate crime enforcement.

COMPLIANCE INSIGHT 3.1: EVEN A LEGEND IS NOT ABOVE COMPLIANCE

Normally, a retailer worries about shrinkage from shoplifting and theft by employees. Sometimes, it is not just the lower-level employees who commit these crimes, but also executives paid millions of dollars a year and responsible for corporate oversight.

Thomas Coughlin was once one of Wal-Mart's most revered and respected leaders. A legend at the company, a close friend and hunting partner of Wal-Mart founder Sam Walton, Coughlin was also one of Walton's protégés. Over a 27-year career, Coughlin worked in almost all aspects of the company's business, eventually rising to be the company's number two executive.[a] But, even someone who did sizable charitable work and inspired high regard from both executives and rank-and-file employees can still succumb to greed and arrogance.

Coughlin stole up to $500,000 from the retailing giant by submitting false expense reports and by misusing company gift cards. In 2004, Coughlin requested 51 $100 Wal-Mart gift cards, to be given as prizes to "All-Star" employees. Instead of giving them out, Coughlin used them himself to pay for items such as puppy chow, vodka, three twelve-gauge shotguns, CDs, contact lenses, and food, even though he made over $6 million a year. In other instances, he directed employees to file false expense reports and pocketed the money to pay for personal expenses. Coughlin made the purchases, and then had his employees submit the purchases as legitimate business expenditures. Wal-Mart found questionable transactions totaling between $100,000 and $500,000 over a period of seven years; because the transactions were masked as legitimate business expenses, internal investigators had trouble figuring out an exact dollar loss. Coughlin defrauded the company to pay for dog care, hunting vacations, custom-made alligator boots, and a camouflage hunting vehicle.[b]

This whole scheme came to light thanks to an alert Wal-Mart employee. In January 2005, after Coughlin tried to use one of the gift cards, a sales clerk called the home office asking for help in processing the transaction. A home office staffer noticed the card was supposed to be used by "All-Star" employees only and "could not understand why Coughlin would be trying to redeem it."[c] The employee alerted the company, who began an internal investigation. Wal-Mart tracked Coughlin's purchases and eventually led to the discovery of the fraud and to Coughlin's resignation. Wal-Mart then rescinded Coughlin's retirement plan, froze millions of dollars in benefits, and sued him to recoup the lost money.[d]

In 2006, Coughlin pleaded guilty in federal court to charges of wire fraud and tax evasion, while one of his deputies pleaded guilty to three counts of wire fraud.[e] Wal-Mart's former vice chairman was sentenced to 27 months of home confinement and five years probation, and was ordered to pay $400,000 in restitution. The judge, in meting out the sentence, said Coughlin had already been punished by the publicity surrounding the case and the possibility of losing his retirement benefits.[f] The government appealed the sentence as too lenient and a federal appeals court agreed. The court said giving Coughlin home detention rather than prison "does not fall within the range of reasonableness." As of the writing of this book, a new sentencing hearing has not been scheduled.

What can be learned from this betrayal? This illustrates both the importance of monitoring and of vigilance. Coughlin's scheme was detected by an observant and resourceful employee who recognized something was amiss and alerted the proper individuals in the company. However, it should be noted that it was only luck that Coughlin was caught when he was. Had the sales clerk not called the home office, who knows how much longer the fraud would have continued? Furthermore, while Wal-Mart maintains an extensive internal control system, it did not appear to be focused as strongly on higher levels of the corporation, as the system did not flag the false transactions. This may be because of Coughlin's high stature and reputation. As he had a great deal of authority, these transactions were not questioned. This is something all companies must be aware of. Even the most senior and respected employees could be found to be defrauding the company, so compliance programs must monitor all levels of the organization equally in order to be fully effective.

Coughlin also pressured other Wal-Mart employees to assist him in his scheme. Fearful of being fired, they *neither* stood up to him *nor* reported his actions. A company must put into place measures to allow for anonymous reporting of unethical behavior, but more importantly a company must foster an environment where a whistleblower knows he or she will not be retaliated against for coming forward. All the hotlines in the world are useless if an employee feels that management will punish him or her for reporting the misdeeds of a valuable member of the organization.

The sad irony here is that Coughlin should have known better. One of his first positions in Wal-Mart was as a loss prevention officer, so he dealt first hand with theft and the impact of poor ethical conduct. As a tough-minded Wal-Mart executive once said, "Anyone who is taking money from associates and shareholders ought to be shot...That greed will catch up with you."[g] The executive who said this? Thomas Coughlin.

---

[a]James Bandler and Ann Zimmerman, "A Wal-Mart Legend's Trail of Deceit," *Wall Street Journal*, April 8, 2005, A1.
[b]Ibid; James Bandler and Ann Zimmerman, "How Gift Cards Helped Trip Up Wal-Mart's Aide," *Wall Street Journal*, July 15, 2005, B1; "Former Wal-Mart Exec Sentenced for Theft," *Associated Press*, August 8, 2006.
[c]James Bandler and Ann Zimmerman, "How Gift Cards Helped Trip Up Wal-Mart's Aide," *Wall Street Journal*, July 15, 2005, B1.
[d]"Ex-Exec's Benefits Frozen Amid Probe," *Seattle Times*, April 16, 2005, E4; Ann Zimmerman and Kris Hudson, "Wal-Mart Sues Ex-Vice Chairman," *Wall Street Journal*, January 7, 2006, A1.
[e]James Bandler, "Former No. 2 at Wal-Mart Set to Plead Guilty," *Wall Street Journal* January 7, 2006, A1.
[f]"Former Wal-Mart Exec Sentenced for Theft," *Associated Press*, August 8, 2006.
[g]James Bandler and Ann Zimmerman, "A Wal-Mart Legend's Trail of Deceit," *Wall Street Journal*, April 8, 2005, A1.

This newer memo intended to alleviate many of the concerns engendered by application of the previous memo's principles while still maintaining stiff penalties for offenders and a strong anti-corporate crime outlook. The Thompson Memo's policies, while recognized for their effectiveness, faced criticism, particularly from corporations and the defense bar, for their rigid application and sometimes heavy handed tactics from Justice Department lawyers. Critics felt the government had too much power and sometimes unchecked influence over defendant corporations. However, the most persistent criticism involved the pressure put on organizations to waive the attorney-client privilege.[37]

The attorney-client privilege protects confidential communications between an attorney and a client or prospective client. An ancient legal protection, the privilege allows for frank and open discussions with an attorney without fear of the information becoming public. The Thompson Memo told prosecutors, when assessing the level of cooperation, to consider the corporation's willingness to waive the attorney-client privilege with respect to its internal investigations and communications between employees and counsel.[38]

These disclosures were a boon for the government, and often led to damaging material being turned over. Corporations had to do everything possible to demonstrate their cooperation was "authentic," by turning over significant amounts of privileged information and sharing all the results of internal investigations, or else risk the possibility of an indictment which could well destroy the company.[39] Waiving the privilege also opened up the door for future litigation, as those future litigants would have access to the information provided to the government, which they otherwise would not. Additionally, the pressure to turn over culpable employees has led to concerns that corporations, in an attempt to avoid the dreaded indictment and to insulate themselves from liability, will paint the employees as having gone "rogue" and will offer up lower and mid-level executives as scapegoats. This may lead to termination and public humiliation of individuals who would not be seen as culpable had a more precise and thorough investigation been done.[40]

The McNulty Memo took these criticisms to heart, as it announced changes in Department of Justice (DOJ) policy that aimed to placate corporate executives, the defense bar, as well as concerned citizens and law enforcement personnel. As then-Deputy Attorney General Paul McNulty stated in the cover letter to the memo:

We have heard from responsible corporate officials recently about the challenges they face in discharging their duties to the corporation while responding in a meaningful way to a government investigation. Many of those associated with the corporate legal community have expressed concern that our practices may be discouraging full and candid communications between corporate employees and legal counsel.[41]

In recognition of these challenges, McNulty announced a shift in DOJ policy, away from regular requests for "voluntary disclosure" of privileged materials. Instead of regular, blanket requests for waivers, henceforth waiver requests would be rare and only done as specifically needed. "Prosecutors may only request waiver of attorney-client or work product protections when there is a legitimate need for the privileged information to fulfill their law enforcement obligations."[42] A legitimate need must go beyond convenience or the desirability of the information; it must be something that is needed and cannot be otherwise obtained, given the totality of the circumstances. Now, to obtain privileged material a prosecutor must make a special request to and get approval from his or her respective United States Attorney.[43] Waiver will not be a prerequisite to a finding that a company has cooperated with a government investigation. Of course, waiver is looked upon favorably and is still encouraged. A corporation volunteering to provide privileged information without being asked could reap great benefits. As George Stamboulidis, former Chief of the Long Island Division of the U.S. Attorney's Office for the Eastern District of New York and current head of the White Collar Defense and Corporate Investigations practice group at the law firm of Baker Hostetler, stated in an article he coauthored, "Something as seemingly trivial as relieving the prosecutor of the burden of submitting a memo to her boss for authority [to request privileged information], could prompt her to recommend a lighter punishment or forgo the indictment entirely."[44]

Despite some adjustments, the overall Justice Department policy remains intact. Cooperation with government investigations remains of paramount importance, as prosecutors will not tolerate obstruction or cover-up efforts. A high value is placed on companies' internal investigation. Rather than "doing the government's job for it," these investigations are the most effective way to combat violations. A quicker response can be had, rather than waiting for a government investigation. Moreover, an internal response is superior and more effective at catching misconduct than the government and regulatory action.[45]

Prosecutors are given wide latitude in making charging decisions—the decisions are left to their discretion, but the memo provides general guidance for handling of corporate crimes, listing factors to be evaluated in charging decisions. Part of the decision involves analysis of the corporation's *pre-existing* compliance program and its remedial actions. Compliance Insight 3.2 describes the factors to be considered by prosecutors when potentially charging a corporation with criminal violations.

Beyond outlining Justice Department policy, the McNulty Memo also gives executives and corporations guidance on what to expect and what to do should a violation be uncovered. When examining this guidance, the value of a strong compliance program becomes apparent. As outlined above, cooperation is highly valued. In fact, it is in a corporation's best interest to cooperate. How many companies have been damaged not so much by their misconduct, but rather by their efforts to cover it up? This cooperation is crucial to rooting out the true culprits, as the corporation itself is in the best position to discover and evaluate relevant evidence. In return, the company may well receive more lenient treatment from the government, or at least be in a better position to negotiate a more favorable plea bargain. The corporation must be willing to identify the culprits within the corporation, even if it includes senior management.[46] If a company

COMPLIANCE INSIGHT 3.2: CHARGING A CORPORATION: FACTORS TO BE CONSIDERED

The McNulty Memo lists nine factors specifically to be considered by prosecutors when assessing the criminal culpability of corporations, in addition to the typical considerations, such as the strength of the evidence and the likelihood of conviction. In conducting an investigation, determining whether to bring charges, and negotiating plea agreements, prosecutors must consider:

- The nature and seriousness of the offense, including the risk of harm to the public, and applicable policies and priorities, if any, governing the prosecution of corporations for particular categories of crime;

- the pervasiveness of wrongdoing within the corporation, including the complicity in, or condoning of, the wrongdoing by corporate management;

- the corporation's history of similar conduct, including prior criminal, civil, and regulatory enforcement actions against it;

- the corporation's timely and voluntary disclosure of wrongdoing and its willingness to cooperate in the investigation of its agent;

- the existence and adequacy of the corporation's *pre-existing* compliance program;

- the corporation's remedial actions, including any efforts to implement an effective corporate compliance program or to improve an existing one, to replace responsible management, to discipline or terminate wrongdoers, to pay restitution, and to cooperate with the relevant government agencies;

- collateral consequences, including disproportionate harm to shareholders, pension holders and employees not proven personally culpable and impact on the public arising from the prosecution;

- the adequacy of the prosecution of individuals responsible for the corporation's malfeasance; and

- the adequacy of remedies such as civil or regulatory enforcement actions.[a]

---

[a]Paul J. McNulty, "Principles of Federal Prosecution of Business Organizations," *Department of Justice*, December 2006 ("McNulty Memo"), 4, www.usdoj.gov/dag/speech/2006/mcnulty_memo.pdf.

appears to be shielding culpable employees, it will be very damaging to the company's position.[47] While it may be a natural instinct to want to protect them, why should a company do so? These executives are people who have damaged the company and its reputation, and defied their fiduciary duties by putting their own interests ahead of the company's. In the end, a company's actions must be able to demonstrate to the prosecutor's satisfaction "that the corporation's focus is on the integrity and credibility of its remedial and disciplinary measures rather than on the protection of wrongdoers."[48]

The existence of a compliance program, prior to the alleged misconduct, is a factor to be analyzed by prosecutors throughout the investigatory process. It is a factor that cuts both ways: the commission of an offense in the face of a compliance program may suggest that management does not fully support the program, or a strong program may demonstrate a substantial and consistent good faith effort to achieve compliance, which will benefit the company's chances.[49] Compliance Insight 3.3 details the factors critical to the government's evaluation of a compliance program.

Even though the government may reduce a sentence based on an effective compliance program, a company can't count on it.[50] The main role of a compliance program should be to root out misconduct and seek to prevent it, rather than serve as a mere negotiation tactic at the prosecutorial bargaining table. It should never be what the McNulty Memo calls a "paper program." A prosecutor will examine the company's true commitment to compliance, beyond the superficial appearance of the program. Among the factors that will be examined are: the design and implementation of the program; sufficient staff to audit, document, analyze, and utilize the results of the company's compliance efforts; whether the company's employees are adequately informed about them and whether they are convinced of the company's commitment to it.[51] "This will enable the prosecutor to make an informed decision as to whether the corporation has adopted and implemented a truly effective compliance program that, when consistent with other federal law enforcement policies, may result in a decision to charge only the corporation's employees and agents."[52]

EVALUATING THE SEABOARD CRITERIA IN MITIGATING ENFORCEMENT ACTIONS

One of the benefits of an effective compliance program is the strong possibility of reduced criminal liability in case of a compliance failure by self-reporting to government regulators and prosecutors. In some instances, self-reporting can even result in no action being taken by the authorities against either the culpable company or official. This was the case with

COMPLIANCE INSIGHT 3.3: CRITICAL FACTORS IN EVALUATING AN EFFECTIVE COMPLIANCE PROGRAM

The Justice Department understands that no program, no matter how well-designed or well-supported, could possibly prevent or catch every potential violation. Following this understanding, the McNulty Memo counsels prosecutors in their evaluation of compliance programs to look beneath the surface of a program to assess whether it is merely a "paper program" or whether the company demonstrates a true commitment to compliance. Fundamentally, a prosecutor should ask: "Is the corporation's compliance program well designed?" and "Does the corporation's compliance program work?"[a] In answering these questions, prosecutors must consider:[b]

- Comprehensiveness of the compliance program.
- Extent and pervasiveness of the criminal conduct.
- Number and level of the corporate employees involved.
- Seriousness, duration, and frequency of the misconduct.
- Any remedial action taken by the corporation, including restitution, disciplinary action, and revisions to corporate compliance programs.
- Promptness of any disclosure of wrongdoing to the government and the corporation's cooperation in the investigation.
- Effectiveness of corporate governance mechanisms in detecting and preventing misconduct, including looking at the independence of directors, the amount and quality of information they receive, the quality of the corporation's internal audit function, and the board's adherence to the *Caremark* requirements of a reasonable and sufficient information and reporting system.[c]

---

[a]Paul J. McNulty, "Principles of Federal Prosecution of Business Organizations," *Department of Justice*, December 2006 ("McNulty Memo"), 14, www.usdoj.gov/dag/speech/2006/mcnulty_memo.pdf.
[b]Ibid.
[c]For more information on the *Caremark* decision and its compliance impact, please see "The *Caremark* Case" section in Chapter 4.

Seaboard Corporation beginning with an internal investigation in 1999 and ending with a SEC Report of Investigation and related findings in 2001.

Seaboard Corporation (Seaboard) is a multi-faceted international business involved in food production and processing, commodity trading, containerized shipping, and electrical power production. The company is headquartered in Shawnee Mission, Kansas with over 10,000 employees in worldwide locations. Founded in 1918, it is a publicly traded company on the American Stock Exchange as well as a Fortune 100 company with annual net sales in excess of $2.6 billion. On its homepage, Seaboard states: "We are committed to deliver extraordinary value to our customers across all of our business lines with the highest degree of integrity, honesty, and sound business judgment."

In the introduction to their Code of Ethics site, they further state, "Seaboard Corporation, its subsidiaries and affiliates, strictly adhere to the principles of fairness and ethical conduct. We are committed to the highest standards of personal and professional conduct."[53] Seaboard has a relatively short code that consists of one page plus an addendum of five additional pages on conflict of interest and insider trading policies and prohibitions. Although short, it obviously works as evidenced by the company's actions in an internal probe and the subsequent very positive SEC determination.

In late 1999, Seaboard began an investigation of a division controller for booking improper entries in the financial statements that overstated deferred costs and understated expenses. A concern raised over these unusual entries by other employees resulted in an inquiry by the internal audit department. The controller subsequently confessed to her manager in July 2000 that she had been making these false accounting entries for five years resulting in over $7 million in accounting discrepancies.

Seaboard's management quickly notified the board of directors of the incident and that its financial reports had been misstated due to the controller's actions. The board retained an outside law firm to conduct a thorough investigation of the entire matter. In short order, the controller was fired as were two other employees who failed to adequately supervise her. Seaboard issued a public statement that it would be restating its financial statements for a five-year period due to the controller's action, and self-reported the matter to the SEC.[54]

The SEC conducted its own investigation and confirmed the findings of Seaboard's internal investigation that the controller had violated securities laws. Seaboard fully cooperated and assisted in the SEC investigation. As the SEC stated in its Report of Investigation dated October 23, 2001:

The company pledged and gave complete cooperation to our staff. It provided the staff with all information relevant to the underlying violations. Among other things, the company produced the details of its internal investigation, including notes and transcripts of interviews with Meredith (the controller) and others; and it did not invoke the attorney-client privilege, work product protection or other privileges or protections with respect to any facts uncovered in the investigation.

The company also strengthened its financial reporting processes to address Meredith's conduct–developing a detailed closing process for the subsidiary's accounting personnel, consolidating subsidiary accounting functions under a parent company CPA, hiring three new CPAs for the accounting department responsible for preparing the subsidiary's financial statements, redesigning the subsidiary's minimum annual audit requirements, and requiring the parent company's controller to interview and approve all senior accounting personnel in its subsidiaries' reporting processes.[55]

As a result, the SEC decided not to take any action against Seaboard. The SEC explained how the company's swift and transparent actions including self-reporting, benefited investors and the SEC's enforcement program. As a result of this case, the SEC issued four key factors and related criteria that they would consider in determining whether or not to "credit self-policing, self-reporting, remediation, and cooperation" in deciding whether to take reduced action or no action against others in future enforcement actions.[56] The following are the SEC's four key factors in this regard:

- **Self-policing:** The establishment and ongoing maintenance of an effective compliance program strongly supported by executive management and the board of directors where issues and allegations are properly escalated and fully investigated.
- **Self-reporting:** As a result of effective self-policing and determination of violation of the code of conduct, the organization then promptly and effectively discloses the violation(s) to the public, government regulators, and law enforcement as appropriate.
- **Remediation:** The appropriate disciplinary process for those found to have violated the organization's code of conduct as well as the strengthening of internal controls to mitigate repeat misconduct or other violations.
- **Cooperation:** Full and complete cooperation with the SEC and other law enforcement agencies including providing all relevant documentary and testimonial evidence related to the violations and investigation at hand.

The following are the SEC's related criteria and questions to be asked and answered by an organization:

1. What is the nature of the misconduct involved? Did it result from inadvertence, honest mistake, simple negligence, reckless or deliberate indifference to indicia of wrongful conduct, willful misconduct, or unadorned venality? Were the company's auditors misled?
2. How did the misconduct arise? Is it the result of pressure placed on employees to achieve specific results, or a tone of lawlessness set by those in control of the company? What compliance procedures were in place to prevent the misconduct now uncovered? Why did those procedures fail to stop or inhibit the wrongful conduct?
3. Where in the organization did the misconduct occur? How high up in the chain of command was knowledge of, or participation in, the misconduct? Did senior personnel participate in, or turn a blind eye toward, obvious indicia of misconduct? How systematic was the behavior? Is it symptomatic of the way the entity does business, or was it isolated?
4. How long did the misconduct last? Was it a one-quarter, or one-time event, or did it last several years? In the case of a public company, did the misconduct occur before the company went public? Did it facilitate the company's ability to go public?
5. How much harm has the misconduct inflicted upon investors and other corporate constituencies? Did the share price of the company's stock drop significantly upon its discovery and disclosure?
6. How was the misconduct detected and who uncovered it?
7. How long after discovery of the misconduct did it take to implement an effective response?
8. What steps did the company take upon learning of the misconduct? Did the company immediately stop the misconduct? Are persons responsible for any misconduct still with the company? If so, are they still in the same positions? Did the company promptly, completely, and effectively disclose the existence of the misconduct to the public, to regulators, and to self-regulators? Did the company cooperate completely with the appropriate regulatory and law enforcement bodies? Did the company identify what additional related misconduct is likely to have occurred? Did the company take steps to identify the extent of damage to investors and other corporate constituencies? Did the company appropriately recompense those adversely affected by the conduct?
9. What processes did the company follow to resolve many of these issues and ferret out necessary information? Were the Audit Committee and the Board of Directors fully informed? If so, when?

10. Did the company commit to learn the truth, fully, and expeditiously? Did it do a thorough review of the nature, extent, origins, and consequences of the conduct and related behavior? Did management, the board or committee consisting solely of outside directors oversee the review? Did company employees or outside persons perform the review? If outside persons, had they done other work for the company? Where the review was conducted by outside counsel, had management previously engaged such counsel? Were scope limitations placed on the review? If so, what were they?

11. Did the company promptly make available to our staff the results of its review and provide sufficient documentation reflecting its response to the situation? Did the company identify possible violative conduct and evidence with sufficient precision to facilitate prompt enforcement actions against those who violated the law? Did the company produce a thorough and probing written report detailing the findings of its review? Did the company voluntarily disclose information our staff did not directly request and otherwise might not have uncovered? Did the company ask its employees to cooperate with our staff and make all reasonable efforts to secure such cooperation?

12. What assurances are there that the conduct is unlikely to recur? Did the company adopt and ensure enforcement of new and more effective internal controls and procedures designed to prevent a recurrence of the misconduct? Did the company provide our staff with sufficient information for it to evaluate the company's measures to correct the situation and ensure that the conduct does not recur?

13. Is the company the same company in which the misconduct occurred, or has it changed through a merger or bankruptcy reorganization?[57]

The SEC's approach in the Seaboard case underscores the importance of an effective compliance program and the rewarding of good behavior. The many aspects of Seaboard's compliance program worked well beginning with the escalation of questionable accounting practices by vigilant employees, the response of internal audit, involvement of management, an internal investigation, referral to the board, disciplinary action for those culpable, self-reporting, cooperation with the government, and then correcting deficiencies and enhancing internal controls. There is no guarantee that this approach and result will happen in all instances of compliance failures but the precedence is there. The SEC's four key factors and related criteria are additional tools in the compliance toolkit to be used by every organization in enhancing compliance.

NOTES

1. David A. Skeel, Jr., "Icarus and American Corporate Regulation," *The Business Lawyer*, November 2005, 155.
2. Ibid., 156.
3. Robert G. Caldwell, "The Social Significance of American Panics," *Scientific Monthly*, April 1932, 303.
4. David Skeel, *Icarus in the Boardroom: The Fundamental Flaws in Corporate America and Where they Came From*, (New York: Oxford University Press, 2005), 40. Like Enron, Cooke used questionable financial practices to fund his supported venture and to keep it afloat. Furthering the Enron connection, Skeel compares Jay Cooke to Ken Lay, noting that Cooke had close ties at the time to President Ulysses S. Grant. In fact, Grant was at Cooke's house the night the ventures collapsed.
5. Skeel, "Icarus and American Corporate Regulation," 160.
6. Ibid, 165.
7. The idea of government regulating business, though passé nowadays, was in fact a radical notion at the turn of the century. This was the so-called *Lochner* era, named for a Supreme Court decision striking down a New York law that limited the hours one could work, on the basis that it interfered with economic rights, even though it was intended to prevent worker exploitation. Economic rights were treated then just the same as the rights of speech, religion, and so forth, and were just as inviolate. Courts responded fiercely against any attempt by reformers to regulate business conduct.
8. President Theodore Roosevelt's State of the Union Address, December 2, 1902, 53, www2.hn.psu.edu/faculty/jmanis/poldocs/uspressu/SUaddressTRoosevelt.pdf.
9. M.L. Ramsay, *Pyramids of Power*, (New York: Da Capo Press, 1975), 45–47.
10. Ramsay, *Pyramids of Power*, 90–94.
11. Hon. Richard D. Cudahy and William Henderson, "From Insull to Enron: Corporate (Re)Regulation After the Rise and Fall of Two Energy Icons," *Energy Law Journal*, March 2005, 73.
12. Skeel, *Icarus in the Boardroom*, 88.
13. Skeel, "Icarus and American Corporate Regulation," 156.
14. Ramsay, *Pyramids of Power*, 75.
15. Skeel, "Icarus and American Corporate Regulation," 160–61. Unfortunately, due to changing times and loosening regulations, Enron was able to do precisely that.

16. Ibid., 162.
17. Charles J. Walsh and Alissa Pyrich, "Corporate Compliance Programs as a Defence to Criminal Liability: Can a Corporation Save Its Soul?," *Rutgers Law Review*, Winter 1995, 649.
18. Stephany Watson, "Fostering Positive Corporate Culture in the Post-Enron Era," *Tennessee Journal of Business Law*, Fall 2004, 12–13.
19. Martin T. Biegelman and Joel T. Bartow, *Executive Roadmap to Fraud Prevention and Internal Control: Creating a Culture of Compliance*, (Hoboken, NJ: John Wiley & Sons, 2006), 318.
20. Walsh and Pyrich, *Corporate Compliance Programs*, 653.
21. Ibid.
22. Dr. John D. Copeland, "The Tyson Story: Building an Effective Ethics and Compliance Program," *Drake Journal of Agricultural Law*, Winter 2000, 315.
23. Watson, "Fostering Positive Corporate Culture," 13.
24. Renae Merle, "$998,798 Paid for Two 19-Cent Washers," *Seattle Times*, August 17, 2007, A17.
25. Defense Industry Initiative on Business Ethics and Conduct, www.dii .org/Statement.htm.
26. National Commission on Fraudulent Financial Reporting, *Report of the National Commission on Fraudulent Financial Reporting*, (October, 1987), 1, ("The Treadway Report"), www.coso.org/publications/ NCFFR_Part_1.htm.
27. Nancy Frank and Michael Lombness, *Controlling Corporate Illegality: The Regulatory Justice System*, (Cincinnati: Anderson Publishing Co., 1988), 162.
28. Supplemental Report on Sentencing Guidelines for Organizations, (August 30, 1991), 6, www.ussc.gov/corp/OrgGL83091.PDF.
29. Biegelman and Bartow, *Executive Roadmap*, 50.
30. Diana E. Murphy, "The Federal Sentencing Guidelines for Organizations: A Decade of Promoting Compliance and Ethics", *Iowa Law Review*, 2002, 710, www.ussc.gov/corp/Murphy1.pdf.
31. *United States v. Caputo*, No. 03 CR 0126 (N. Dist. IL 2006), 24.
32. *United States v. Ebbers*, 458 F.3d 110, 129–30 (2d Cir. 2006).
33. *United States v. Leahy*, 464 F. 3d 773 (7th Cir. 2006).
34. *Caputo*, 27.
35. *Caputo*, 27–28.
36. Biegelman and Bartow, *Executive Roadmap*, 87–88.
37. George A. Stamboulidis and Jamie Pfeffer, "A Quarter Century after *Upjohn*, in Our Current Culture of Waiver, Do Privileges Still Exist?" Coursebook for the 21st Annual National Institute on White Collar Crime, 2007, P-37, www.bakerlaw.com/PublicDocs/News/Articles/

LITIGATION/ABA%20Stamboulidis%20Pfeffer%20March%202007 .pdf.

38. Larry D. Thompson, "Principles of Federal Prosecution of Business Organizations," Department of Justice, January 2003, 37–38, www .usdoj.gov/dag/ctft/corporate_guidelines.htm.

39. Stamboulidis and Pfeffer, "A Quarter Century After Upjohn," P-37–38.

40. Christopher A. Wray and Robert K. Hur, "Corporate Criminal Prosecution in a Post-Enron World: The Thompson Memo in Theory and Practice," *American Criminal Law Review*, Summer 2006, 1181–82. One of this article's authors, Christopher Wray, is in a unique position to critique the Thompson Memo. He worked in the Justice Department as Principal Associate Deputy Attorney General when the Memo was released. In fact, Thompson's preamble to the Memo states that all comments regarding the Memo be directed to Wray.

41. Paul J. McNulty, "Principles of Federal Prosecution of Business Organizations," Department of Justice, December 2006 (the "*McNulty Memo*"), www.usdoj.gov/dag/speech/2006/mcnulty_memo.pdf.

42. *McNulty Memo*, 7.

43. Waiver requests are divided into two categories. Category I covers purely factual information, which may or may not be privileged, relating to the underlying misconduct. This includes factual interview memoranda, timelines, organizational charts created by counsel, witness statements, copies of key documents, etc. When analyzing the request, the United States Attorney must consult with the Assistant Attorney General for the Criminal Division before approving it. Category II, which includes attorney-client communications and non-factual attorney work product, is only reached when the purely factual information available provides an incomplete basis to conduct a thorough investigation. This type of information includes legal advice given to the corporation before, during, and after the underlying misconduct. Category II information should only be sought in rare circumstances, and will be available in even fewer cases. Before requesting it, the U.S. Attorney must receive written authorization from the Deputy Attorney General. *McNulty Memo*, 8–10.

44. Stamboulidis and Pfeffer, "A Quarter Century After Upjohn," P-49.

45. Wray and Hur, "Corporate Criminal Prosecution," 1171.

46. *McNulty Memo*, 7.

47. Ibid., 11.

48. Ibid., 15.

49. Ibid., 12–13.

50. *See* Frank O. Bowman III, "Drifting Down the Dnieper with Prince Potemkin: Some Skeptical Reflections About the Place of Compliance

Programs in Federal Criminal Sentencing," *Wake Forest Law Review*, Fall 2004, 685 (questioning the effectiveness of compliance programs, comparing them to "overpriced insurance," and arguing that they have little to no impact on sentencing, and almost never directly lead to a reduced sentence).

51. *McNulty Memo*, 14.
52. Ibid.
53. Seaboard Corporation, www.seaboardcorp.com/about.aspx.
54. *In the Matter of Gisela de Leon-Meredith, Respondent*, Securities and Exchange Act of 1934 Release No. 44970, October 23, 2001, United States Securities and Exchange Commission, www.sec.gov/litigation/admin/34-44970.htm.
55. Securities and Exchange Act of 1934 Release No. 44969, Report of Investigation, October 23, 2001, United States Securities and Exchange Commission, www.sec.gov/litigation/admin/34-44970.htm.
56. Ibid.
57. Ibid.

CHAPTER 4

Caremark and Sarbanes-Oxley: Enhancing Compliance

"Glass, china, and reputation are easily cracked, and never mended well."

Benjamin Franklin

There are many reasons to have a world-class compliance program. One important reason is to monitor and positively influence behavior in a company to achieve desired results. Some of these reasons reflect practical realities, that not all employees will independently follow the rules, and that the presence of bad employees, if left unchecked, can negatively influence others around them. Other reasons reflect the legal framework in which companies must operate. The law, by placing a premium on solid corporate governance, provides many reasons to operate a truly effective compliance program. As discussed in the previous chapter, the Federal Sentencing Guidelines for Organizations explicitly mandate that prosecutors take into account the existence or lack thereof of an effective compliance program, providing opportunities for reduced sentences if such a program exists. Beyond the Guidelines, other laws and regulations give companies strong incentives and reason to put a compliance program in place or to ensure that an existing program is as effective and runs as smoothly as it can be.

In fact, there are situations where a company is legally required to have a compliance program and the company's leadership can be liable for the failure to put one in place. Court decisions, in conjunction with strong efforts by the federal government, have moved the issue of compliance to the forefront of corporate law. By establishing stiffer penalties for violators and in stepping up enforcement of existing laws and regulations, the legal system has created an even greater incentive for compliance. Recognizing that existing rules have not fully stemmed the tide of corporate scandal, the government and courts have continued to push forward with strict interpretations of the law, and will continue to do so, in an effort to change this behavior.

Compliance failures can subject a company and its directors to substantial penalties and legal actions by the government and by shareholders. Court decisions, as reflected in the seminal *Caremark* case and in the last decade's worth of corporate law jurisprudence, have put directors' actions under the microscope, and if they are found not to have complied with the law, they can suffer serious consequences. Courts have focused on the good faith, or many times the lack thereof, in directors' actions. The duty of good faith by corporate leaders is an important part of the analysis, playing a large role in the courts' decisions. Furthermore, stock exchanges such as the New York Stock Exchange and NASDAQ have enacted corporate governance rules as a listing prerequisite. A company that does not meet these requirements will not be allowed to be traded on these exchanges.[1] Additionally, federal laws, including the Sarbanes-Oxley Act, mandate a complex compliance structure for publicly-traded companies.

Other laws, such as the USA PATRIOT Act, establish stringent requirements for companies, requirements that can only be met through the efforts of a compliance program. The Foreign Corrupt Practices Act (FCPA) falls into this category. Laws such as these are important in setting out a framework for a company's own compliance programs. By following what judges have said in court cases, a company can put itself in a safe harbor by meeting these minimum standards. These laws set out the standards for a company, in many cases explicitly stating what the minimum requirements for a compliance program are. A company must be aware of what is permissible and what is not—not always an easy feat. This is particularly important when a company does business overseas or has offices in foreign countries. United States-based companies must be acutely aware of the FCPA and the PATRIOT Act anti-money laundering provisions, both of which are heavily enforced by the government. The FCPA, in particular, has gotten stepped up enforcement while at the same time court decisions have extended its reach and what conduct can be prosecuted. The FCPA is discussed at length in Chapter 6 while more information on anti-money laundering is in Chapter 7. With all of these trends, a company has almost no choice but to focus on compliance.

THE *CAREMARK* CASE

One of the most important court decisions in this area is the 1996 *Caremark* case. While the case is over a decade old by now, and did not have as great an impact as intended, it is still an important legal milestone. As a bit of background, *In Re: Caremark International, Inc. Derivative Litigation (Caremark)* involved a lawsuit by shareholders against Caremark, a health care services company. The shareholders, in their derivative suit, alleged violations of federal and state laws and regulations by Caremark employees, including illegal payments to doctors to distribute specific Caremark-marketed drugs. These payments, which amounted to kickbacks, led to serious investigation and indictments against the company and two of its officers, among others. Following this, the shareholders filed suit in Delaware; due to the large number of companies incorporated in that state, Delaware's courts are often at the forefront of corporate law. The crux of the suit alleged that the directors failed to appropriately monitor their employees, and as a result the company suffered significant financial losses, including civil and criminal fines. The shareholders could not proceed on the typical theories of a breach of the duty of care in the directors' actions or for a conflict of interest, as the evidence did not support either approach. Instead, the suit alleged liability for failure to monitor. Essentially, the case asked, "What is the board's responsibility with respect to the organization and monitoring of the enterprise to assure that the corporation functions within the law to achieve its purpose?"[2]

Chancellor William Allen of the Delaware Court of Chancery recognized this theory, novel at the time, as a legally valid one. In short, directors have a responsibility to make a good faith effort to ensure that the law was being followed and to take measures towards that end. In beginning, to answer the question raised by the Caremark shareholders, Chancellor Allen noted the increasing role of compliance, via federal law, in the corporate world. "Modernly, this question has been given special importance by an increasing tendency, especially under federal law, to employ the criminal law to assure corporate compliance with external legal requirements, including environmental, financial, employee and product safety, as well as assorted other health and safety regulations....The [Federal Sentencing] Guidelines offer powerful incentives for corporations today to have in place compliance programs to detect violations of law, promptly report violations to appropriate public officials when discovered, and to take prompt, voluntary remedial efforts."[3] While federal regulation of corporations through criminal prosecution has become well-established since *Caremark*, particularly in the post-Enron era, and the Guidelines' link to compliance is well-known, Chancellor Allen's words still ring true today.

Caremark began to lay out the standards against which the directors would be judged, and how the monitoring function requirement may be fulfilled. "[C]orporate boards may satisfy their obligation to be reasonably informed concerning the corporation, [by] assuring themselves that information and reporting systems exist in the organization that are reasonably designed to provide to senior management, and to the board itself, timely, accurate information sufficient to allow management and the board, each within its scope, to reach informed judgments concerning both the corporation's compliance with the law and its business performance."[4]

The decision establishes, though with some substantial hedging, that this monitoring duty is to be included as part of a director's overall obligation to the company. For a director, his or her "obligation includes a duty to attempt in good faith to assure that a corporate information and reporting system, which the board concludes is adequate, exists, and that failure to do so under some circumstances, may, in theory at least, render a director liable for losses caused by non-compliance with applicable legal standards."[5] The decision also gave companies substantial flexibility in how to meet this standard. Recognizing that no two companies are alike and thus no two compliance programs will be alike, the judgment allows decision-makers at companies to decide for themselves, in good faith, what will suit their particular business. While they must adhere to the law, the exact method of how this is to be done is left to the individual companies.

> *Obviously the level of detail that is appropriate for such an infor-mation system is a question of business judgment. And obviously too, no rationally designed information and reporting system will remove the possibility that the corporation will violate laws or regulations, or that senior officers or directors may nevertheless sometimes be misled or otherwise fail reasonably to detect acts material to the corporation's compliance with the law. But it is important that the board exercise a good faith judgment that the corporations' information and reporting system is in concept and design adequate to assure the board that appropriate information will come to its attention in a timely manner as a matter of ordinary operations, so that it may satisfy its responsibility.*[6]

This set forth a duty to act in good faith to ensure the creation of an adequate corporate information system—a compliance program.

Despite all of this language about director obligations and the duty to monitor, the decision also established a very high standard for liability and made it easy for directors to meet this obligation. So long as the board of directors made a good faith effort to install a compliance program, the duty will be fulfilled. This is seemingly the only requirement; it does not matter under *Caremark* that the board's efforts failed or that the compliance program did not work, so long as they tried. In fact, the decision states that "only a sustained or systematic failure of the board to exercise oversight—such as an utter failure to attempt to assure a reasonable information and reporting system exists—will establish the lack of good faith that is a necessary condition to liability."[7] Applying this high standard for liability, Chancellor Allen found that the Caremark board did not fail in their duty to monitor, as there was no evidence of lack of good faith in the exercise of their monitoring duties or that they consciously permitted violations of the law by the corporation.[8]

Under the *Caremark* standard for compliance programs, a board must create a timely and accurate reporting system containing legal compliance and business information, which flows back to the board in the ordinary course of business. Given the decision's frequent mentions of the Sentencing Guidelines, such a program should also satisfy, at minimum, the Seven Steps.[9] The case did not create an independent duty of good faith for corporate directors, but courts will analyze whether or not the directors did in fact exercise their required duties, particularly the duty of care, in good faith. Courts applying this standard address procedural violations in terms of good faith; they focus on whether the director's actions established the lack of good faith that is a necessary condition to liability.[10]

CAREMARK: A CRITICAL LOOK BACK

Delaware's courts decided the *Caremark* case over a decade ago. It was intended to promote enhanced corporate governance and to ensure greater stability and compliance among America's corporate leadership. Unfortunately, it did not achieve that goal. Within a few years of the decision, corporate scandal after corporate scandal dominated the news, each more reprehensible than the last. Was *Caremark* nothing more than "an empty triumph of form over substance," as some commentators have described it?[11]

The Delaware court decided *Caremark* as an attempt to fill a widening gap between federal and state corporate law, of which Delaware had been at the forefront for most of the century. Federal law had taken a much greater role in corporate regulation, particularly with the passage of the Organizational Sentencing Guideline amendments to the Federal Sentencing Guidelines and other Congressional enforcement. *Caremark* did upgrade the law, but due to the limitations in the decision, it did not achieve the revolution in corporate governance that it sought. Though it did not have the desired effect, the decision did have a great impact, as a much-discussed and analyzed case, particularly when one looks at the volumes of law review articles, commentaries, and symposia devoted to the topic.

Caremark's failure to achieve its goal was caused by its mix of lofty aspirations but minimal expectations. The decision had high aspirations, but they were not appropriately enforced. It was too easy to fulfill the requirements without actually achieving what was intended, that being full legal and ethical compliance. Though it created a fiduciary obligation to assure that a legal compliance mechanism existed within the organization, a doctrinal and practical dilemma still exists.[12] Only the most egregious violations would be deemed to have violated the standard. Thus, as long as a director could reasonably plead that he or she acted in good faith, he or she would escape liability, no matter how badly the decision hurt the company. Many directors, concerned with their own personal financial liability, designed programs with the goal of avoiding liability, rather than actually preventing corporate misconduct.[13] In their view,

> *[t]he more actions taken by the corporation to create compliance procedures and regimes, the better record for liability preclusion upon judicial review. This led to a substantial increase in the size and scope of corporate compliance activities and ultimately the creation of vast compliance bureaucracies within the organization. As the motivation for these actions was primarily liability-driven, their actual impact on corporate activities was questionable.*[14]

This feature of the decision had the opposite effect of what it intended. It led to a dangerous form of board passivity. "In terms of compliance, boards were lulled into thinking they had done their job, that their company had an effective oversight regime simply because funds had been expended on ethics and compliance officers and consultants who developed compliance programs and information and reporting systems of Byzantine structure and complexity."[15] This focus on procedure did not see more effective board compliance oversight and fewer violations of law. It did not provide the proper incentives for compliance along with the procedures. The only incentive it gave was for directors to create a labyrinthine web of procedures so as to protect themselves from shareholder lawsuits. It did not motivate them to actively root out offenders or to impose tight enough controls to monitor and prevent their harmful actions.

After the decision, corporate boards rushed to create compliance mechanisms that served to limit the directors' and the corporations' legal liability, but in actuality did little else. They did not do anything to affect culture change or to instill proper ethical values. Returning to the two-tiered compliance idea from Chapter 1, these corporations stayed only at the first level, not fully embracing the values of compliance. As stated earlier, a company that gives the appearance of compliance but does not truly believe in it or practice it is a dangerous thing.

Nevertheless, *Caremark* did correctly emphasize the board's responsibility to ensure proper corporate behavior.[16] The board's compliance goal should be long-term success of the company, involving ethical behavior and strict adherence to the law, rather than the use of compliance mechanisms as ways to insulate itself from liability or to falsely assuage outsiders' concerns regarding the company's practices. Furthermore, the board and the executive suite need to pair these ethical practices with the proper tone from the top, resonating throughout, thus affirming the company's commitment to compliance.

Despite all of these factors working against it, *Caremark* still has relevance and importance. The rules stated in the case have been applied by two different federal courts,[17] while Delaware has reaffirmed *Caremark* in recent rulings.[18] The Delaware Supreme Court in *Stone v. Ritter* stated that while directors do not have an independent duty of good faith to go along with their duties of care and loyalty, good faith is an important part of the analysis in determining whether liability will attach. The *Stone* Court linked the good faith requirement with the duty of loyalty, which obligates a director to act in the best interests of the company and not to put his or her own interests before the company's. "Where directors fail to act in the face of a known duty to act, thereby demonstrating a conscious disregard for their responsibilities, they breach their duty of loyalty by failing to discharge that fiduciary obligation in good faith."[19] In restating the *Caremark* standard for director oversight liability, the Court stated that "the directors utterly failed to implement any reporting or information system or control, or having implemented such a system or controls, consciously failed to monitor or oversee its operations thus disabling themselves from being informed of risks or problems requiring their attention."[20]

Caremark remains important, as it shows the importance of ethics and compliance in a court's examination. While courts may not impose liability often for failure to monitor, they are increasingly willing to take these complaints, and to examine a corporation's internal workings and its compliance program at trial. Furthermore, other states have followed Delaware's lead in examining compliance issues in the courtroom. This case also emphasized the importance of the Federal Sentencing Guidelines at a time when they were not as prominent. Through repeated references, the decision raised awareness of the Guideline's impact and importance.

This decision began the change in law seen now, with an increased emphasis on legal compliance and the internal workings of a business. As in many of the high profile prosecutions of the last few years, a company's internal culture can play a big role in the trial, particularly with the board's oversight responsibility and how it follows the law, or doesn't. Moreover, shareholders will allege a lack of good faith in failing to monitor in their lawsuits. Companies have to be prepared to answer those charges by showing the compliance program, how it functioned, and how the board of directors emphasized and supported it, to show that they acted in good faith in their actions. By not having a functioning compliance program, shareholders could say that it was *per se* a breach by the board of directors and seek money damages against them. This might be a worrisome proposition now, especially as companies are cutting back on paying the legal bills of their executives, particularly if there is a concurrent federal investigation and prosecution. Companies are more than willing now to serve up their own executives in order to save the company itself from harm.

While *Caremark* and the enactment of the Sentencing Guidelines did not readily change behavior or stop scandals, one can argue now that companies are more ready to change and put into place effective compliance programs. Organizations now have a market incentive to do so because of the negative image of scandal-ridden companies. When evaluating the resources and effort put into compliance, the legal reasons for compliance have to be kept in mind, but a company also has to ask itself what kind of company does it want to be?

SOX RECONSIDERED

The Sarbanes-Oxley Act, or SOX as it is commonly known, is undoubtedly one of the most controversial pieces of legislation in American history, no small feat in and of itself.[21] Passed in July 2002, it responded to a crisis of corporate scandals and eroded investor confidence in the financial markets. The Act contained a myriad of sections, covering such things as auditor independence, corporate responsibility, improved internal controls, and enhanced financial disclosures. It created a strong and independent Public Company Accounting Oversight Board, to oversee audits of public companies that are subject to securities laws. SOX promoted auditor independence by prohibiting an auditor from performing a number of non-audit related services, so as to avoid conflicts of interest. Companies must also create a system for whistleblowers to report misconduct, and the company must respond appropriately to such reports. CEOs and CFOs of public companies must certify the disclosures they make in periodic reports. Personal loans from companies to executives are banned. Additionally, a raft of enhanced civil and criminal penalties gives the Act significant teeth to punish corporate misconduct.[22]

A company must confirm management's responsibility for establishing and maintaining an adequate internal control structure and procedures for reporting, as well as evaluating the effectiveness of these controls and procedures. The company's public accountants must attest to and report on the management assessment as part of the audit engagement. In the financial disclosures, a company must also report any material changes to prior financial reports, as well as all material off balance sheet transactions.[23]

Given the years that have passed since SOX's enactment, it is time to look back at it and examine the criticisms leveled against it. Critics say the Act is too expensive and inefficient and call for it to be severely reworked or even discarded. Supporters fear that any changes to SOX's stringent provisions will encourage more corporate malfeasance.

SOX is admittedly an easy target, given its high profile. Commentators have hammered at the high cost of SOX compliance, publishing numerous screeds against it.

A typical editorial seethes about its high cost, complains that it stifles innovation, drives away foreign business, while briefly acknowledging the positive effects of its reforms. It usually ends by calling for either a repeal of the law or significant changes to it. The persistent theme of these commentators is money. They see compliance only as a burden, approaching it solely from a bottom-line perspective. Since compliance, no matter how effective, does not readily translate into quantifiable numbers, the danger exists that its benefits can be seemingly outweighed by its costs.

The unremitting focus on costs alone is a wrong-headed approach to both compliance and SOX commentary. This leaves the impression that these people care only about money and not on reform. In short, they appear to mirror the very executives whose behavior SOX sought to rein in in the first place. They do not seem to appreciate that one of the reasons a company may be making money is due to the economic reforms put into place, and the internal compliance efforts carried out by the company itself. The most puzzling aspect of the criticism is the cry that Congress overreacted by passing SOX. The country faced a wave of corporate scandals and executive malfeasance, and a tough response was needed. Corporations needed better oversight to ensure they would not repeat the mistakes of their scandal-ridden brethren. SOX is far from perfect, and sensible changes have been made to make it more effective. However, a purely cost-based examination of it accomplishes little, as there are many aspects of SOX that should be analyzed to truly determine how best to improve corporate accountability, rather than money alone.

A common SOX worry is "regulatory overkill": too much red tape and overly burdensome procedures stifling the economy and the stock market, driving investors and companies elsewhere. For instance, "policy makers and business groups have argued that post-Enron regulatory burdens have made U.S. markets less competitive—citing as proof that many foreign companies list their shares in London instead of New York."[24] Another point of contention is the high cost of SOX compliance, particularly Section 404, which "requires company management to develop a process to monitor internal controls over financial reporting,"[25] but does not give management guidelines on how to perform this function.

Despite the furor, a closer look indicates that SOX's impact is not as damaging to business as claimed. A 2007 study refutes the claim that foreign companies prefer to list their stock in London rather than New York because of the regulatory burden. The decline in new foreign listings is due to other factors, none having to do with SOX. In fact, the "research also found that investors are willing to pay a sizable premium for foreign-company shares listed in the U.S. in return for meeting tough U.S. regulatory standards. Foreign-company stocks in London received no similar premium...."[26] Some of the companies listing overseas would never pass the ethical and regulatory hurdles needed to demonstrate their compliance commitment and financial stability for listing in America.

Another criticism points to the drop in IPOs as proof of SOX's harm.[27] The increase in foreign IPO listings, and the drop in American IPOs, may be partly traced to the increased investment, infrastructure building, and overall economic boom happening in many previously underdeveloped nations. It would seem rational that many new companies in growing countries would choose to list in an index closer to home, rather than in the United States. While there are fewer IPOs now than during the 1990s, this cannot be blamed on SOX. As many 1990s tech investors undoubtedly remember, multitudes of hot IPOs soon flamed out and the companies went bankrupt. Few of the big-time IPOs remain as successful businesses today. A drop in their number was inevitable. SOX cannot be blamed for stifling the growth of new business, as billions of dollars in venture capital funds still finance Silicon Valley start-ups.

Additionally, while SOX compliance is expensive, the costs have fallen and the SEC has taken steps to address this issue. The cost of Section 404 compliance has fallen every year from 2003 to 2006. Compliance costs in 2006 fell 23% from the prior year, and 35% from the first year. The reductions in costs came as companies became more efficient with internal reviews.[28] Though overall costs have fallen, external review costs remain high. Thus, the SEC issued new guidelines for SOX compliance to make it more cost-effective, particularly for smaller companies.

Essentially, the reforms allow for an individual tailored response to the requirements, rather than a one-size-fits-all approach. The guidelines outline steps that executives may take to adjust their evaluations based on the needs and requirements of their individual businesses.[29] It allows for a scaleable evaluation, and is a more cost-benefit type approach that will particularly benefit smaller businesses, especially those who in the past would have been unable to shoulder the regulatory burden. The guidelines also merge the two separate opinions, one on controls and the other on management's

COMPLIANCE INSIGHT 4.1: THE IMPACT OF SOX

"Sarbanes-Oxley is a textbook case of how regulation should ideally work in a democracy: A scandal is addressed through strong legislative reaction, followed by fine-tuning by relevant agencies.... Is it any wonder that variations are being adopted in Japan, France, China, Canada, and other countries around the world?"[a]

- The United States' S&P 500 has increased 67% between July 30, 2002 (the date that President Bush signed the Sarbanes-Oxley Act into law) and June 30, 2007. This translates into a $4.2 trillion market value.[b] There is no denying that SOX had a major impact on this return of investor confidence in the financial markets.

- Although critics complain about the estimated $6 billion that U.S. companies spent in 2006 for SOX compliance, this pales in comparison with the $60 billion that investors lost due to the Enron corporate fraud.[c]

- Section 404 of SOX is working. Far fewer companies today are experiencing internal control weaknesses. While there were 97 companies reporting material internal control weaknesses in the first year of Section 404 reporting, that number was down to 55 in the third year of Section 404 reporting ending April 1, 2007.[d]

- Although the number of companies restating their financial results has increased each year since the enactment of SOX, it now appears that the numbers are beginning to come down. In the first half of 2007, there were 698 restatements as compared to 786 in the first half 0f 2006.[e]

- In but one of many examples from all over the United States, Invitrogen Corp., a biotechnology firm in Carlsbad, California has this to say about the benefits of Sarbanes-Oxley: "Sarbanes-Oxley helped to spur other changes that made Invitrogen a better-run business. Directors meet more often without executives present. Multiple ombudsmen field employee complaints. Ethics training is more rigorous. And Chief Executive Greg Lucier requires his lieutenants to take more responsibility for their results."[f]

---

[a]Thomas J. Healey, "Sarbox Was the Right Medicine," *Wall Street Journal*, August 9, 2007, A13.
[b]Ibid.

ᶜIbid.
ᵈGregory Jonas, Marc Gale, Alan Rosenberg and Luke Hedges, "The Third Year of Section 404 Reporting on Internal Control," Moody's Investor Service, May 2007, http://papers.ssrn.com/sol3/papers.cfm?abstract_id=985546.
ᵉJoann S. Lublin and Kara Scannell, "Critics See Some Good From Sarbanes-Oxley," *Wall Street Journal*, July 30, 2007, B1.
ᶠIbid.

process for assessing those controls, into one single opinion, as another way to reduce costs.

The Act's authors, former Senator Paul Sarbanes and former Representative Michael Oxley, reaffirmed their support for it and its goals. Oxley points out that SOX has resulted in greater confidence among investors, pointing to the tremendous increase in the Dow Jones industrial average, for instance, since the bill was passed.[30] Sarbanes echoed these comments about improved investor confidence. In his view, the Act markedly improves corporate accountability, and by removing many conflicts of interests, "[c]hecks and balances are working again and the watchdogs are functioning as watchdogs."[31] To further counter the argument that SOX has inhibited U.S. markets relative to foreign ones, he points out that other countries are moving in a similar direction, with higher standards and other provisions similar to SOX. He sees the money spent on compliance as a capital investment: expensive at first, particularly for a very good system, but something that will pay off and cost less in subsequent years. SOX is a necessary burden, a cost that must be paid to ensure that companies are held to a high standard and that people can invest their money with confidence.[32]

Overall, the law has done far more good than harm and should not be weakened by legislative reforms. Even those who criticize its cost and burdensome aspects acknowledge the greater boardroom accountability it produced and how it has helped to spur further changes within companies to help them avoid future scandals. Boards can now address and solve internal problems "before they fester and explode."[33] Institutional shareholders have benefited, as disclosure and certification requirements have helped to reassure investors and restore their confidence in the integrity of companies' financial statements. Even though many companies had to restate financial results in the years immediately following the law's passage, that practice is much less common now as companies have fixed old problems and avoided new ones. Many more companies quickly escalate discovered financial issues and handle them immediately.[34] Thanks to the reforms put into place, these usually minor issues can be handled quickly. Companies can constantly fine-tune their procedures to ensure their compliance efforts are as robust as they can be.

ADDITIONAL COMPLIANCE LAWS AND STANDARDS

In building a compliance program, an organization will encounter a wide variety of different laws, regulations, and standards. Some will give guidance on how to best construct a program or establish the minimum requirements required by the law. Others include industry standards or organizational certification requirements. As the topic of compliance is so broad, this book cannot possibly cover every aspect or every law. For example, the areas of health care, environmental impact, workplace safety, and financial privacy regulations have specific compliance requirements. The False Claims Act, the Health Insurance Portability and Accountability Act of 1996, the Gramm-Leach-Bliley Act, known as the Financial Modernization Act of 1999, and the compliance requirements related to the Office of Foreign Assets Control of the U.S. Department of the Treasury that enforces economic and trade sanctions against targeted foreign countries, are but a few of the many acts and regulatory provisions requiring compliance programs. This book has tried to cover many key points but the world of compliance is so vast that no book could hope to be truly comprehensive in anything less than several volumes. Understanding compliance from the concepts discussed in this book provides the basis for effective compliance no matter what particular regulation or law applies.

NOTES

1. For more information on the NYSE listing rules, please see Martin T. Biegelman and Joel T. Bartow, *Executive Roadmap to Fraud Prevention and Internal Control: Creating a Culture of Compliance*, (Hoboken, NJ: John Wiley & Sons, 2006), 90–94.
2. *In re Caremark International Inc. Derivative Litigation*, 698 A.2d 959, 968–69 (Del. Ch. 1996).
3. Ibid., 969.
4. Ibid., 970.
5. Ibid.
6. Ibid.
7. Ibid., 971.
8. Ibid., 972.
9. Stephany Watson, "Fostering Positive Corporate Culture in the Post-Enron Era," *The Tennessee Journal of Business Law*, Fall 2004, 20.

10. Thomas Rivers, "How to Be Good: The Emphasis on Corporate Directors' Good Faith in the Post-Enron Era," Note, *Vanderbilt Law Review*, March 2005, 644.
11. Charles M. Elson and Christopher J. Gyves, "In Re Caremark: Good Intentions, Unintended Consequences," *Wake Forest Law Review*, Fall 2004, 692.
12. Ibid., 701.
13. Ibid.
14. Ibid.
15. Ibid., 702.
16. Ibid., 692.
17. The Sixth Circuit applied the *Caremark* rule in 2001 in *McCall v. Scott*, 239 F.3d 817 (6th Cir. 2001), and the Seventh Circuit did so in 2003 with *In re Abbot Laboratories Derivative Shareholder Litigation*, 325 F.3d 795 (7th Cir. 2003).
18. *Stone v. Ritter*, 911 A.2d 362 (Del. 2006).
19. Ibid., 370.
20. Ibid.
21. For more information on the background of Sarbanes-Oxley and its provisions, see Martin Biegelman and Joel Bartow, *Executive Roadmap to Fraud Prevention and Internal Control: Creating a Culture of Compliance*, (Hoboken, NJ: John Wiley & Sons, 2006), 63.
22. Biegelman and Bartow, *Executive Roadmap*, 64–71.
23. Biegelman and Bartow, *Executive Roadmap*, 71.
24. Greg Ip, "Maybe U.S. Markets are Still Supreme," *Wall Street Journal*, April 27, 2007, C1.
25. Kara Scannell, "Softening a Sarbanes-Oxley Thorn," *Wall Street Journal*, April 5, 2007, C2.
26. Ip, "U.S. Markets Still Supreme," C1.
27. *See, e.g.*, Robert E. Grady, "The Sarbox Monster," *Wall Street Journal*, April 26, 2007, A19. This editorial blames Sarbanes-Oxley for causing a "precipitous drop" in the number of venture capital-backed startup companies and "killing that job-creating engine." Ibid.
28. Kara Scannell, "Costs Fall Again for Firms to Comply with Sarbanes," *Wall Street Journal*, May 16, 2007, C7.
29. Siobhan Hughes, "Sarbanes-Oxley is Eased," *Wall Street Journal*, May 24, 2007, C8.
30. Alison Grant, "Corporate Reforms Working, Says Law's Co-Author," *Newhouse News Service*, appeared in Seattle Times, April 22, 2007, F1. The Dow Jones was a little over 7000 when the bill was passed and was over 12,500 in 2007 when the interview took place. Ibid.

31. Dick Carozza, "Sarbanes-Oxley Act Revisited: An Interview with Sen. Paul S. Sarbanes," *Fraud Magazine*, May/June 2007, 36.
32. Ibid.
33. Joann S. Lublin and Kara Scannell, "Critics See Some Good From Sarbanes-Oxley," *Wall Street Journal*, July 30, 2007, B1.
34. Ibid.

CHAPTER 5

CA's Compliance Rebirth: Don't Lie, Don't Cheat, Don't Steal

"Have the courage to say no. Have the courage to face the truth. Do the right thing because it is right. These are the magic keys to living your life with integrity."

W. Clement Stone

It's not often that a person or an organization gets a second chance to right an awful wrong. But redemption and positive change can occur, even from the wreckage of corporate fraud and scandal. Such is the case with CA, Inc. (formerly Computer Associates), which is a major technology company with worldwide operations. CA suffered through several years of a very public government investigation, media headlines of accounting fraud at the highest levels, prosecutions and convictions of many in their executive leadership, and a negative impact on their reputation and shareholder value.

The fact is that CA did not have a compliance program when the massive accounting fraud was occurring. There is a strong argument to be made that if an effective program had been in place, this chapter would not be necessary. Yet, the very positive changes that CA subsequently made provide learning points and best practices for other organizations. Ultimately, CA endured a very painful process and survived as a company, albeit a much changed and better one.

CA is one of the world's largest information technology management software providers. They develop, market, deliver, and license software products that allow their customers to manage systems, networks, security, storage, applications, and databases securely and dynamically. Their goal is to help people and organizations realize the full power of IT to drive business by unifying and simplifying IT management. The company serves more than

99% of the Fortune 1000 companies as well as government agencies, educational institutions, and numerous companies in varied industries. It was founded in 1976 and is a global business leader with operations in 45 countries. Headquartered in Islandia, New York, it is listed on the New York Stock Exchange with a market capitalization of $14.40 billion. The company was originally named Computer Associates but changed its name to CA, Inc. in February 2006.

THE "35-DAY MONTH" ACCOUNTING FRAUD

In 2002, the FBI, SEC, and United States Attorney's Office in Brooklyn, New York started an investigation into accounting practices at CA. The investigation ultimately uncovered a massive accounting fraud perpetrated by many of CA's senior executives from at least the 1990s through 2001. The government also found compelling evidence that company executives attempted to cover-up and conceal the fraud and obstruct the investigation through the destruction of evidence and making false statements to government investigators and others.

In the early stages of the investigation, the government came to the conclusion that certain CA executives were not being totally cooperative in producing documentary evidence and asked the Board of Directors to start its own investigation. CA's Audit Committee agreed and in July 2003 hired the law firm of Sullivan & Cromwell to conduct an internal investigation of the allegations of accounting fraud. By early fall, the internal investigation confirmed the allegations and the existence of a "35-day month" practice. In October 2003, the company announced that it "found improper booking of sales."[1]

In December 2003, Sullivan & Cromwell expanded its investigation to include obstruction of justice by senior executives. Subsequently, investigators hired by the Audit Committee turned over evidence including e-mails, documents, and results of internal interviews where executives had lied. The Board of Directors then fired or forced out several executives including the general counsel.[2] CA knew that the level of cooperation, the replacement of "responsible management," and the "pervasiveness of the criminal conduct" were all factors that the government used in determining whether to charge the company criminally.[3] CA provided the results of its internal investigation to the government.

The government investigation found that employees conducted a fraudulent accounting practice known internally as the "35-day month" because company accountants would extend the booking of revenues in the final month of a fiscal quarter several days beyond the actual end of the month to prematurely recognize added revenue.[4] In Fiscal Year 2000 alone, CA prematurely recognized more than $1.4 billion in revenue.[5] The internal investigation conducted by CA discovered that executives "snipped date-stamps off faxed documents and added fake dates to contracts" to hide the fraud from their external auditors.[6]

In the early months of 2004, four former senior executives including the CFO pleaded guilty to securities fraud and obstruction of justice charges. The securities fraud charges involved "a long-running, company-wide scheme to backdate and forge licensing agreements in order to allow the company to meet or exceed its quarterly earnings projections during multiple fiscal quarters."[7] The obstruction of justice charges related to "the defendant's lying to the government investigators and concealing evidence of the securities fraud."[8] The United States Attorney who was prosecuting the case stated that the guilty pleas of executives and their allocutions to their crimes "demonstrate the corrupt culture in CA's management."[9]

On September 22, 2004, former CEO Sanjay Kumar was indicted on securities fraud and obstruction of justice charges for his role in the massive conspiracy. On the same day, CA agreed to a Deferred Prosecution Agreement and also to pay $225 million into a restitution fund for investors to settle the SEC lawsuit and avoid criminal prosecution. By agreement, payments were made in $75 million increments over an 18-month period and all payments have now been made. The company's agreement with the government included accepting responsibility for its criminal conduct and continued cooperation with the government.[10]

As part of the Deferred Prosecution Agreement, CA agreed to the appointment of new management, the addition of independent members to the board of directors, and the appointment of an independent examiner to review compliance with the terms and conditions of the agreement with the government. CA would continue implementing remedial steps throughout the organization to establish an effective compliance program to ensure that fraud does not recur. In return, CA received a deferred prosecution for the criminal conduct of its former officers, executives, and employees.[11]

In the criminal proceeding brought against CA by the United States Attorney's Office, CA made the following stipulation of facts as to the criminal conduct that prior management had engaged in:

The central goal of the 35-day month practice was to permit CA to report that it met or exceeded its projected quarterly revenue and earnings when, in truth, CA had not met its projected quarterly revenue and earnings. As a result of the practice, CA reported falsely to investors and regulators during multiple fiscal quarters, including each of the four quarters of CA's fiscal year 2000, that it had met or exceeded its consensus estimates. In fact, during each of the four quarters of fiscal year 2000, CA improperly recognized and falsely reported hundreds of millions of dollars of revenue associated with numerous license agreements that had been finalized after the quarter close. In so doing, CA made misrepresentations and omissions of material fact that were relied upon by members of the investing public.[12]

In all, eight former CA senior executives including the CEO, CFO, General Counsel, Executive Vice-President of Sales, and Head of Financial Reporting pleaded guilty to securities fraud and/or obstruction of justice charges. Kumar received the longest sentence of 12 years in prison and an $8 million fine. CA had to restate $2.2 billion in revenues.

THE DEFFERED PROSECUTION AGREEMENT

The signing of the Deferred Prosecution Agreement with the government on September 22, 2004, not only resolved the government's investigation but started an intensive and critical process of transforming CA and building a compliance program. Deferred prosecutions operate similar to probation in the sense that they give the offender an opportunity to reform and avoid prosecution; they have been particularly applied in the corporate setting. Under a deferred prosecution agreement (DPA), the prosecutor charges the corporation, but agrees to defer the prosecution, in exchange for an admission of wrongdoing, an honest and significant commitment to rehabilitation, and the removal of offending executives from within the company's ranks.[13] If the corporation follows the agreement, cooperates with authorities, and has been sufficiently rehabilitated, the prosecutor may dismiss the case. If the corporation breaches the agreement, the prosecutor can move forward on an indictment, putting the corporation in jeopardy. Though they cannot face jail time, corporations are highly susceptible to convictions, as it may result in license forfeitures or the loss of valuable government contracts, as with CA. Thus, prosecutors can achieve their goals of installing satisfactory compliance programs and removing unscrupulous employees while the company can avoid crippling punishment.[14]

CA acknowledged and accepted responsibility for the violation of law through the conduct of certain executives, officers, and employees related to the filing of materially false and misleading financial reports with the SEC, and obstruction of justice. As CA stated on their Web site after the signing of the DPA, "This marked the end of a troubling period in CA's history, as well as the beginning of a new era of opportunity for the company. The company has accepted full responsibility for the illegal conduct that occurred at CA, and has agreed to implement controls and governance measures to ensure that such past practices are never repeated. Our obligation to ensure the highest standards of integrity throughout CA is more important than any business objective or other consideration."[15]

CA posted the various requirements of the DPA on their Web site and over time updated it with the progress it made on the agreement. In compliance with the DPA, CA's Board of Directors and current senior management have taken numerous remedial steps in response to the misconduct that was discovered including:

- Terminating CA officials and employees responsible for improper accounting, inaccurate financial reporting, and obstruction of justice
- Terminating CA officials and employees who refused to cooperate with CA's internal investigation or who took steps to obstruct or impede the investigation
- Appointing new management including a CEO, CFO, head of world-wide sales and General Counsel
- Continuing obligation of cooperation
- Payment of restitution to CA shareholders
- Corporate reforms including:
  - Adding independent directors to the Board of Directors and undertaking corporate governance reforms
  - Ensuring that no less than 2/3 of the board members will be independent
  - Establishing a compliance committee of the Board of Directors
  - Establishing a disclosure committee
  - Inclusion of the Compliance Committee's report on the CA Web site
  - Establishing new comprehensive records management policies and procedures
  - Implementing best practices for recognition of software licensing revenue
  - Establishing a comprehensive Compliance and Ethics Program
  - Providing ethics and compliance training for all CA employees to minimize the possibility of future violations of law
  - Appointing an independent, senior-level Chief Compliance Officer
  - Amending senior executive compensation plan
  - Reorganizing the Finance Department
  - Reorganizing and enhancing the Internal Audit Department
  - Establishing a written plan to improve communication with government agencies
  - Enhancing current hotline reporting[16]

Among the many steps implemented by CA was the appointment of an Independent Examiner to examine CA's compliance with the terms and conditions of the DPA as well as the Final Judgment resulting from the SEC's civil action. The Independent Examiner at the conclusion of his term will report on CA's compliance with instituting "best practices" including "(1) practices for recognition of software licensing revenue; (2) internal accounting controls; (3) implementation of a new 'enterprise resource planning' information technology system; (4) the adequacy of the Internal Audit Department; (5) ethics and compliance policies; and (6) management policies and procedures."[17]

CA also appointed a Chief Compliance Officer; appointed a Restitution Fund Administrator for the $225 million investor restitution fund; selected two companies for their Worldwide Enterprise Resource Planning Transformation; established a Disclosure Committee; and appointed a new Chief Controller, Chief Accounting Officer, and Director of Records and Information Management.

CA'S FIRST CHIEF COMPLIANCE OFFICER

Patrick J. Gnazzo is Senior Vice President, Business Practices and Chief Compliance Officer at CA. He joined the company in January 2005 and is the first Chief Compliance Officer (CCO) that CA has had. Gnazzo is responsible for developing and implementing a comprehensive compliance and ethics program. He also oversees government regulatory compliance and the establishment of a records and information management program. Prior to joining CA, Gnazzo served as Chief Compliance Officer at United Technologies Corporation (UTC) for ten years. As Vice President for Business Practices at UTC, he built and led an ethics program that is among the best in the world. He managed more than 260 business practices officers worldwide who supported the implementation of the company's ethics and compliance programs for all of its 200,000 employees in 180 countries.

Gnazzo held several other significant positions at UTC, including Vice President for Contracts and Deputy General Counsel at UTC's Pratt & Whitney division; Vice President and Government Liaison; President of United Technologies International; Vice President and Litigation Counsel; and Vice President for Government Contracts and Compliance. These other positions at UTC provided Gnazzo a strong understanding of UTC's business as well as business risks that set the stage for his later role as their Chief Compliance Officer.

Prior to joining UTC in 1981, Gnazzo served as the Chief Trial Attorney and Director of the U.S. Department of the Navy's litigation division. He has served on the board of directors of the Ethics Officers Association and is a frequent lecturer on ethics and compliance. He earned his law degree from Cleveland State University and his undergraduate degree from John Carroll University.

In CA's case, bringing in an experienced thought leader in compliance such as Gnazzo was the best thing they could do. His blend of business acumen and reputation for compliance excellence was needed for several reasons. More than just meeting the requirements of the DPA, Gnazzo would provide needed reassurance to investors, employees, and the government. More importantly, he knew that building a compliance program isn't easy, especially at a company trying to come back from major compliance failures. "The challenges to developing an ethical culture are great. In the first place, cultural change takes time," said Gnazzo. "Culture can't happen overnight. You can write the values overnight, but culture is not imbedded until you act on the values enough times that you're known for it."[18]

When CA was looking for its first CCO, they retained a well-known recruiter. This recruiter knew Gnazzo and reached out to him for possible candidates for the position. Gnazzo was happy to oblige and provided the recruiter with several names of very qualified candidates. After the conversation, Gnazzo got to thinking about this truly unique and challenging opportunity at CA. He had been at UTC for many years at that point and had built a world-class compliance program that was running quite smoothly. He was contemplating retirement but he kept thinking about how infrequently one gets the chance to build a compliance program from scratch, as was the need at CA. The more Gnazzo thought about it, the more he knew that this was the challenge he wanted. He called the recruiter and told of his strong interest in the position. The rest is history.

When Gnazzo joined CA, his plan was to gradually build the compliance program at CA so that it would be permanently embedded. "I want to institutionalize compliance and ethics within CA," said Gnazzo. "To make it part of the company's fabric and something that no one CEO or anyone else can ever take away." He knew that in order to achieve a successful and lasting compliance program, it had to be much more than simply using a check-the-box-and-it's-done approach. It is management's responsibility to drive a culture of compliance and build it element by element until all employees understand every one of the program's components.

UNFETTERED ACCESS

Gnazzo had ten years of compliance experience at UTC before joining CA. His program at UTC was well-respected and was a model for other organizations. He also knew what to expect in building and maintaining a state-of-the-art program. Having "unfettered access" and being able to "buttonhole any manager from the CEO down" was absolutely necessary for Gnazzo. And he got it at CA. He has a direct reporting line to the Audit and Compliance Committee of the Board of Directors. This total access provides Gnazzo with the ability to walk into anyone's office and ask a probing question or fix a potential problem quickly. Gnazzo meets regularly with the Senior Leadership Team, the Executive Leadership Team, the CFO, the General Counsel, the external auditor KPMG, and anyone else as necessary. Being an executive officer with an office on CA's executive row also sent a strong message internally and externally about how much compliance was now valued at the company. The many messages that CA and Gnazzo sent out about the program established his presence and reinforced the importance of compliance.

In determining the ability of a CCO to make a difference, Gnazzo suggests that one look at where an organization's ethics officer sits. An ethics officer may report to a general counsel, but who actually presents the periodic compliance report to the audit committee is very telling. Gnazzo recommends that it be the CCO. It's important to note that in a survey conducted by the Ethics and Compliance Officers Association (ECOA), less than 10% of public companies have a CCO with a direct reporting line to the board.

BUILDING THE COMPLIANCE PROGRAM

Having a reputation as a leader in compliance made it easier for Gnazzo to build the program and walk into any office anywhere in the world at CA and ask questions. For any company rebuilding after a compliance failure, a true best practice is to bring in a solid, experienced compliance professional. Someone who has developed and managed a world-class compliance program brings immediate stature, respect, and ability to a new program. And no one sees this better than an organization's employees. I have seen this effect at other companies where the CCO is a respected person in the field. I witnessed this impact firsthand when I was at a meeting at another company. The CCO for this company is a former federal prosecutor and previously was a CCO at another organization. He had many years of experience and was a thought leader in compliance. After he spoke on an aspect of compliance, I heard an employee comment on how lucky that company was to have someone with his experience. I also saw how this person and others in the audience looked at him with respect and awe. This is the impact that Gnazzo has at CA.

"There was a culture shock at CA," said Gnazzo. "Their prior executives failed them [the employees] and as result everyone was tarred with a broad brush. New people came to CA with new ways of doing things. Yet, the employees thought they were doing it right before." Gnazzo knew that employees needed strong leadership and reassurance that they would be provided guidance on right from wrong and that their company would never again fail them.

Much needed to be done in building CA's compliance program. Gnazzo realized that employee understanding and buy-in was needed from the beginning. Early on, he held a webcast where he explained to employees what he and his compliance team would be doing in the coming months. He also told them that he would be providing them periodic updates on his progress. This lessened uncertainty among employees and gave them confidence that CA would emerge a far better and compliant company.

CA had an existing code of conduct but it needed revamping. The code was rarely distributed and employees were never trained on their responsibilities relative to the code. In addition, employees did not know who to reach out to if they wanted to report a fraud issue or other compliance concern. Ironically, the only hotline available to report violations of the code rang on the desk of the company's former General Counsel. This was the same General Counsel who pleaded guilty to obstruction of justice and conspiracy to commit securities fraud and was subsequently sentenced to two years in prison. Thus, the hotline had to be overhauled. The hotline needed to be outsourced to a third party vendor for independence and accountability. Gnazzo's experience served him well. When CA created its hotline, there was a concern among executives that they would be inundated with issues. They weren't. True to Gnazzo's experience, most of the calls received were human resource related. Still, a significant number of potential allegations of misconduct were reported. A hotline is not a panacea, but it is a necessary tool and an element in a robust compliance program.

Gnazzo advised that both the NYSE and NASDAQ require a company listed on their stock exchanges to have a code of conduct but there is no requirement that an organization have someone to actively manage the code of conduct. At CA, their Code was completely reviewed and revised. This will be an ongoing process as the compliance department has ownership for managing the Code.

CA understands that an organization's core values are the foundation of a successful compliance program. First, focus groups of employees were formed to learn what values were important to employees. The employees weighed in on what they felt the core values should be. Then the Senior Leadership Team (SLT) met to review these findings and align and finalize the core values. Subsequently, the SLT results were sent back to employees for their feedback. The SLT wanted to send a strong message about the importance of the core values. Only then were the new core values communicated to employees worldwide.

CA used a survey to learn where it had strengths and where there were opportunities for improvement. The survey showed that 94% of employees have read and understand the Code of Conduct and what it means to them. The survey showed that employees considered that 85% of the SLT, the top 40 CA executives, was ethical in their actions and words. The survey looked at employees' direct managers as well. 86% of the employees stated that their manager acts in accordance with high ethical and compliance standards. The survey's weakest point was that employees did not feel they were getting a consistent message from the SLT and this was addressed.

CA'S REVISED CODE OF CONDUCT

CA's Code of Conduct is entitled "Business Practice Standards of Excellence: Our Code of Conduct" and it is very compelling. The new executive leadership revised the code as a framework to assist employees in recognizing and responding to workplace or ethical dilemmas. They were also clear to explain that the code was not "all encompassing" to cover every potential issue an employee may face. It sends an important message to employees that the code is "a starting point with very clear avenues of escalation" for them to use when faced with ethical issues. As CA's CEO John Swainson states in the introduction to the code, "We have a shared responsibility to make compliance and good business practices part of the fabric of CA." He goes on to say, "we've developed the enhanced Code of Conduct—'Our Code of Conduct.' We use the word 'our' rather than CA because we are the people who will make this Code a true reflection of all that is good about the company. After all, we **are** the company."

Many other aspects of the code are also excellent. In the introduction, the CEO names Pat Gnazzo as the Chief Compliance Officer and asks each employee to contact Gnazzo or any member of his team if there are any questions or concerns either about the code or related issues. The code comes right out and states, "the fundamental business rules for all CA employees are: Don't Lie, Don't Cheat, and Don't Steal." It's especially effective when this declaration is said in such direct and clearly understandable terms. In the Core Values section of the code, I also like that they state, "values provide perspective in the best of times and the worst."

CA also revised their Core Values to include Innovation, Excellence, Teamwork, Integrity, and Performance. CA states "added to the equation, and at the forefront, is Integrity." CA further adds that "we are honest in all interactions" and "we earn our reputation by adhering to the highest ethical standards and conduct." Gnazzo explained that integrity was not specifically listed in the original core values but was always a given. It's just that after the government investigation, it was necessary to articulate integrity in clear terms and detail it as a core value. CA's management made a decision that integrity needed to be put front and center in light of what had happened at the company. When the new Code was finalized, a copy was placed on all employees' desks for them to read and confirm that they had read it and would comply with it.

CA's Code highlights important elements of compliance throughout the document that provide robust content in a best practices code. The following are selected examples from CA's Code:

- All of our ethical rules and principles are built on CA's shared goals and core values.
- CA expects all employees to read and understand the Code. Employees who have questions about the Code should feel free to raise such questions with his/her manager, local Human Resources representative, and/or a member of the Business Practices and Compliance organization. It is the obligation of every employee to report suspected violations of the Code to management utilizing the avenues discussed in the "CA's Commitment to Transparency" section of the Code.
- Each year, CA will require all employees to acknowledge his/her understanding of the Code and to report any perceived and/or actual conflicts of interest.
- Violations of the Code may result in disciplinary action, up to and including dismissal.
- Compliance with the Code is the responsibility of every CA employee. CA encourages all employees to bring issues and concerns forward to management without fear of retaliation.
- CA will not tolerate **any** retaliation against any employee who raises a question or concern about CA's business practices or for utilizing the CA Helpline. Employees must understand, however, that using these communication channels to report a wrongdoing will not absolve the employee from accountability for personal involvement in such wrongdoing.
- CA's Commitment to Transparency: Our obligation is to create a corporate culture of transparency and accountability.
- Compliance with the law is mandatory.
- Because CA conducts its business in over 100 countries, laws, local customs, and social standards differ greatly from one place to the next. CA's policy is to abide by the national and local laws of the countries in which it operates, unless such laws or practices violate U.S. law. Every

CA employee has the responsibility to understand and abide by the local laws and rules that apply where they are conducting CA business.

- If you find yourself with a compliance or ethical dilemma, remember you are not alone. Contact your Manager, your Human Resources Representative, the Business Practices and Compliance Organization, Worldwide Law Department or call the CA Helpline.
- Obviously, the Code cannot address all possible compliance or ethical dilemmas as a CA employee may encounter in his/her career at CA. (CA then lists numerous business situations and potential compliance violations that an employee may encounter in the course of his/her career such as antitrust, financial reporting, human resource related, and conflicts of interest.) Remember, these may not be the only compliance or ethical dilemmas that may be encountered.
- CA does not offer or pay bribes to government officials.
- CA employees working outside the U.S. should be aware that payments of bribes to foreign government officials violate the Foreign Corrupt Practices Act (FCPA) and may also violate local laws outside the U.S. In addition, the FCPA requires CA to maintain proper accounting controls and keep detailed records about all financial dealings with governments, including payments of any kind.
- CA also discourages "facilitating payments" that are made to help ensure that public officials perform tasks they are supposed to perform as part of his/her normal job functions (such as issuing licenses or permits). All facilitating payments must be reviewed and approved by a member of the Worldwide Law Department and accurately recorded in the appropriate financial record as a "facilitating payment."
- As a publicly traded U.S. company, CA must comply with various securities laws, regulations and reporting obligations. U.S. federal laws and CA's associated policies and procedures require that CA disclose accurate and complete information regarding its business, financial condition, and results of operations. Inaccurate, incomplete, or untimely reporting will not be tolerated and may result in legal liability.
- The fundamental rule for financial reporting is: do nothing that would mislead or misinform anyone about CA's finances.[19]

CA has done an excellent job in reinvigorating their Code of Conduct. Others think so too. *Ethisphere Magazine*, in their Q2 2007 edition, conducted a benchmarking exercise of the codes of conduct of 50 financial services and technology companies. The benchmarking considered eight elements including public availability, tone at the top, readability and tone, non-retaliation, commitment to stakeholders, risk topics, learning aids, and presentation and style. CA came away with a superb overall rating of A-.

Ethisphere Magazine commented that CA's code is "a very well-written code with strong layout. It's obvious that CA has invested heavily in their ethics and compliance program (not surprisingly)."[20]

JOINING THE DEFENSE INDUSTRY INITIATIVE

As a further demonstration of a commitment to compliance excellence, Gnazzo decided that CA needed to join the Defense Industry Initiative (DII). The DII was organized in 1986 by 32 major defense contractors who pledged to adopt and implement a strong code of business ethics. The formation and role of the DII was covered in Chapter 3 and is further discussed in Appendix C. CA does business with the government and the compliance issues there are just as great as doing business elsewhere. Gnazzo saw several important opportunities in joining the DII. The DII is an organization that promotes best practices in the area of defense industry compliance. According to Gnazzo, once an organization joins and gives a public endorsement of the importance of the DII, it's not easy to then leave. It reinforces tone at the top of CA. Gnazzo added that DII holds an annual best practices meeting where cutting-edge benchmarking is shared with the many members. Gnazzo's action is but another best practice that all companies doing business with the government should consider.

CA'S TONE AT THE TOP

Gnazzo believes that tone at the top is a critical element of every compliance program. "Human beings mirror their leaders," he states. Yet, this message is so important that it must be communicated by more than just senior level executives and in a number of ways. "The message of compliance can't be only delivered by the Chief Compliance Officer, the CEO, or the CFO; it must also come from the managers." This is especially true in operations outside the United States where the country manager is the face and voice of company leadership. They are the ones that local employees interact with and look to for direction. A strong message of compliance from such a person and other managers in a country or region can do much to embed ethical practices and compliance.

Tone at the top can and must also be measured in a number of ways. Employee surveys, polls, compliance with code of conduct training by employees, managers and executives, compensation reviews where compliance is measured, and commitment to training for all employees are but a few of the ways to measure both tone at the top and a commitment to compliance. Other measurement indicators include the amount of money budgeted for compliance, the number of people assigned to compliance, having a compliance log of all issues communicated, investigated, and resolved.

Executives are measured in many ways. Included are how they support the compliance and ethics program, how responsive they are to requests for investigative support, whether they give out appropriate disciplinary action, and how they work with legal and human resources. As much as 10% of executive compensation is based on how they handle and respond to compliance requirements, whether they have completed the required ethics training, how they communicate the importance of the Code of Conduct to their organization, and how they demonstrate tone at the top. At CA, executives receive the same training as any other employee and they are expected to complete each and every training course as required. There are no exceptions. Taken as a whole, these measurements provide a good indicator of tone at the top. Of note, the Ethics and Compliance Officers Association has reported that fewer than 10% of U.S. based corporations tie executive compensation to the measurement of ethics and compliance.

Reinforcing the importance of training, Gnazzo hired a Director of Training Awareness and Communication. This position has responsibility for promoting awareness of CA's compliance program throughout the company. This Director develops and conducts training around CA's various ethics and compliance initiatives such as the Code of Conduct and Conflict of Interest Policy.

The DPA also required a comprehensive overhaul of the company's document retention policies and procedures. In response, Gnazzo hired a Vice President in Charge of Records and Information Management. This position is responsible for ensuring that CA's records and documents are created, retained, and disposed of properly. Having an efficient, effective, and compliant records management policy ensures that the company meets its business needs as well as complies with all legal and regulatory requirements.

Gnazzo also leads the newly created Enterprise Risk Management group at CA as Chief Risk Officer. He believes that risk and compliance go hand-in-hand. If organizations identify the various risks they potentially can face, they are less likely to hide them. The purpose of their Enterprise Risk Management group is to empower employees to identify risk early on. The NYSE requires its listed companies to have a policy on financial risk approved by the audit committee.

RESPONSE TO VIOLATIONS OF BUSINESS PRACTICES

CA has a very professional and predicable process for responding to allegations of misconduct and conducting internal investigations. Previously, the company had no full-time investigators to respond to allegations of fraud and compliance failures. Gnazzo believes that companies must bring in professional investigators to conduct and resolve issues of fraud and non-compliance. He described how beneficial it was to hire John McDermott as a compliance investigator. McDermott was a career United States Postal Inspector who joined CA in June 2006. McDermott was both a respected fraud investigator and manager of a team of federal investigators for many years in New York. McDermott investigated some of the most complex and highly-publicized fraud cases in New York including fraudulent financial accounting cases. He was uniquely qualified for a role in CA's compliance program and has become a key member of the team. Gnazzo explains how by adding experienced professionals such as McDermott, organizations gain credibility and compliance effectiveness.

Every issue that is reported is documented in CA's matter management log, which is a Web-based case management system. This includes all allegations, inquiries, and government requests. They keep metrics on the number of cases, location of cases, types of cases, status of cases, the level and position of subjects of allegations, the losses from each case, and other key metrics. Gnazzo uses this reporting tool in preparing quarterly presentations to the Audit and Compliance Committee of the Board.

ENSURING FUTURE COMPLIANCE

A question posed to Gnazzo was how he would respond to an employee at CA who asked how he would ensure that what happened would never again occur. Gnazzo stated that the best assurance is open communication and to provide many avenues of communication to employees to ask questions and escalate concerns. He explained that non-compliance can be stopped by providing employees and others outside the company an opportunity to break the chain if fraud and corruption exist.

Gnazzo explained that what happened at CA was a massive conspiracy involving numerous senior executives. No one broke the chain so the fraud lasted for many years. CA didn't have a compliance program or the culture that may have been able to either prevent it from happening in the first place or at least catch it earlier. The executives who were asked about the fraud all lied and covered it up. They lied to the board. They lied to company attorneys. They even lied to federal prosecutors. They weren't caught until one executive finally stopped lying. This executive hired a former federal prosecutor as his attorney and when he was questioned by federal agents and prosecutors, finally admitted he was lying all along. He confirmed the huge accounting fraud at CA. That broke the chain of lying and obstruction of justice and opened the door for acceptance of responsibility and subsequent rebirth.

A well-communicated hotline, a strong and independent audit committee, a professionally staffed human resources department, an ombudsperson program, and an effective compliance program are all key elements for successful communication of compliance issues, according to Gnazzo.

The Ombudsperson Program is another option for employee communication at CA. It provides another platform for employees to raise concerns to someone who will maintain their confidentiality while ensuring the issue is escalated to management. In addition to a hotline, having a long-term, well-respected, thoroughly trained, and trusted employee who will listen to an employee's problem provides yet another communication option. An employee may be more likely to speak to someone of this stature than call a hotline. As Gnazzo said, there were many people involved in the 35-day month accounting fraud. "That couldn't have happened if CA had had the proper compliance attitude. The best insurance that this massive fraud will never happen again is open communication and resources to escalate issues."

The ongoing message to employees at CA is that the compliance department is a lifeline for them to ask any and all questions at any time. It constantly reminds management to always include compliance in their daily work. The message also sent is that there is a personal responsibility for compliance and that the results are measured.

Gnazzo believes in communicating violations of business conduct with employees but it must be done in a productive way. CA does not believe in "public hangings" of employees involved in fraud and policy violations. Employees who have been terminated for cause or given other disciplinary action are not publicly named or otherwise identified. Instead, CA uses details of the transgressions in training scenarios to better educate employees by showing how others have violated CA's Code of Conduct.

Side letters are another area that CA's compliance program has addressed. Side letters are after-the-fact changes to contracts including terms, conditions, and agreements that are not specifically detailed in the original contract and can result in potential financial and litigation risk. Gnazzo advised that the importance of understanding the "four corners of every contract" is one way to lessen the problem of side letters. CA requires that employees complete an attestation that no side letters are incorporated into a contract. In addition, CA educates its employees on the risks that side letters pose. It also sends out letters to customers asking for follow-up on the aspects of the contract so that it is clear that there were no side letters included in deals.

BUSINESS PRACTICE OFFICERS

Gnazzo knew that there are different standards of business practices in foreign countries, cultural sensitivity issues, and different legal and employee requirements in those countries that had to be dealt with. In response, he created 87 part-time Business Practice Officers (BPO) in CA offices worldwide to improve compliance. These are in addition to Gnazzo's compliance team based in the company headquarters in New York. The BPOs act as regional compliance deputies in countries where CA operates. Their role is to share information with management and employees, help organize town hall meetings, discuss best practices with human resources and legal departments, and provide compliance awareness and education. The BPOs serve as a local connection for employees to ask questions and raise concerns.

The BPOs were identified and vetted by the compliance department and then thoroughly trained in various ethics and compliance areas such as handling conflict of interest issues. The BPO role is a collateral duty for those assigned and they spend about 10–15% of their time on compliance activities. They do not conduct investigations but collect information used by compliance investigators. As Gnazzo explained, they are not expected to act as "police" and initiate investigations, but they are there to put a local face on the corporate message of ethics and compliance.

COMPLIANCE AND ETHICS LEADERSHIP COUNCIL PROGRAM ASSESSMENT

To further assess CA's ethics and compliance program, Gnazzo had a detailed assessment completed using the Compliance and Ethics Program Assessment Wizard. The Program Assessment Wizard was created by the Corporate Executive Board's Compliance and Ethics Leadership Council (CELC) and is a comprehensive measurement and benchmarking system for compliance and ethics program performance. For more information on the Program Assessment Wizard, please see the related section in Appendix C.

The CELC and the Program Assessment Wizard gave CA superior grades in all but two of their 28 criteria. Among the areas where CA was rated with high performance were program structure and oversight, standards and procedures, program measurement and monitoring, allegation reporting and investigations, communications, and discipline and incentives. The only areas marked for improvement were training for the Board and identifying risk. CA is actively addressing both.

PAT GNAZZO'S FIVE BEST PRACTICES FOR A WORLD-CLASS COMPLIANCE PROGRAM

Gnazzo provided his five best practices for a world-class compliance program but he qualified it by saying that there are other important aspects too.

1. The head of compliance needs to be "seen at the table" with other top executives. That's everyone with a "c" at the beginning of their title. The person must have complete access to everyone at the company, no matter their level, and not have to make an appointment to meet. The CCO must be highly visible at the company and have significant experience and standing in the field.
2. The CCO must be independent with a solid reporting line to the audit committee and a dotted line to the general counsel.
3. The company must have an open communication program where anyone can report an allegation or issue through many different channels and have it addressed quickly.
4. The company must have a strong investigative response and process for allegations. The compliance department must have skilled investigative professionals who know how to obtain and analyze information, conduct interviews, report on findings and improve the compliance and ethics program.
5. Having Business Practice Officers embedded in offices worldwide is also a best practice.

In addition, Gnazzo believes that not just the audit committee but also the entire board needs to be heavily involved in compliance. All board members need to know the CCO and interact with him or her. They must thoroughly understand how the compliance program works. Gnazzo finds some topic or issue to discuss in order to get before the entire board each year. He interacts closely with each member. This puts the compliance program on par with all the other business operations and programs at CA.

It is clear that the CCO is a valuable part of the equation for compliance excellence. A world-class CCO needs a variety of knowledge, skills, and abilities. Business acumen is an absolute requirement. Experience in business and being able to understand the particular business operation and model at their company is a factor for success for a CCO. A CCO who can meet with a business division president and talk the same language is a tremendous asset to the compliance program's standing. When a CCO needs to meet with a business division president and can talk the same language, there is a greater understanding and benefit. Adding business knowledge to compliance expertise is critical for a successful CCO.

Gnazzo's experience in two business roles at UTC prior to becoming the CCO was a major factor in his ability to build a world-class program at CA. Having management experience and leading people are also important. Being an effective communicator and being able to speak to large audiences and deliver important messages are other absolute necessities. Being comfortable in one's skin and being able to step up in a crisis are other key qualifications.

Gnazzo has other recommendations for CCOs to follow. Become a thought leader in the field of compliance. Join professional compliance organizations and participate in roundtable sessions and sharing of best practices. Speak and write on the various topics of compliance.

A NEW ERA OF OPPORTUNITY

CA has had an impressive turnaround since the issuance of the DPA. The compliance program that CA developed is a major factor. Gnazzo's experience, credibility, and reputation as well as CA's strong commitment made ethics and compliance the foundation for their revival. On May 21, 2007, CA announced that it had satisfied the terms of the DPA. The Independent Examiner's report dated May 1, 2007 to the United States Attorney's Office stated that CA had "complied with" the DPA. As a result, the Federal Judge assigned the case dismissed all pending charges against CA. CA will no longer be under the close scrutiny of the government to ensure a commitment to ethics and compliance. "Our efforts won't stop because we have met the requirements of the DPA," said President and CEO John Swainson. "We will continue to demand a high level of transparency, ethical behavior, and integrity from our entire organization."

This DPA was one of the first instituted by the Department of Justice in which the required reforms were so specific. CA spent hundreds of millions of dollars in complying with the DPA. The improved controls and processes have made a real difference. Now, the question is whether the changes that CA instituted will become a part of the company's DNA. Gnazzo sees this as an opportunity to reinforce the message of compliance and acting with integrity and accountability even when the government is not looking over their shoulder so closely. In fact, Gnazzo eagerly looks to the future as the true test of the new CA and its compliance rebirth. As Gnazzo states, "the measure of a company's success is how it deals with trouble, not that it never had any trouble to begin with."

NOTES

1. Steve Hamm, "A Probe—and a Bitter Feud," *Business Week*, April 12, 2004, 78.

2. Martin T. Biegelman and Joel T. Bartow, *Executive Roadmap to Fraud Prevention and Internal Control: Creating a Culture of Compliance*, Hoboken, NJ: John Wiley & Sons, Inc, 2006, 335.

3. Charles Forelle and Joann S. Lublin, "Kumar Gives Up Leadership Posts Under Pressure," *Wall Street Journal*, April 22, 2004, A1.

4. Charles Forelle, "Ex-CFO at Computer Associates To Enter Plea in Accounting Probe," *Wall Street Journal*, April 8, 2004, A1.

5. Charles Forelle, "CA Ex-Executives Plead Guilty, Call Fraud Pervasive," *Wall Street Journal*, April 9, 2004, A3.

6. Ibid.

7. Second Year Report to the President, Corporate Fraud Task Force, July 20, 2004, www.usdoj.gov/dag/cftf/2nd_yr_fraud_report.pdf.

8. Ibid.

9. Charles Forelle, "CA Ex-Executives Plead Guilty," A3.

10. Biegelman and Bartow, *Executive Roadmap*, 335–37.

11. Deferred Prosecution Agreement between the Government and CA posted on the CA Investor Relations Web site, September 22, 2004, http://investor.ca.com/phoenix.zhtml?c=83100&p=irol-govdeferred.

12. Stipulation of Facts, www.ca.com/about/dpa/exhibit_c_stipulationoff acts.pdf.

13. Benjamin M. Greenblum, "What Happens to a Prosecution Deferred? Judicial Oversight of Corporate Deferred Prosecution Agreements," *Columbia Law Review*, October 2005, 1863.

14. Ibid.

15. CA's Deferred Prosecution Agreement, Investor Relations and Corporate Governance site, CA, Inc., http://investor.ca.com/phoenix.zhtml?c=83100&p=irol-govdeferred.

16. Ibid.

17. "Court Appoints Attorney Lee S. Richards Independent Examiner for Computer Associates International, Inc.," SEC Press Release 2005–37, March 16, 2005, www.sec.gov/news/press/2005–37.htm.

18. Gregory J. Millman, "Black and White Fever: The State of Business Ethics," *Financial Executive Magazine*, May 2006, 26.

19. "Business Practices Standards of Excellence: Our Code of Conduct," available at www.ca.com/XXX.

20. Douglas Allen, "50 Codes of Conduct Benchmarked: How Does Your Organization Stack Up?," *Ethisphere Magazine*, Q2 2007, www.ethisphere.com/Ethisphere_Magazine_0207/50-codes-Q2.

CHAPTER 6

The International Landscape of Compliance

"Your beliefs become your thoughts. Your thoughts become your words. Your words become your actions. Your actions become your habits. Your habits become your values. Your values become your destiny."

Mahatma Gandhi

In today's shrinking world, a whisper uttered in New York is heard in Beijing. A deal made in Delhi is felt in London. A company based in the United States often has subsidiaries in dozens of other countries. The world economy is quickly growing at breakneck speed. The BRICs—the emerging economies of Brazil, Russia, India, and China—are expected to be dominant forces in the global economy by the middle of this century if not sooner. It seems that nothing short of an extinction level event will stop this explosive growth. Yet, there are other forces besides natural disasters, armed conflicts, and environmental issues that can severely derail business efforts and hinder the flattening of the world.[1] Corruption, corporate fraud, and scandal are the end products of an ineffective corporate compliance program and can lead to business failure.

Compliance goes beyond the borders of the United States with the globalization of business. International compliance is a necessity because of a confluence of several important factors. The global nature of companies with subsidiaries, affiliates, and vendors all over the world provide great opportunity but also great risk. U.S. law reaches all around the world and covers the actions of U.S. corporations and their employees no matter where they are. Illegal actions relating to the Foreign Corrupt Practices Act or the USA PATRIOT Act can have major implications. There are harsh penalties for those who violate the anti-bribery provision of the Foreign Corrupt Practices Act. Third party liability is another major concern as companies are liable for the actions of people it hires, be they direct employees or agents. The solution is a strong compliance program to ensure everyone knows what the rules are, what's going on, and to keep track of who's doing what. These themes will span this and the following chapter, illustrating the importance of truly worldwide compliance.

THE FOREIGN CORRUPT PRACTICES ACT

Bribery and corruption are unfortunate elements of the dark side of business. Illegal payments by public and private corporations to foreign government officials to induce business dealings have long been an unscrupulous practice. These bribes, usually in the form of cash but not exclusively, are illegal and have been outlawed by the United States for many years. A rash of bribery and corruption cases in the 1970s, and a Congressional focus resulted in the enactment of the Foreign Corrupt Practices Act (FCPA) in 1977. Violations of the FCPA have always been taken very seriously by prosecutors in the United States. Since the passage of the Sarbanes-Oxley Act, there has been a renewed focus on investigations and prosecutions involving FCPA violations. Thus, compliance with the provisions of the FCPA is more important than ever.

The FCPA prohibits individuals and companies from "corruptly making use of the mails or any means or instrumentality of interstate commerce in furtherance of an offer, promise, authorization, or payment of money or anything of value to a foreign official for the purpose of obtaining or retaining business for, or directing business to, any person or securing any improper advantage."[2] Furthermore, the FCPA also requires "issuers not only to refrain from making corrupt payments to foreign government officials, but also to implement policies and practices that reduce the risk that employees and agents will engage in bribery."[3] The books and records provision of the FCPA requires certain corporations to create and maintain books, records, and accounts that fairly and accurately reflect company transactions. The knowing falsification of company records is also prohibited.[4] Penalties include both civil and criminal sanctions against the company and culpable employees.

The purpose of this provision is to put teeth into the statute. Logic tells us that companies probably will not accurately record bribe payments to foreign government officials but if they do, the evidence is there for the government to obtain. If companies omit or falsify transactions to hide the bribe payments, they also face legal peril. The strength of the FCPA gives great leverage to the government in investigating and prosecuting bribery and corruption schemes. Violators are damned if they do and damned if they don't. The best way to avoid punishment is not to do the crime in the first place.

The following case is an interesting study of both an initial compliance failure and a subsequent turnaround by instituting compliance requirements. There are many lessons to be learned from the experiences that this company went through. The lack of an effective compliance program contributed to a long-standing policy of paying bribes to foreign nationals. The development of a compliance program helped to expose a history of wrongdoing. The implementation of a robust compliance program helped the company restore its reputation.

SCHNITZER STEEL AND THE FCPA

Schnitzer Steel Industries, Inc. (SSI) is an old and proud company with its roots in the United States' Pacific Northwest. The company was started by a Polish immigrant named Sam Schnitzer in Portland, Oregon in the early 1900s. In 1906, Sam saw a great business opportunity in scrap metal, and started collecting and selling it. In a few years, he and a partner, H. J. Wolfe, owned two companies, Alaska Junk Company and Schnitzer & Wolfe Machinery Company. Sam continued to grow the enterprise over the years and brought his five sons into the family business. In the 1950s, the Schnitzer family bought out the Wolfe family for sole control of the business now called Schnitzer Industries. Sam died in 1952 and left the business to his sons to run. Four sons continued to do so, with one son leaving the family business in the mid-1950s to build his own real estate business. In 1962, a Portland newspaper columnist called Sam "a brilliant immigrant who began with a sack on his back, a horse and wagon, and whose portrait hangs in the board room of the fine Schnitzer Building."[5]

Over the years, SSI continued to grow its business in the United States and internationally through internal growth and by acquiring other companies. In 1993, SSI announced that it was taking its privately owned business public with an initial public offering. In Oregon newspapers, there was speculation that a conflict between different generations of the Schnitzer family on running the business resulted in the decision to go public.[6] Even after SSI went public, the Schnitzer family controlled 95% of the voting shares. Sam's sons and their sons-in-law controlled the majority of executive positions at SSI. The company was a fixture in Oregon with the Schnitzer family one of the wealthiest in the state, and doing much in the way of philanthropy and civic affairs.

After going public in 1993, SSI went on an acquisition spree that significantly boosted the amount of scrap metal processed annually; revenue jumped. Millions of dollars more were spent on expansion and increasing capacity to process scrap metal. A journalist for a Portland business publication at the time wrote that the acquisitions were "an indication of the aggressiveness of the younger generation of the Schnitzer clan.... The conservative and low-profile generation that succeeded founder Sam Schnitzer has been replaced by a more aggressive crop of business people."[7] The journalist had no way of knowing at the time that his words would be a harbinger of events that would become public more than a decade later.

Today, SSI is one of the largest recyclers of ferrous metals in the United States. Its three business segments include metals recycling, steel manufacturing, and an auto parts business. The company is headquartered in Portland, Oregon, and its common stock is listed on the NASDAQ. The company has over 3,200 employees and revenue of $1.855 billion for the fiscal year ended August 31, 2006.

The FCPA Violations and Subsequent Discovery

In doing research for this chapter, I had the good fortune to meet a former employee of SSI who provided me valuable information and insight on both the company and how the compliance failures occurred. This person worked at SSI for a number of years during the period in question. I am protecting the confidentiality and identity of this person and will only refer to this person as a "Confidential Source" (CS) throughout this chapter. CS was in no way involved in the criminality and only learned of it when the general population of employees was told of the internal investigation resulting from the FCPA violations. CS was in a unique position and was able to provide me with thoughts and opinions on what happened and why. It is a snapshot in time. CS has taken me through a period where the lack of an effective compliance program brought forth significant and painful changes in a very old and proud company.

By going public in 1993, SSI now had the capital to grow its business. In 1995, SSI acquired a privately held scrap metal recycler in Tacoma, Washington that was the largest scrap metal recycler in the state, as well as a leading scrap metal exporter to Asian markets. It had two subsidiaries that SSI renamed SSI International Far East, Ltd. (SSI Korea) and SSI International, Inc. (SSI International). SSI Korea was based in South Korea. While this acquisition greatly improved SSI's ability to collect and process far greater amounts of scrap metal, there was a sinister side effect according to the CS. It seems that, unknown to SSI at the time of the acquisition, the acquired company had a practice of paying bribes to foreign government officials in Asia to secure business. Unfortunately, this practice continued after the acquisition by SSI.

The discovery of this bribery years later demonstrates the importance of instituting effective compliance programs. With the advent of Sarbanes-Oxley and an increased focus on compliance, SSI started a compliance program. Prior to this, SSI did not have a formal code of conduct that employees were required to read and sign off on. SSI prepared a new code of conduct with an ethics policy that was provided to employees to read and sign that they understood and would follow the policies contained therein.

About the summer of 2003, representatives of SSI's legal and human resources departments went to the Tacoma subsidiary and presented the compliance policies to employees there. One of the senior employees advised that after reading the policy about bribery and kickbacks, he could not sign the code of conduct. He explained that he was probably doing what was prohibited, and therefore, was in violation of the policy. As a result of this startling discovery, SSI started an internal investigation. Ultimately, the Board of Directors retained a Washington, DC law firm with experience in FCPA issues to conduct a thorough investigation. The investigation uncovered the full extent of the bribery and corruption that had been going on since the acquisition. Subsequently, a disclosure of this illegal activity was made to the Department of Justice and the SEC.

The Conspiracy

According to the SEC, "employees and agents of SSI International and SSI Korea made improper cash payments to managers of scrap metal customers [businesses] owned, in whole or in part, by the Chinese government. These payments were intended to induce those managers to purchase scrap metal from Schnitzer."[8] SSI "paid over $205,000 in improper payments to managers of its government-owned customers in China in connection with 30 sales transactions" and their "gross revenue for those transactions totaled approximately $96 million"[9] As a result, SSI "earned $6,259,104 in net profits on these sales."[10]

SSI paid two types of kickbacks to its foreign customers. One was a "standard" kickback of between $3,000 and $6,000 per shipment of scrap metal. The money for these payments came from the revenue earned on the scrap metal sales. The other type of kickback was referred to internally as either a "refund" or "rebate." To pay these refunds, the general managers of steel mills would overpay SSI for the steel purchases. Then, they would "personally recover the overpayment," usually in amounts ranging from $3,000 to $15,000. SSI would wire money for these illegal payments to secret bank accounts in South Korea that were opened by the head of SSI Korea. The heads of SSI Korea and SSI International then would use these funds to make cash payments to the managers of their customers. Besides cash payments, other gifts such as jewelry, gift certificates, golf outings, and condominium timeshares were provided as bribes and kickbacks.[11]

SSI Korea also acted as a broker for Japanese scrap metal companies that sold scrap metal to China. They made payments to managers at these steel mills on behalf of the Japanese companies and earned commissions for facilitating the illegal payments. SSI didn't restrict their bribery to government officials. They also made improper payments to privately owned steel mills in China and South Korea. The true nature of these illegal payments was concealed in the company's books and records by being falsely described over the years as "sales commission," "commission to the customer," "quality claims," "discounts," "customer relations," "refunds," or "rebates."

During the period 1995 to 2004 when SSI was making these illegal payments in violation of the FCPA, the company "provided no training or education to any of its employees, agents, or subsidiaries regarding the requirements of the FCPA" and "failed to establish a program to monitor its employees, agents, and subsidiaries for compliance with the FCPA."[12] The failure of thorough due diligence in the merger and acquisition phase further contributed to SSI's financial and reputational damage.

By May 2004, as a result of the internal investigation, SSI's compliance department learned more details of the bribery and kickbacks. Although a senior executive then prohibited any further illegal payments, this person "nonetheless authorized Schnitzer employees to pay at least two additional bribes that Schnitzer previously had promised private customers. The same senior executive also authorized Schnitzer employees to increase entertainment expenses in lieu of cash payments to its private and government-owned scrap metal customers."[13] What was this senior executive thinking? More importantly, why was this person ever elevated to a senior executive position, let alone be an employee of the company? SSI Korea also destroyed incriminating documents after the start of the investigation but prior to SSI's order to employees to preserve all related documents.

In prosecuting SSI Korea for conspiracy, wire fraud, and FCPA violations, the United States Attorney for the District of Oregon wrote the following in the Criminal Information that SSI Korea pleaded guilty to:

From in or about 1995 through in or about August 2004, in the District of Oregon and elsewhere, defendant SSI Korea did unlawfully, willfully, and knowingly conspire and agree with Officer A,

Officer B and other persons, known and unknown to commit the following acts against the United States: to violate the Foreign Corrupt Practices Act by the use of the mails and of means and instrumentalities of interstate commerce corruptly in furtherance of an offer, payment, promise to pay, and authorization of the payment of money, and anything of value to foreign officials for the purpose of: (I) influencing acts and decisions of such foreign officials in their official capacities; (II) inducing such foreign officials to do and omit to do acts in violation of the lawful duty of such officials; (III) securing an improper advantage; and (IV) inducing such foreign officials to use their influence with foreign governments and instrumentalities thereof to affect and influence acts and decisions of such governments and instrumentalities in order to assist defendant SSI Korea in obtaining and retaining business for and with, and directing business to SSI Korea and Schnitzer Steel....To further violate the Foreign Corrupt Practices Act by knowingly falsifying the books, records, and accounts that were required, in reasonable detail, to accurately and fairly reflect the transactions and dispositions of the assets of Schnitzer Steel, an issuer within the meaning of the FCPA.[14]

Officer A is believed to be former employee Si Chan Wooh who subsequently pleaded guilty to his involvement in this conspiracy. Officer B as well as the other persons mentioned have not been identified or criminally charged as of the writing of this book.

SSI's Remedial Efforts

As part of its settlement with the government, SSI agreed to a number of remedial actions to improve its compliance program. They include:

- The hiring of a compliance consultant for a period of three years to review and evaluate SSI's internal controls, record-keeping, and financial reporting policies and procedures relating to FCPA provisions as well as applicable foreign bribery laws.
- Full cooperation with the compliance consultant and providing full access to all applicable books and records, operations, and personnel.
- Evaluation by the compliance consultant of SSI's policies and procedures to determine if they are reasonably designed to detect and prevent violations of the FCPA and prepare a report of findings to be submitted to the SEC and DOJ.

- Adoption by SSI of all recommendations of the compliance consultant. SSI can propose alternative policies designed to achieve the same purpose or objective for ones that may be unduly burdensome, impractical, or costly. If the compliance consultant does not agree to the alternative policy, SSI must abide by the original recommendations.

On October 16, 2006, SSI finalized settlements with the DOJ and SEC over the FCPA violations. SSI Korea pleaded guilty to violations of the FCPA's anti-bribery and books and records provisions and was fined $7.5 million. SSI received a Deferred Prosecution Agreement (DPA) and a $7.7 million penalty in disgorgement and interest. In its 2006 Annual Report, SSI advised that it had settled proceedings with the DOJ and the SEC. They stated that "The Company had a past practice of making improper payments to the purchasing managers of nearly all of the Company's customers in Asia in connection with export sales of recycled ferrous metal."[15] The DOJ agreed to the DPA for SSI and the guilty plea for SSI Korea because of the company's commitment to a number of significant remedial actions and compliance improvements including the following:

- voluntary disclosure to the DOJ and SEC of the FCPA violations;
- extensive internal investigation by SSI's Board of Directors, the retaining of experienced outside counsel, and the sharing with the government of the results of that investigation;
- extensive cooperation with the DOJ and SEC;
- appropriate disciplinary actions including the replacement of certain senior management; and
- remedial steps including retaining an experienced compliance consultant and the creation of an effective compliance program to protect against future FCPA and other compliance failures.

On June 29, 2007, Si Chan Wooh, the former Schnitzer Steel Executive Vice President and head of SSI Korea, pleaded guilty to conspiracy to violate the FCPA. In his allocution to the guilty plea in federal court, Wooh admitted that he and others made illegal payments to government-owned customers in China for almost ten years. Between September 1999 and August 2004, Wooh paid more than $200,000 in bribes to managers of government-owned businesses in China. The Department of Justice also announced that Wooh was cooperating in the continuing criminal investigation leading to the possibility of further prosecutions of members of the conspiracy.[16] In Compliance Insight 6.1, an official from the Department of Justice opines on the FCPA and SSI.

COMPLIANCE INSIGHT 6.1: ASSISTANT ATTORNEY GENERAL ALICE S. FISHER ON COMBATING CORRUPTION

Alice S. Fisher is an Assistant Attorney General with the United States Department of Justice in Washington, DC. In an address before the American Bar Association's National Institute on the Foreign Corrupt Practices Act on October 16, 2006, Fisher provided important commentary on the FCPA and related compliance programs. While she was speaking to an audience of attorneys, she was also speaking to a much broader group of business leaders. She stated:[a]
"Corruption is the linchpin of so many different global problems. It undercuts democracy and the rule of law. It stifles economic growth and sustainable development. It destabilizes markets. And it creates an uneven playing field for U.S. companies doing business overseas."
Fisher explained that strong FCPA enforcement encouraged other governments to step up their own anti-corruption efforts, as well as made sure "that your competitors do not gain an unfair advantage when competing for business overseas. And we are ensuring the integrity of our markets at home so that investors will continue to invest in your companies."
In emphasizing the importance of cooperation with Justice Department investigations, she described the Schnitzer Steel case. She pointed to the company's "exceptional cooperation," which paid strong dividends in allowing it to receive a deferred prosecution agreement and pay a far lower criminal fine, based on a Department recommendation, than what it would have received otherwise.
Assistant Attorney General Fisher also emphasized four FCPA policy issues including voluntary disclosures, compliance consultants, the FCPA opinion procedure, and transactional due diligence.

VOLUNTARY DISCLOSURES

"When serious FCPA issues do arise, we strongly encourage you and your clients to voluntarily disclose those issues. I know that there is a concern out there that there is not enough certainty in the voluntary disclosure process. And frankly, there are good reasons for that.... But what I can say is that there is *always* a benefit to corporate cooperation, including voluntary disclosure, as contemplated by the Thompson memo.[b] The fact is, if you are doing the things you should be doing—whether it is self-policing, self-reporting, conducting proactive risk assessments, improving your controls and procedures, training on the FCPA, or cooperating with an investigation after it starts—you will get a benefit. It may not mean that you or your client will get a complete pass, but you will get a real, tangible benefit."

When a company voluntarily discloses FCPA violations, in some cases it results in a guilty plea, but in other cases the company has not been prosecuted at all. With this in mind, Fisher underscored there is a *real* benefit to voluntary disclosure and cooperation.

COMPLIANCE CONSULTANTS

In several recent FCPA decisions, such as Schnitzer Steel, the Department required the offending company to "hire a compliance consultant to review the company's system of FCPA internal controls." She then listed some of the factors taken into account when deciding to require a compliance consultant: "the strength of the company's existing management and compliance team, the pervasiveness of the problem, and the strength of the company's existing FCPA policies and procedures."

"And when we do require a monitor, we will make every effort to tailor the scope of the monitor's work in appropriate cases. That being said, there are plainly many circumstances where a compliance consultant is an essential component of any deferred prosecution agreement. Those are cases where the company has simply taken a 'cookie cutter' approach to FCPA compliance, or has a 'paper' program without any real substance to it."

OPINION PROCEDURE

Fisher outlined the FCPA opinion procedure, which she hopes will encourage companies to talk to the DOJ before they commit an FCPA violation. Under the opinion procedure, a company or individual can request an opinion on a proposed business transaction or conduct, before undertaking it. When the Department issues the opinion, the conduct or transaction is presumed to be FCPA-compliant. "Over the years," Fisher noted, "the FCPA opinion procedure has generally been under-utilized, with only a handful of opinions being requested each year. But as Assistant Attorney General, I want the FCPA opinion procedure to be something that is useful as a guide to business."

DUE DILIGENCE

The opinion procedure may also be useful in the context of joint ventures, mergers, and acquisitions, "when the FCPA due diligence turns up potential problems with the foreign counterpart. Transactional due diligence in the FCPA context is good for business." This was on display in GE's merger with InVision Technologies, Inc. "In that case, investigations by DOJ and the SEC revealed that InVision paid bribes in [Thailand] in connection with sales of its airport security screening machines. InVision ultimately accepted a deferred prosecution agreement (DPA) and paid an $800,000 fine."

Thanks to GE's due diligence, it discovered the conduct before completing the merger, and avoided potential successor liability. "Although GE entered into a separate agreement with the Department to ensure InVision's compliance with the DPA, think of the potential consequences to GE if they had not performed thorough due diligence in that case."

---

[a]The quotes and material in this section come from the prepared remarks of Alice S. Fisher, Assistant Attorney General, United States Department of Justice, at the American Bar Association's National Institute on the Foreign Corrupt Practices Act, Omni Shoreham Hotel, Washington, DC, October 16, 2006. Transcript of prepared remarks found at http://skaddenpractices. skadden.com/fcpa/.
[b]The Thompson Memo is the informal name of the Department of Justice's "Principles of Federal Prosecution of Business Organizations." This speech was given prior to the Department of Justice issuance of the McNulty Memo which updated Department of Justice guidance on criminally charging businesses as previously detailed in the Thompson Memo.

METCALF AND EDDY CIVIL FCPA SETTLEMENT

Metcalf & Eddy International Inc., a Massachusetts-based environmental engineering firm, was convicted in 1999 of violating the FCPA for unlawfully providing travel and entertainment expenses to an Egyptian public official. The official was the chairman of a committee that was involved in contract negotiations for a sewage upgrade project in Egypt that Metcalf & Eddy would work on. He received, along with his family, trips to the United States and a per diem that amounted to 150% above the rate allowed by law. Metcalf & Eddy paid for the flights, including first class upgrades, and almost all the travel and entertainment expenses, even though the official had already received the funds to pay for his expenses. Moreover, Metcalf & Eddy failed to accurately record these transactions, furthering the prosecution's case that the company knowingly violated the law.[17]

The civil settlement in this case required Metcalf & Eddy to institute an FCPA compliance program. This case set the standard for what the government expects in such a program, and has been repeatedly followed in other cases. The standards laid out establish the minimum requirements that should be met when creating an FCPA compliance program.[18]

At minimum, an effective FCPA compliance program includes the following elements:

- Clear FCPA policy, establishing compliance standards and practices to be followed by employees, consultants, and agents. These standards and practices must be reasonably capable of reducing violations and ensuring compliance.
- Assignment of one or more senior officials to be responsible for oversight of the compliance program. The official shall have the authority and responsibility to implement and utilize monitoring and auditing systems to detect criminal conduct, and when necessary, bring in outside counsel and independent auditors to conduct investigations and audits. The officials should make any necessary modifications to the program to respond to detected violations and to prevent further similar violations.
- Creating and maintaining a committee to review the hiring of agents, consultants, or other representatives to do business in a foreign country, and the related contracts. The committee will also review all prospective joint venture partners, to ensure FCPA compliance, and the due diligence done in selecting the prospective partner. The committee has a continuing responsibility to ensure subsequent due diligence in retaining other agents and consultants by the joint venture. This committee should be independent and not to be influenced by the company officials involved in the transactions at issue.
- Clear corporate policies to make sure that the company does not delegate substantial discretionary authority to individuals that the company knows or should know are likely to engage in illegal activities.
- Clear corporate procedures to assure that the necessary precautions are taken to make sure the company only does business with reputable and qualified individuals. The policy must require that evidence of the due diligence performed be maintained in the company's files.
- Communicating FCPA policies, standards, and procedures to employees; requiring regular training on the FCPA and other applicable foreign

bribery laws to officers and employees involved in foreign projects. Agents and consultants hired in connection with foreign business should also be given appropriate training, as soon as is practicable.

- Implementation of appropriate discipline measures, including as necessary, discipline of individuals who fail to detect violations of the law or of the company's compliance policies.
- Establishing a reporting system whereby suspected criminal conduct may be reported, without fear of retribution, and without having to report directly to immediate superiors.
- Including in all foreign business contracts provisions banning foreign bribery. No payment of money or anything of value will be promised, offered, or paid, directly or indirectly to any foreign official, politician, political candidate, or similar individual, to induce them to use their influence or to obtain an improper advantage in a business dealing. All contracts must include a provision that all prospective agents agree not to retain any sub-agents or representatives without prior written consent of a senior company official; any breach of this provision terminates the contract.

Furthermore, an effective FCPA compliance program should also include:

- Periodic review, at least once every five years, of its corporate policies and FCPA compliance program, to be conducted by independent legal and auditing firms retained for such purpose.
- Prompt investigation and/or reporting of any alleged violations of the FCPA or other applicable foreign bribery laws by the company, its officers, agents, or other personnel, and of any joint venture in which the company is a participant.

Newer cases have added an additional requirement:[19]

- The company, using objective measures, must determine the regions or countries in which it does business that pose higher risks of corruption, and then on a periodic basis, conduct rigorous FCPA audits of its operations in such areas. The audits shall include detailed audits of the operating unit's books and records, audits of selected agents, consultants, and joint venture partners and interviews with relevant employees, consultants, agents, etc.

The importance of having an effective FCPA compliance program is heightened by increased FCPA enforcement in the last several years, and the widening of its scope and the severity of its penalties.[20] The Department of Justice and the SEC have attacked foreign corruption the same way they have confronted domestic corporate scandals. Court decisions have also furthered these efforts, by upholding the government's broad interpretation of the FCPA, such as *United States v. Kay*.[21] The government has wide latitude in enforcing the FCPA's provisions and can harshly punish violators as appropriate.

A case that illustrates the government's increased efforts is the case of the Monsanto Corporation. An employee of the agri-business giant bribed an Indonesian official to induce him to repeal a law that Monsanto deemed burdensome. Even though the bribery appeared to result solely from the actions of a single employee operating without authorization, Monsanto's internal controls discovered the misconduct and punished it, and voluntarily reported the incident to the government, the SEC still proceeded with the case. However, because of the existence of Monsanto's compliance program and its cooperation, it received a deferred prosecution agreement.

After the *Kay* decision and the Monsanto settlement agreement, "it is clear that, subject to the FCPA's limited exceptions, any illicit payment to a foreign official can run afoul of the law, regardless of whether the company has a potential contract on the horizon."[22] Furthermore, officials at the DOJ and the SEC have repeatedly dismissed the idea of a "rogue employee" defense. Regardless of the fact that an individual employee acting alone in contravention of company policy caused the violation, the company is still liable for the breach. The DOJ and SEC take the position "that any FCPA problem must be the result of some deficiency in a company's internal controls."[23]

Even though the government has prosecuted companies such as Monsanto who have working compliance programs and voluntarily reported misconduct, this still underscores the need for an effective compliance program. For one, compliance programs can always be improved and strengthened to increase their effectiveness. Additionally, the government's stepped-up prosecutions of FCPA violators have put corporations on notice that their wrongdoing will be found out and severely dealt with, particularly if they do not have a compliance program that meets the minimum standards and do not cooperate.

The complete lack of an FCPA compliance program can doom a company, as was the case with the Titan Corporation, a San Diego-based military intelligence and communications firm. An SEC complaint alleged, among other FCPA violations, that "Titan funneled approximately $2 million, via its agent in Benin, towards the election campaign of Benin's then-incumbent President... Titan made these payments to assist the company in its development of a telecommunications project in Benin and to obtain the Benin government's consent to an increase in the percentage of Titan's project management fees for that project."[24] After consenting to the entry of final judgment, Titan agreed to pay $28.4 million, at the time the largest FCPA penalty ever, which included disgorgement of profits stemming from the illicit payments. A merger deal with Lockheed Martin also fell through after the discovery of the violations.[25] Most importantly, the SEC took the company to task for its failure to have any sort of compliance program or to even make any sort of substantial compliance effort at all.

> *In its 23 years of existence prior to 2004, Titan has never had a FCPA compliance program or procedures. Titan's only related "policy" is a statement in Titan Corporation's Code of Ethics, which all Titan employees were required to sign annually, stating "employees must be fully familiar with and strictly adhere to such provisions as the Foreign Corrupt Practices Act." Titan did not enforce that policy nor did it provide its employees with any information concerning the FCPA.*[26]

This complete absence of compliance efforts undoubtedly factored into the harsh penalties that Titan suffered. The government treats harshly those companies that make no efforts at compliance, and will take that into account when punishing them.

However, the presence of an effective FCPA compliance program and cooperation with the government, while it will not preclude prosecution, will help to reduce the penalties faced by a company. In dealing with self-reporting of FCPA violations, the government has seemingly followed the cooperation standards laid out by the Thompson and McNulty memos.[27] By voluntary reporting and cooperating with the investigation, a company stands a much greater chance of escaping with a deferred prosecution agreement and lessened penalties than otherwise could have been achieved.

THE CHALLENGE OF IMPLEMENTING CORPORATE COMPLIANCE IN FOREIGN ISSUERS

Pedro Fabiano is an international expert with more than 15 years experience conducting fraud investigations and compliance audits, designing fraud prevention, anti-money laundering (AML), and ethics compliance programs, and providing consulting services in multi-industry and multi-partner environments in the United States and Latin America. He is a Certified Fraud Examiner and Certified Public Accountant and is based in Buenos Aires, Argentina.

Fabiano was elected to the Board of Regents of the Association of Certified Fraud Examiners (ACFE) for the period 2002–2004. In 2005, he was designated an ACFE Fellow. The Fellow Program was established to recognize outstanding achievements, significant contributions, and exceptional service to the field of fraud examination. He is also President and cofounder of the Argentina Chapter of the ACFE, the only Chapter in Latin America.

He is a frequent lecturer at universities and for professional organizations on the topics of corporate governance, information security, loss prevention, fraud auditing, and AML. Most recently, he has developed and conducted the seminar entitled *Auditing and Fraud in Financial Institutions: A Global Regulatory Perspective*, for the Central Bank of Argentina.

Based on his wealth of experience, Fabiano provides a unique perspective on compliance challenges outside the United States with an emphasis on Latin America in the following question and answer session:

Q: What has been the impact on foreign private issuers as a result of the recent changes to laws and regulations in the United States in relation to corporate governance and fraud prevention?

A: The recent changes to laws and regulations in the United States with respect to governance and fraud prevention have had a considerable impact on foreign private issuers and also on subsidiaries of U.S. registered entities. A combination of Sarbanes-Oxley's (SOX) greater focus on internal controls, the increased penalties for Foreign Corrupt Practices Act (FCPA) books and records violations as a result of SOX, and a continued aggressive U.S. government policy to target international business bribery, has resulted in a significant level of FCPA enforcement activity since 2002.

For example, in April 2006, the SEC instituted cease and desist proceedings against Oil States International, Inc. (OSI) for violations of the books and records and internal controls provisions of the FCPA, arising from certain payments made through its HWC subsidiary. The SEC stated that OSI, through certain employees of HWC, provided approximately $348,350 in improper payments to employees of Petroleos de Venezuela, S.A., an energy company owned by the government of Venezuela.

It is important to highlight that there is no general exemption from the U.S. securities laws for foreign private issuers. If their securities are offered or traded in the United States, they need to concern themselves with these laws. The Montedison S.P.A. case represented the first time the SEC sanctioned a foreign issuer that had no operations in the United States. This Italian company, whose senior management fraudulently overstated company income by at least $398 million from 1988 through early 1993, was ordered by the U.S. District Court for the District of Columbia to pay a civil penalty of $300,000 for violating the antifraud, financial reporting, and books and records provisions of federal securities laws. The order was the result of a settlement between the SEC and Montedison in which Montedison neither admitted nor denied liability for the allegations in the complaint. The SEC had filed the complaint in 1996 and was settled in 2001.

The FCPA, which was enacted in 1977, is usually associated with its prohibitions against foreign bribery. The provisions of the FCPA relating to bookkeeping and internal controls receive less publicity but are much more likely to form the basis of a government proceeding against companies subject to the Act. The most common FCPA enforcement mechanism is a civil action by the SEC under the accounting provisions and not a criminal charge by the Department of Justice ("DOJ") or even a civil action by the SEC under the anti-bribery provision. The SEC has, in fact, used the FCPA in several cases to prosecute wrongdoers who have not engaged in bribery of foreign officials, but whose actions technically violate the Act's accounting requirements, much like the federal government has used tax laws to prosecute organized crime figures whose other crimes cannot be proven.

Since the passage of SOX in 2002, the accounting provisions have assumed even greater importance because officers now are required to certify the integrity of their companies' financial statements and assess the adequacy of internal controls. As a result, companies are more frequently uncovering accounting-provision violations in connection with internal SOX reviews and are self-reporting these violations to regulators in hopes of mitigating penalties for noncompliance.

Several SOX provisions have contributed to the increase in self-reported FCPA cases, but two in particular, Sections 302 and 404, have fundamentally changed the approach companies take in preventing, detecting, and responding to fraudulent accounting practices. These provisions place responsibility for detecting fraudulent behavior and inadequate record-keeping in the highest levels of management. In response to Sections 302 and 404, certifying officers are demanding greatly enhanced scrutiny of the adequacy of internal controls and procedures and other fraud-prevention measures, the natural consequence of which is an increase in the number of FCPA violations discovered internally and self-reported to regulators. Moreover, certifying officers have a strong incentive to prevent and detect fraud. Under SOX Section 906, a criminal provision closely related to Section 302, a manager who willfully certifies a periodic report filed with the SEC that omits the requirements of the accounting provisions of the FCPA faces criminal penalties of up to 20 years in prison and/or fines of up to $5 million.

Q: How important are foreign issuers in the U.S. stock markets?

A: Roughly 1,200 foreign companies are listed on U.S. exchanges. The New York Stock Exchange (NYSE) has 450 foreign issuers, NASDAQ has about 300, and the remaining foreign companies trade on over-the-counter exchanges.

Listing on the U.S. markets carries a lot of prestige and as investor interest in non-U.S. securities grows, the NYSE is committed to listing companies that demonstrate the highest standards of corporate governance and financial strength. In 2005, the NYSE continued to be the leading market for non-U.S. companies. As of December 31, 2005, the NYSE listed more than 450 non-U.S. companies, from 47 countries, representing a total global market capitalization of $7.9 trillion. The market capitalization of the 17 mainland Chinese companies on the NYSE increased to $329 billion, and the NYSE added its ninth listed company from India in 2005.

Latin America had 89 companies listed in the NYSE by the end of 2005. The majority of these companies were headquartered in Brazil (35 companies), Chile (18), Mexico (17), and Argentina (12). These companies cover several industries including: telecommunications, gas distribution/transportation, oil/gas exploration, water utility, electric utility, and banking.

Q: What are the key characteristics of the business environment in Latin America that affects corporate governance and fraud prevention?

A: Based on my experience, the business environment in most countries in Latin America has two main general characteristics: a poor or not properly enforced legal and regulatory framework and a very high concentration of ownership and control. Countries in Latin America share a common legal origin: the European civil code tradition. But the legal and judicial commonalities within the region extend as well to the approaches taken to enforcement of laws and contracts. In general, the incidence of civil litigation is small in comparison to European and North American patterns, with greater emphasis placed on administrative and criminal judicial actions. Private dispute resolution mechanisms, such as mandatory arbitration, are comparatively new and largely untested.

In many emerging economies of the region, the vast majority of people do not trust one another. For example, the distrust surrounding the enforceability of contracts leads to large portions of the population believing that negotiations are not over even after a contract is signed. This can result in side letters and other agreements not detailed in the contract but still enforceable. As a result, transaction costs to protect one party from the other in such circumstances are much higher.

A confusing, burdensome, or even unfair legislative and regulatory framework increases the cost of establishing a business, discourages investors, and provides a fertile ground for corruption. In some countries, certain critics even believe that regulations are intentionally drafted in a confusing manner to provide officials with more discretion. Under such circumstances, responsible business conduct is frequently discarded in favor of survival, or the law is bent or interpreted to fit the circumstances.

Even where laws and regulations are well drafted, they are often enforced unevenly—or ignored by the population—in practice. The failure to enforce the legislative and regulatory framework, or to comply with it, contributes to confusion, places the law-abiding enterprise at a competitive disadvantage, discourages investors, and extends a climate of corruption.

Many firms are directly or indirectly controlled by one of the numerous industrial, financial, and mixed corporations that operate in Latin American economies. A mixed corporation is a group of firms linked to each other through ownership relations and controlled by a local family, a group of investors, or by a foreign company. The dominant shareholders, through complex structures including the use of pyramids, cross-holdings, and dual class shares, usually control these entities. High ownership concentration and mixed corporation structures also significantly affect the composition of boards. Most board members in Latin American companies are related to controlling groups through family ties, friendships, business relationships, and labor contracts.

The lack of transparency that typically characterizes intra-group transactions and the absence of independent-level firm decision-making are now increasingly seen as obstacles to cost-effective financing. In the course of the past few years, a number of groups have begun to segregate their operations and more clearly separate the activities, financing, and governance of group member companies. How groups re-direct themselves, and the mechanisms they put into place in response to calls for greater transparency and independent management of business lines, are important elements of the evolution of a market economy in the region.

Despite massive privatization of state-owned companies, the state is still an important shareholder in many large companies throughout the region. In addition, in many cases, the privatization process importantly shaped the configuration of the ownership and control structures of the privatized companies.

Finally, Latin American capital markets have recently experienced a wave of mergers and acquisitions where ownership of the largest domestic companies has been transferred to foreign companies. Also, during the last ten years many of the largest Latin American companies have been on the U.S. markets through the *American Depositary Receipt* (ADR) program, while domestic trading has contracted, presenting lower turnover ratios and a very low level of new equity issues.

Q: What are the main obstacles faced by U.S. subsidiaries and foreign issuers in implementing U.S. standards in Latin America?

A: Getting international employees to embrace U.S. standards is a great challenge, which consists of making people in remote parts of the world feel like they are part of one enterprise, global in nature.

Cultural issues are always an obstacle. A good example is the implementation of a hotline. People in many parts of the world are uncomfortable having an anonymous method of reporting a problem, especially in places where there has been a history of repression or abuse. There is a real cultural aversion to that. In some Latin American companies, although a variety of anonymous reporting mechanisms have been properly implemented, they have not received any complaints during the first two years of existence.

A common cultural difference is the attitude toward hiring relatives. In some countries, it is expected that owners and managers will hire relatives as a matter of course. In others, hiring relatives is discouraged or, in some circumstances, prohibited.

Another obstacle we often encounter is that local executives and employees consider that the extension of U.S. regulatory directives into those countries is, to some extent, an expression of American hegemony. Frequently, this creates or encourages a feeling of anti-Americanism. As a result, the initial efforts in educating overseas workers about U.S. compliance can be really hard. I was recently contracted to conduct a training program in a Latin American company listed on the NYSE, and found that the employee's initial reaction was "this is a U.S. problem." But the employee's attitude changed significantly when I explained that the company has voluntarily decided to become a listed entity in the United States and that this decision resulted in important benefits for the stakeholders and some specific compliance requirements. This dramatic change of attitude showed me that the employees had not been properly and timely informed about the basic obligation of a foreign issuer. This situation also demonstrates that, besides training, effective "top-down" communication is an essential element in any compliance effort.

The implementation of the FCPA in emerging market economies is also a major challenge. For example, although no society openly *approves* paying or accepting bribes, in countries where government employees receive lower than subsistence-level pay, "expediting fees" (also known as "grease or facilitating payments") often become unapproved but *accepted* behavior under local custom. In such countries, bribery is so common that even law enforcement officials pay bribes to gain their positions.

Q: Considering the cultural issues and the business environment, what would be your general recommendations for a successful compliance approach in Latin America?

A: A thorough analysis and assessment of the country's legal framework and its enforcement, and the local business practices would be the suggested first step in designing a successful compliance strategy.

Given the country and industry differences found, it appears to be a mistake to expect all corporate compliance programs to look alike. Careful thought should be given to tailoring the policy to the particular firm, industry, and country. Large multinational firms operating in a number of countries need to consider the general applicability of a code of ethics or ethics training that was developed in the country in which the firm's headquarters is located. If ethical concerns differ by country, then imposing a set of standards developed for one country on another country may be counterproductive. Similarly, expatriates working for multinational firms need to be aware that their own perception of ethical issues may not match that of their native fellow employees.

The design and implementation of a global compliance program requires extreme sensitivity to local norms, values, and standards. The program must recognize that management policies, standards, and procedures will be open to interpretation at all levels of the enterprise. For example, a shallow approach to ethical business conduct only condemns bribes and threatens to punish those who pay or accept them. However, a global compliance program takes a comprehensive approach. It recognizes such accepted behavior as part of the obstacles facing the enterprise and addresses such issues systemically. In other words, it addresses them at their roots by examining hiring processes, compensation schemes, and training and education; by instituting monitoring, auditing, and reporting mechanisms; and by influencing the legislative or regulatory processes.

In dealing with employees' reluctance to accept the SOX/FCPA provisions, training becomes essential. The first important message to communicate during training is that they are part of a larger global enterprise, and that in this world of globalized technology and information, inappropriate conduct will ultimately be exposed. It is highly unlikely that bribery and corruption going on in one part of the world will not eventually be discovered in another part of the world. The second, and not less important message, is that all their reputations are at stake, and a company's most important asset is its reputation; once we lose that, it is very hard to recover it.

Finally, it is essential to convince executives and employees that the SOX/FCPA provisions should not be viewed as more than just another bureaucratic measure through which businesses are forced to jump. Instead, the provisions are highly effective tools that businesses can use to prevent and detect fraud. Sound accounting practices and internal controls often are the best defense against fraud, especially in certain foreign countries where regulators take a less rigorous approach in enforcing rules related to financial reporting. Accordingly, domestic companies with operations outside the United States and foreign issuers are strongly advised to make SOX/FCPA compliance a high priority in their global business strategies.

Q: Based on your experience, what specific best practices and strategies have been implemented by successful companies?

A: The most common best practices and strategies adopted by companies in Latin America include:

- The establishment of a clear, written job description for the compliance officer, approved by senior management, and the board. This job description is effectively communicated to all levels of the organization.
- The assignment of primary compliance responsibilities to business departments (marketing, operations, finance, etc.) as compared to those areas mainly involved in supporting compliance functions (legal, human resources, etc). These responsibilities are commonly documented in a "Compliance Responsibility Chart," which is an integral part of the Compliance Program.

- The Compliance Program requires that the business and supporting departments prepare quarterly reports for the Compliance Officer. The Compliance Officer prepares quarterly summary reports and an annual assessment for the Board.
- The Internal Audit Plan includes the review of the supporting documentation and evaluation of the reliability of the quarterly compliance reports issued by the departments.
- Senior management and board members demonstrate their commitment to compliance by attending training sessions and sharing successful compliance experiences with the employees.
- Strong formal and informal communication channels have been developed between Internal Audit, Security, and the compliance executive.

NOTES

1. Author Thomas L. Freidman coined the phrase "The World is Flat," which is also the title of his best-selling book that examines how the playing field of the world is being leveled through technology, competition, and innovation.
2. Title 15, United States Code, Section 78dd-3.
3. *United States v. SSI International Far East, Ltd,* defendant, criminal information unsealed on October 16, 2006, United States District Court, District of Oregon, 24.
4. Ibid.
5. Schnitzer Steel Industries, Inc. Company History, www.fundinguniverse.com/company-histories/Schnitzer-Steel-Industries-Inc-Company-History.html.
6. Ibid.
7. Ibid.
8. *In the matter of Schnitzer Steel Industries, Inc.,* Respondent, Order Instituting Cease-and-Desist Proceedings, Making Findings, and Imposing a Cease-and-Desist Order Pursuant to Section 21C of the Securities Exchange Act of 1934, Securities and Exchange Commission Release No. 54606, October 16, 2006, www.sec.gov/litigation/admin/2006/34–54606.pdf.
9. Ibid.
10. Ibid.
11. Ibid.
12. Ibid.
13. Ibid.

14. *United States v. SSI International Far East, Ltd,* defendant, criminal information unsealed on October 16, 2006, United States District Court, District of Oregon, 5–6.

15. Schnitzer Steel Industries, Inc. 2006 Annual Report, November 9, 2006, 22, /library.corporate-ir.net/library/87/870/87090/items/225808/2006AR.pdf.

16. "Former Senior Officer of Schnitzer Steel Industries Inc. Subsidiary Pleads Guilty to Foreign Bribes," United States Department of Justice Press Release, June 29, 2007, www.usdoj.gov/opa/pr/2007/June/07_crm_474.html.

17. Transparency USA Toolkit, www.transparency-usa.org/Toolkit1c.html.

18. *United States of America v. Metcalf & Eddy, Inc.* (D. Mass No. 99CV12566-NG).

19. *See, e.g., United States of America v. Monsanto,* Deferred Prosecution Agreement (Dist. D.C. 2005), www.corproatecrimereporter.com/documents/monsantoagreement.pdf.

20. William B.F. Steinman and Kathleen M. Hamann, "Expanding Risks Under the Foreign Corrupt Practices Act," *Government Contract,* September 25, 2006, www.pogolaw.com/articles/2054.pdf. ("[T]here were more FCPA cases brought in 2004 and 2005 than in the prior 26 years combined.").

21. *See United States v. Kay,* 359 F.3d 738 (5th Cir. 2004) (holding that when Congress enacted the FCPA, it intended to cast a "wide net over foreign bribery.").

22. Steinman and Hamann, "Expanding Risks Under the Foreign Corrupt Practices Act."

23. Ibid.

24. *SEC v. The Titan Corporation,* Complaint, Civ. Action No. 05–0411 (JR) (Dist. DC March 1, 2005), 1–2.

25. Fred Shaheen and Natalia Geren, "Penalties Get Tougher for FCPA Violations," *National Defense,* September 1, 2005, 50.

26. *SEC v. Titan,* 16.

27. Michael T.Burr, "Corporations Caught in Rising Tide of FCPA Enforcement," *Inside Counsel,* November 2005, www.insidecounsel.com/issues/insidecounsel/15_168/regulatory/214–1.html.

CHAPTER 7

Compliance Programs and Anti-Money Laundering Efforts

By Marc B. Sherman, Laura Connor, and David Meilstrup*

I n the past, a documented and reasonably functional compliance program was adequate. Today that is not enough; the compliance program must also be effective. There is no better example of this than with money laundering. The threat of money laundering has become a serious concern for both governments and businesses of many nations. In the United States, money laundering has long been used in criminal enterprise, including narcotics trafficking. While the late 1990s brought money laundering investigations and prosecutions greater attention, it was the aftermath of the September 11, 2001, attacks that brought it to the forefront. The global proliferation of anti-money laundering (AML) laws and worldwide investigations have been utilized by authorities to confront the growing specter of international terrorism.

The enforcement of AML laws, however, does not only impact terrorism and narcotics trafficking, areas traditionally associated with money laundering. Vigorous international law enforcement and the breadth of the current anti-money laundering statutes put domestic and international businesses at risk of inadvertently violating the various laws that are at the heart of today's anti-money laundering effort. To aid in the fight against money laundering and terrorist financing activity, the United States government enacted the USA PATRIOT Act[1] ("PATRIOT Act" or "Act"), which

---

*This chapter was written by three forensic accounting professionals highly experienced in AML issues. I deeply appreciate their willingness to contribute their unique insights and expertise to this book.

amends the Bank Secrecy Act (BSA)[2] and allows for better prevention, detection, and prosecution of money laundering and terrorist financing.

Money laundering has long been used to hide the proceeds of crime and prevent detection and prosecution of certain illegal activity. The ability to move and hide the proceeds of crime through the financial system facilitates criminal activity and frustrates the ability of law enforcement to combat crime, and more recently, terrorist financing. In order to help prevent and detect money laundering in the financial system and the underlying criminal and terrorist activity, certain compliance requirements have been imposed on banks and other businesses. As part of compliance, the laws and regulations impose obligations on financial institutions to monitor customer transactions and report suspicious activity.

WHAT IS MONEY LAUNDERING?

Money laundering is the process of filtering "dirty" money (criminal proceeds) through a series of transactions in order to disguise or prevent detection of the source of the money.[3] The "dirty" funds are laundered to give them the appearance of proceeds from legitimate activity. By definition, money laundering consists of three separate independent steps: placement, layering, and integration.

Placement, as the name would imply, is the placing of unlawful cash proceeds into commerce, whether through deposits or other means. *Layering* consists of the separating of the criminal proceeds from their source of origin through many layers of complex financial transactions. Such transactions can include converting cash into monetary instruments, wire transfers, stocks, bonds, and letters of credit or by purchasing valuable assets, such as art and jewelry. Finally, *integration* is the use of seemingly legitimate transactions to disguise the laundering of criminal proceeds back to the criminal.

Money laundering can involve a variety of transaction types, but historically has involved a few common schemes, including structuring,[4] the Black Market Peso Exchange, Mexican bank drafts, and factored third-party checks. The Black Market Peso Exchange is the most common means of money laundering in the Western Hemisphere, used most prevalently by drug traffickers. The proceeds from illegal drug sales in the United States are "bought" by a peso broker in exchange for pesos, at a discounted exchange rate. The dollars in the United States are then re-sold for pesos to South American businessmen, again at a discount. The businessmen use the laundered U.S. dollars to purchase goods in the United States and illegally import them into their home countries.[5] At the conclusion of the transaction, the drug trafficker has pesos, the foreign businessman has U.S. purchased goods for his business, the broker has a commission for brokering the currency exchange, and the U.S. dollar drug proceeds are inserted (laundered) into the legitimate stream of commerce.

Since the enactment of the PATRIOT Act, money laundering has become a concern for all individuals and entities conducting business within or through U.S. borders. In the United States, both the Internal Revenue Service and the Department of Justice have divisions that investigate suspected money laundering crimes.[6]

BANK SECRECY ACT

Money laundering as a means to enable other criminal activity has been a favorite of the international criminal culture for decades, and therefore, a productive target for law enforcement. The United States Congress passed the Bank Secrecy Act in 1970[7] with the main purpose of preventing financial institutions from being used as unwitting intermediaries for criminal activity. The law was expected to reduce illegal activity by removing an implementation device and by providing law enforcement with another means to more easily detect criminal schemes. To accomplish this, the BSA mandates that financial institutions[8] file certain reports with the government relating to their customers' use of currency and monetary instruments. The law also requires that the institutions maintain specific records for possible use in criminal, tax, and regulatory proceedings.[9] A financial institution's compliance with the BSA results in a paper trail that is useful in better identifying and tracing money laundering activities, which in turn, is expected to lead to identification and prosecution of the related underlying criminal activity. This includes narcotics trafficking, terrorism, and other types of white collar and organized crime.

Because money laundering is such an active tool for the profiting from and disguising of illegal activity, the government takes it very seriously as evidenced by the number of money laundering convictions from 1996 through 2000. In fact the number of convictions was clearly on the rise even prior to the September 11, 2001, terrorist attacks and the enactment of the PATRIOT Act. (See Compliance Insight 7.1).

Reporting Requirements

The BSA requires financial institutions to report many types of transaction activity. *Currency Transaction Reports* (CTRs) are required to be filed by a financial institution with the United States Treasury Department for any cash deposits, cash withdrawals, exchanges of currency, or other transfers

COMPLIANCE INSIGHT 7.1: DEFENDANTS CONVICTED ON MONEY LAUNDERING COUNTS (1996–2000)

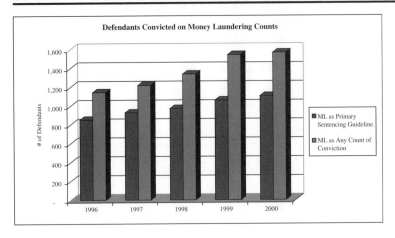

	1996	1997	1998	1999	2000
ML as Primary Sentencing Guideline	853	929	973	1,061	1,106
ML as Any Count of Conviction	1,145	1,219	1,338	1,542	1,565
Total Defendants Convicted of Money Laundering	**1,998**	**2,148**	**2,311**	**2,603**	**2,671**

Source: U.S. Sentencing Commission[a]

[a]"2002 National Money Laundering Strategy"; *Department of the Treasury & Department of Justice*; July 2002, 27.

of cash in excess of $10,000. A financial institution must treat multiple currency transactions as a single transaction if they are conducted by or on behalf of the same individual and total more than $10,000 in cash received or disbursed during one business day.

Suspicious Activity Reports (SARs) must be filed to report any suspicious activity that may relate to the violation of any laws or regulations. Specifically, SAR filing requirements compel banks[10] to file a SAR following the discovery of: any type of insider abuse; violations of federal law when the aggregate amount is $5,000 or more; and transactions in aggregate of

$5,000 or more that may potentially involve money laundering, violations of the BSA, attempts to evade BSA reporting requirements, or have no business or apparent lawful purpose.[11] A bank is required to file a SAR in a timely manner, which in most cases means no later than 30 days from the bank's initial detection of facts that may constitute a basis for suspecting that an activity constitutes "suspicious activity," and in no case more than 60 days.[12] The law imposes similar requirements on non-bank financial institutions as a result of the PATRIOT Act.[13] Other non-bank "financial institutions" now subject to the regulations of the Bank Secrecy Act and its reporting requirements as a result of the PATRIOT Act include mutual funds,[14] insurance companies,[15] securities brokers and dealers,[16] money service businesses,[17] and casinos.[18] All of these classified businesses must now equally comply with the reporting and recordkeeping requirements of the BSA.

The international transport or maintenance of cash or other assets requires United States persons or businesses, including financial institutions that are subject to U.S. jurisdiction and have an interest in, signature, or other authority over one or more bank, security, or other financial account in a foreign country with an aggregate value exceeding $10,000 at any time during the year to file a *Report of Foreign Bank and Financial Accounts* (FBAR). The Financial Crimes Enforcement Network (FinCEN)[19] defines the term "United States person" as "a citizen or resident of the United States, a domestic partnership, a domestic corporation, or a domestic estate or trust."[20]

Record Keeping Requirements

BSA regulations require financial institutions to maintain certain records for a period of five years. The records are to be retained, in part, to allow for the reconstruction of transactions if needed. These recordkeeping requirements include monetary instrument sales records and funds transfer recordkeeping (travel rule) requirements.[21]

In addition to the necessity of filing CTRs on transactions involving cash over $10,000, a bank must maintain records of cash sales of all monetary instruments, including bank checks, drafts, cashier's checks, money orders, and traveler's checks between $3,000 and $10,000, inclusive. These records include evidence of the purchaser's identity and other detailed information. Banks are also required to retain records of all fund transfers of $3,000 or more that it sends, receives, or for which it acts as an intermediary. The type of information that the bank must retain is dependent on its role in the funds transfer process. Also, as the transfer originator or intermediary, the bank is required to pass on certain information to the next bank in the transfer chain.[22]

USA PATRIOT ACT

Since its enactment in 1970, the BSA has undergone several amendments aimed at strengthening its AML and counter-terrorism objectives. Of these amendments, the most significant is itself a new, robust, and somewhat more novel law. On October 26, 2001, President Bush signed into law the Uniting and Strengthening America by Providing Appropriate Tools Required to Intercept and Obstruct Terrorism Act, more commonly known as the USA PATRIOT Act. Title III of the Act strengthens the laws to counter money laundering and makes significant amendments to the BSA.[23] This new law places new and enhanced legal obligations on a variety of businesses in the financial services arena. With this heightened focus on money laundering prevention and detection, even an innocent or unintentional act falling under the definition of "money laundering," unrelated to other criminal activity, may not go as unnoticed as in the past, and may not be dealt with lightly.

The PATRIOT Act is a far-reaching statute that allows for the tracking and intercepting of communications for law enforcement and foreign intelligence gathering purposes.[24] It also provides regulatory authority to the Secretary of the Treasury over U.S. financial institutions to ensure the prevention, detection, and prosecution of foreign money laundering and the financing of terrorism.[25] The Act has also significantly expanded the definition of a "financial institution" to include new types of entities, including all credit unions, a more detailed definition of money transmitters, futures commission merchants, commodity trading advisors, and commodity pool operators.[26] In general, the federal government's powers are strengthened by the Act in three areas: regulations, criminal sanctions, and forfeiture.[27]

Regulations

The PATRIOT Act amends the BSA and expands the Secretary of the Treasury's authority to regulate U.S. financial institutions' activities, especially those activities dealing with foreign individuals and entities. Some of the regulatory changes of the amendments include "special measures" and "enhanced due diligence" requirements to:

- Battle against foreign money laundering,
- prohibit the maintenance of correspondent accounts with foreign shell banks,
- prevent the use of a financial institution's concentration accounts to conceal customer's financial activities, and
- establish minimum new customer identification standards and record-keeping, along with more effective means to verify the identity of foreign customers.[28]

The Act also encourages the sharing of information regarding suspected money laundering and terrorist activities among financial institutions and law enforcement agencies. Most importantly for financial institutions, the Act requires *all financial institutions to implement and maintain an anti-money laundering program.* An effective program would, at a minimum, include a compliance officer; an employee training program; internal policies, procedures and controls; and an independent audit function.[29]

Criminal Sanctions

New crimes were created by the PATRIOT Act, along with amendments to and increased penalties for previously existing crimes. The Act expands money laundering within the United States to include funds that are the proceeds of foreign crimes of violence and political corruption. It also bans the laundering of the proceeds from cybercrime and prohibits supporting terrorist organizations. The penalties for counterfeiting are also increased by the Act and it provides the government with the authority to prosecute overseas fraud involving American credit cards. In addition, the Act permits the prosecution of money laundering in the location that the predicate offense occurred.

Forfeiture

Criminal forfeiture can be ordered by the court as a sanction to an individual or entity convicted of a violation of Title 18 of the United States Code, Sections 1956, 1957, or 1960. A forfeiture finding requires the accused to forfeit to the U.S. government all property (real or personal), that is used for or is the proceeds of the criminal offense. Any property traceable to the assets that are directly involved is also subject to forfeiture.[30] The U.S. Department of Justice has an Asset Forfeiture Program designed to seize the assets that are the proceeds of, or were used to facilitate federal crimes. The Asset Forfeiture Program is funded by an Asset Forfeiture Fund ("Fund") as established by the Comprehensive Crime Control Act of 1984. The Fund is self sustaining—it receives the proceeds of any forfeiture and in turn is used to pay for the cost associated with future investigations and prosecutions.[31]

The PATRIOT Act establishes two new types of forfeitures. First, the Act permits the confiscation of all of the property from an entity or individual who participates in an act of terrorism, either domestic or international. Any property derived from or used to aid domestic or international terrorism can also be confiscated. The Act enables the government to establish a mechanism to acquire long-arm jurisdiction for forfeiture proceedings and allows the United States to enforce foreign forfeiture orders. Lastly, the

Act permits the seizure of correspondent accounts held in U.S. financial institutions for foreign banks that are holding forfeitable assets overseas.[32]

NON-FINANCIAL INSTITUTIONS

While the BSA and the PATRIOT Act govern the actions of "financial institutions," other types of entities should be alert to inadvertent implication in money laundering activities. For example, persons involved in *any* trade or business are required to file an IRS/FinCEN Form 8300 for cash transactions over $10,000, and can face severe penalties for failure to comply, even if not a financial institution subject to the BSA.[33] Rules similar to those under the BSA apply to this form if related cash transactions appear to be structured in a manner intended to avoid a Form 8300 reporting. Violations of the requirement of a Form 8300 filing can be subject to criminal prosecution resulting in penalties up to five years in prison or fines from $250,000 to $500,000 for individuals and corporations, respectively.[34]

COMPLIANCE PROGRAMS

At this point, it should be clear that an anti-money laundering compliance program for financial institutions is no longer optional. The complexity of anti-money laundering compliance has matured over time. In the last 10 years, automated software has been developed and banks have beefed up their AML compliance functions. Today's software programs are sophisticated monitoring systems that look at transactions that come into and out of an institution and look for patterns in activity. Patterns that are out of the ordinary are then signaled for further manual investigation. In addition, the government has put more definition on what it expects from the financial institutions (e.g., the PATRIOT Act provided for enhanced due diligence requirements and "know your customer" [KYC] has become the norm). Many banks kept up with the enhancements and government expectations; however, not all have.

    Even with the banking industry's deep experience in the area of AML compliance, there are several reasons why financial institutions continue to fall under the scrutiny of prosecutors. Non-bank financial institutions are relatively new to the AML compliance game and are short on experience with the regulations and with compliance program implementation. This lack of experience puts these businesses in a position of great risk of legal violations. The government has lost its tolerance for lax compliance, particularly given the link between money laundering and terrorism.[35]

Many financial institutions still have antiquated programs that have not been enhanced to meet the current standards of increased scrutiny. Others have off-the-shelf AML programs that are not customized to the unique attributes of the specific operation. The same way that lax AML programs are not being tolerated, AML programs that are not properly or adequately enhanced and updated are also being targeted as money laundering activity by the government.

Today the government expects effective, well-staffed AML programs. It will no longer accept an institution's compliance efforts that are stuck in the past or otherwise unable to function in the current environment, or that fail to meet the current standards. The government expects financial institutions to keep up with the requirements and the sophistication of the times as the regulations change to combat new methods of laundering money and more craftily conceal criminal and terrorist activity. The penalties for failure to meet the requirements of the BSA and PATRIOT Act can be severe.[36] Today, financial institutions should not rely on their programs' past successes or their view of the "industry norm," nor should they expect that the potentially burdensome cost of enhancing their AML programs will buy them any leniency. These problems will likely affect smaller banks more because of their lack of financial strength, regulatory sophistication, and economies of size, but larger, money center banks, that are large-scale financial institutions that provide numerous financial services on a national or international level, will be affected as well.

Financial institutions often end up in the spotlight of a money laundering investigation through the institution's acceptance of funds associated with criminal law enforcement investigations unrelated to the institution. Large banks have now had decades of time and experience refining their AML programs and many have become reasonably adept at preventing and detecting money laundering activity. That causes illicit money to find another path in an attempt to avoid detection. Because the large banks are more likely today to detect illicit money flowing through their more sophisticated detection programs, tainted money has begun moving through smaller banks, banks new to the U.S. regulatory arena, and non-bank financial institutions that, from a compliance perspective, are less sophisticated. This presents a significant risk to these businesses that are now covered by the AML laws. As time passes, these institutions can expect to see law enforcement money laundering investigators show up on their doorsteps with greater frequency. This throws them into the heart of these investigations and puts their AML compliance efforts under the microscope. Consequently, it has become a necessity that these institutions be informed on the current regulatory environment and be prepared with effective AML compliance programs.

The requirements for financial institutions to implement and maintain an anti-money laundering program is not a hollow mandate. According to the BSA and the PATRIOT Act, financial institutions must implement a compliance program that permits them to monitor and identify suspicious activity, which can then be reported to the Treasury Department in a timely manner. Compliance requirements not only apply to the corporate entity, but also to employees of the institution. The law and the government impose obligations on the institution and the employees to watch over the propriety of customers' activities. The institution can be subject to fines, penalties, and criminal sanctions. In addition, employees can individually be subject to criminal sanctions as well, including jail. Some of the common deficiencies of compliance efforts include lax programs and the continuation of older programs not enhanced to meet current standards, as discussed earlier. The government has proven through its prosecution efforts that an institution's claim that a program is on par with historically common industry practices or that the cost of an enhanced AML program is too burdensome are not acceptable defenses. Effective compliance programs should be viewed as living efforts that need to continually evolve with time and circumstances.

As part of the requirements to establish and maintain an *effective* anti-money laundering program, at a minimum, the institution is required to have a designated compliance officer; an ongoing employee training program; adequate and effective internal policies, procedures and controls; and an independent audit function to test programs.[37] Ultimately, these programs must be designed and function to prevent the institution from actively conducting or unknowingly participating in money laundering. At a minimum, the program must be reasonably designed to capture and identify any activity that is unusual or suspicious. In order to detect unusual (and therefore possibly suspicious) activity, an institution must have an appropriate customer due diligence program in place to "know their customers" and have procedures and systems in place to monitor the customer's account activity for unusual or suspicious transactions. In order to adequately accomplish this requirement, most financial institutions today, especially banks, include as an element of their AML program an automated monitoring system for account activity analysis.

Successful activity monitoring programs consider aspects such as red flag type activity, the customer's business, account profile, and related risks. Better procedures also call for reviews of a customer's total relationship, not simply an account-by-account review. In the face of an unusual transaction, isolated account analysis is viewed by prosecutors today as inadequate to make judgments about the legitimacy of the specific transaction or the customer's activity. When potentially suspicious activity is identified, the institution is then required by the BSA and PATRIOT Act to perform an investigation into the potentially suspicious activity and determine whether it rises to the level that would require the filing of a SAR.[38]

Red Flags

Many types of transactions and conduct can constitute potentially suspicious activity and should signal a red flag to a financial institution. Defining and paying attention to red flags in a monitoring system, or elsewhere, is critical to the proper functioning of an adequate compliance program. Once a red flag is signaled, it requires the institution to further investigate the transaction or activity and determine whether a SAR should be filed. Under certain circumstances, appropriate action by the institution may require that an account be closed or customer relationship terminated. These determinations need to be part of the overall compliance program and made on a case by case basis. Failure to take appropriate (and sometimes strong) action against an account holder (depending on the facts) could weigh negatively against the institution in a criminal money laundering investigation.

The following types of activity are examples of "red flags" that could signal potential suspicious activity. These examples also instinctively point out other necessary elements of a good compliance and customer due diligence program by the very nature of the underlying knowledge needed to spot the red flag. These examples are by no means comprehensive.

1. Activity inconsistent with the customer's business:
   Activity that is inconsistent with a customer's business or stated account purpose should always be a red flag and at a minimum requires appropriate inquiries. Of course, this requires a robust KYC program in order to know and understand the customer's business from the inception of the relationship. An institution needs to protect itself from possible suspicious activity conducted by its customers and also protect its customers from potential fraud attempts. Some examples of potentially suspicious activity that may be inconsistent with the customer's business include a retail business that makes routine check deposits, but rarely makes cash withdrawals for daily operations; a business that frequently deposits large amounts of cash, but checks, or debits on the account are inconsistent with that type of business; and a customer's corporate account that primarily has withdrawals and deposits in cash rather than in checks or wire transfers.
2. Avoidance of reporting or recordkeeping requirements:
   Any attempt by a customer to avoid a bank's (or other institution's) reporting and recordkeeping requirements, as required by the BSA,

should be considered a red flag and be investigated and reported. Common schemes used in attempted avoidance include a customer intentionally withholding part of a cash transaction to keep that transaction under the reporting threshold; a customer who is reluctant to either provide the information necessary to file the report or to proceed with the transaction and have the report filed after being informed of the reporting requirement; and a customer or group who tries to coerce a bank employee into not filing any required recordkeeping or reporting forms.

3. Fund (wire) transfers:
Many types of wire transfers should potentially raise suspicion and be cause for further investigation by an institution. In fact, some of these types of red flag activities may be activities for which automated systems can routinely and easily monitor. Examples of potentially suspicious wire activity for which an institution should monitor, automated or otherwise, include large, round number wires; frequent or large volume of wires to and from offshore banks; payments or receipts with no apparent links to legitimate contracts, goods, or services; and wire activity to or from financial secrecy haven countries without an apparent business reason, or when it is inconsistent with the customer's business or history.

4. Insufficient or suspicious information provided by a customer:
When a bank is presented with incomplete, conflicting, or suspicious information by a potential or existing customer, it should consider this suspicious and perform further inquiries to determine whether a SAR should be filed and the relationship denied or terminated. Common cases of such information include a reluctance by a business that is establishing a new account to provide complete information about the business's purpose, prior banking relationships, names of officers and directors, or its location; a customer's refusal to provide information necessary to qualify for credit or other banking services; a spike in a customer's activity with no, little, or illogical explanation; discovery that the customer's home or business phone is disconnected; and a difference in the customer's financial statements from those of similar businesses.

5. Certain activity or behavior by a bank employee:
Not all suspicious, red flag activity is conducted outside the bank. Some red flag activity is conducted in-house by bank employees, whether it is to aid customer illegal activity or to perpetrate some other type of fraud. There are usually warning signs that are exhibited by bank employees involved in these types of activities, including a lavish lifestyle that cannot be supported by the employee's salary; refusal to conform

to recognized systems, policies, and controls, particularly in private banking; and a reluctance to take a vacation.

6. Other suspicious customer activity:
   Other types of suspicious customer activity include substantial deposit(s) of numerous $50 and $100 bills; frequent exchanges of small dollar denominations for large dollar denominations; a large loan suddenly paid down with no reasonable explanation; deposits or disbursements to countries and jurisdictions outside of the customer's normal geography; money orders or travelers checks, which are numbered sequentially, are in round dollars, or have unusual stamps/symbols on them and are deposited by mail; and the use of loan proceeds in a manner that is not consistent with the stated purpose of the loan.

These red flags are not meant to represent an exhaustive list of activities that suggest possible money laundering, but are rather a sample of common examples of red flag activity. Additionally, as those involved in laundering illicit proceeds alter their methods in new and creative ways in order to avoid detection, additional red flags will arise. AML compliance programs need to be able to adapt to these new methods and recognize additional red flags to incorporate them into their suspicious activity detection efforts.

Internal Controls and the Audit Function

In order to have a truly effective AML compliance program, a financial institution needs to have properly designed internal controls in place and the appropriate, periodic *independent* audit function to test those controls and the program as a whole. Proper controls should cover every aspect of the institution's compliance program, from account opening and acceptance to activity monitoring to employee training and suspicious activity reporting. A good control structure will have separation of key duties; proper level and separation of sign-off approvals for various acceptances such as account opening paper work, account monitoring, wire processing, and credit issues; defined processes for SARs, CTRs, and other reporting requirements; and an incorporation of compliance responsibilities in job descriptions and performance evaluations of employees. However, having the policies and controls is not sufficient; they need to function effectively. A financial institution is also required to have an independent audit function to test its compliance programs.[39] This testing should be independent from the institution's management and compliance department and should, at a minimum, assess the following:

- The overall integrity and effectiveness of the systems, controls, and technical BSA/PATRIOT Act compliance;

- transactions, through test samples, in all areas of the institution (with emphasis on high-risk areas, products, and services) to ensure the institution is following the proscribed regulations and internal policies and procedures;
- the employees' knowledge of regulations and procedures;
- the adequacy, accuracy, and completeness of training programs; and
- the adequacy of the institution's process for identifying and reporting suspicious activity.

The findings of the independent audit testing should be part of the institution's governance and senior management processes and given serious attention by both.

THE RISE OF FOREIGN STATUTES

Historically, the U.S. Bank Secrecy Act and related U.S. anti-money laundering laws were considered the model to emulate. In fact, many other countries were known for not having similar or complementary laws and regulations, which consequently encouraged the use of those countries as money havens and frustrated the ability to investigate U.S. money laundering activity. However, today, many other countries are following the lead of the United States and have recently enhanced their AML efforts and have enacted their own regulations and requirements. The Bahamas, Switzerland, Indonesia, and Colombia are examples of just a few of the countries taking steps to enhance their AML protocols.

Banking havens like the Bahamas and Switzerland have enacted a myriad of statutes and regulations, contributing to the global fight against the facilitation of criminal activity through the use of the financial systems to launder criminal proceeds. In fact, both the Bahamas and Switzerland have enacted significant know-your-customer requirements, have further detailed their requirements for reporting suspicious activity and have increased or plan to increase the types of crimes that are predicate offenses of money laundering, which will include crimes related to terrorism activities.[40]

Indonesia has recently come far in its efforts to improve its anti-money laundering environment. As a result of these ongoing efforts, Indonesia was removed from the Financial Action Task Force's ("FATF") list of Non-Cooperative Countries and Territories ("NCCT") on February 11, 2005, and also from special FATF monitoring one year later. [41] In April 2002, Indonesia passed a law that made money laundering a criminal offense and identified 15 predicate offenses related to money laundering. Indonesia also enacted know-your-customer requirements, currency transaction reporting requirements, and suspicious activity reporting requirements.

Even Colombia, a country where the laundering of drug money permeates its economy and affects its financial institutions, has established banking and anti-money laundering laws that in some areas are more stringent than those in the U.S. In fact, Colombia is viewed as the hemispheric leader in the effort to fight money laundering. Colombia criminalized the laundering of proceeds from various types of criminal activities and it has enacted specific laws to combat some of its specific problem areas. In October 2005, Colombia made it illegal to transport more than the equivalent of $10,000 in currency across its borders, inbound or outbound. This step was done in order to combat the issue of bulk cash smuggling in and out of the country.[42]

As now seen in the efforts of these countries, and others, the U.S. is no longer the lone jurisdiction with significant and improving AML laws and regulations. Advancements in many countries around the world that have historically been magnets for money laundering activity are impressive and noteworthy, and are indicative of the international shift to comply with a stricter stance against money laundering and the underlying criminal activity.

NOTES

1. Public Law 107-56.
2. 31 U.S.C. 5311-5330; 12 U.S.C. 1818(s), 1829(b), and 1951-1959.
3. 18 U.S.C. 1956-1957. Money laundering is a criminal act as defined in Title 18 of the U.S.C.
4. Structuring refers to separating large cash transactions into multiple smaller transactions in order to avoid the requirements of the BSA to file Currency Transaction Reports (CTRs) for all cash or cash equivalent transactions that exceed $10,000.
5. Javier Sarmiento, "Money Laundering: Black Market Peso Exchange: An International Scheme," *Fraud Magazine*, July/August 2007, 24.
6. www.irs.gov; www.doj.gov.
7. 31 U.S.C. 5311-5330; 12 U.S.C. 1818(s), 1829(b), and 1951-1959.
8. The BSA has a narrower definition of "financial institutions"; however, the PATRIOT Act further expands this definition.
9. Regulatory Bulletin RB 18-6, Compliance Activities Handbook, Office of Thrift Supervision, Department of the Treasury, March 31, 2004, 1.
10. The definition of bank in the regulations (even before the PATRIOT Act) is quite broad to mean any depository institution such as a commercial bank, thrift, and credit union.
11. 31 CFR 103.18.
12. Ibid.

13. For example, effective December 22, 2003, the Bank Secrecy Act regulatory requirements of 31CFR 103 were amended to add futures commissions merchants and introducing brokers in commodities to the definition of "Financial Institutions" for the purpose of Suspicious Activity Reporting.
14. 31 CFR 103.15
15. 31 CFR 103.16
16. 31 CFR 103.19
17. 31 CFR 103.20
18. 31 CFR 103.21
19. FinCEN is a U.S. law enforcement agency under the Department of the Treasury.
20. www.fincen.gov/reg_fbar.html.
21. *See, e.g.*, 31 CFR 103.33(g)—The "Travel Rule" requires financial institutions to include certain information in transmittal orders relating to transmittals of funds of $3,000 or more.
22. Ibid.
23. Public Law 107-56. The USA PATRIOT Act also includes laws on the tracking and interception of communications, the ability to detain and remove foreign terrorists within U.S. borders, and surveillance measures regulations.
24. Public Law 107-56. Also see Charles Doyle, "The USA PATRIOT Act: A Sketch"; Congressional Research Service, The Library of Congress, April 18, 2002, 1.
25. Ibid.
26. Public Law 107-56 and 31 U.S.C. 5312(a).
27. Public Law 107-56. Also see Charles Doyle, "The USA PATRIOT Act: A Sketch"; Congressional Research Service, The Library of Congress, April 18, 2002, 3-4.
28. Ibid.
29. Public Law 107-56 and 31 U.S.C. 5318(h)(1).
30. 18 U.S.C. 982.
31. www.doj.gov.
32. Public Law 107-56.
33. "US indicts 23, including two Washington, DC area automobile dealership organizations, salesman, and managers," *Washington Post*, March 12, 1993.
34. IRS/FinCEN Form 8300; www.irs.gov.
35. *See e.g.*, BankAtlantic's Deferred Prosecution Agreement, www.usdoj.gov/usao/fls/PressReleases/Attachments/060426-02.BankAtlanticDPA.pdf.

36. *See, e.g.*, AmSouth Bank's $50 million penalty. (www.usdoj.gov/usao/ mss/documents/pressreleases/october2004/amprsrels.htm, www.fincen .gov/amsouthassessmentcivilmoney.pdf and www.federalreserve.gov/ boarddocs/press/enforcement/2004/20041012/), Riggs Bank's $41 million in criminal and civil penalties (www.usdoj.gov/tax/usaopress/ 2005/txdv050530.html and www.fincen.gov/riggsassessment3.pdf) and BankAtlantic's penalty of $10 million (www.usdoj.gov/usao/fls/Press Releases/Attachments/060426-02.BankAtlanticDPA.pdf).
37. 31 U.S.C. 5318(h)(1) and Public Law 107-56.
38. Even banks that were not governed by the BSA prior to the PATRIOT Act were required to file SARs under other regulations such as 12 CFR 21.11.
39. 31 U.S.C. 5318(h)(1) and Public Law 107-56.
40. *See, e.g.*, Bahamas Security Commission Interim AML and KYC Guidelines - April 2004; The Bahamas Financial Transactions Reporting Act, 2000; The Bahamas Financial Intelligence Act, 2000.
41. The Financial Action Task Force (FATF) is an inter-governmental body whose purpose is the development and promotion of national and international policies to combat money laundering and terrorist financing. www.fatf-gafi.org/pages/0,2987,en_32250379_32235720_1_1_1_1_1, 00.html.
42. Ibid.

About the Chapter Authors

Marc Sherman is a forensic accountant and Managing Director at Huron Consulting Group, an international consulting firm. He is the Fraud, White Collar, and Anti-Money Laundering Services leader for Huron Consulting Group, and is head of its Washington, DC Office. He was previously the National Partner in Charge of the forensic accounting practice at a Big Four accounting and audit firm. Marc has led hundreds of forensic investigations at corporate and financial institutions, both domestically and internationally and has frequently worked as a special consultant to the U.S. Department of Justice Criminal Division, anti-money laundering section, and other law enforcement and regulatory agencies to consult on investigations of suspected money laundering activity and other misconduct. He has also worked for foreign governments to conduct bank fraud investigations and asset recovery throughout the world. His work has included the review and consulting on the effectiveness and adequacy of BSA/AML compliance programs and the elements of those programs. He has authored several chapters on forensic accounting investigations and frequently speaks on the topics of fraud investigations and anti-money laundering. Marc is a CPA, a member of the Maryland and DC Bar, and a Certified Fraud Examiner. He is also on the faculty of Georgetown University where he teaches Forensic Accounting.

Laura Connor is a Manager in Huron Consulting Group's Washington, DC office. Laura provides accounting and financial advice to companies and legal counsel on a variety of issues surrounding financial investigations and litigation. Laura has worked in a variety of industries and has extensive experience assisting government investigators with Bank Secrecy Act/Anti-Money Laundering compliance and fund tracing investigations as well as working with regulators on BSA/AML compliance and fund tracing issues.

David Meilstrup is an Associate in Huron Consulting Group's Washington, DC office. He has conducted investigations into financial and accounting matters, and has assisted counsel in disputes and litigation matters. David's experience spans across a variety of industries, including significant experience with financial institutions in the areas of money laundering activity, BSA/AML compliance, and frauds. David is a Certified Public Accountant, licensed in Virginia.

CHAPTER 8

Interview with an Ethics and Compliance Thought Leader

"To be good is noble. To teach others to be good is nobler ... and no trouble."

Mark Twain

, J.D., LL.M., Ed.D., is an Executive in Residence Center for Leadership and Ethics and Professor of n University. Prior to these positions, Dr. Copeland ident of Ethics and Compliance (1998–2003) at

ı Juris Doctorate from Southern Methodist Univer Agricultural Law from the University of Arkansas, dministration of Higher Education from the Uni ...nsas. He has twice received the American Agricultural Law ssociation's Award of Excellence for Professional Scholarship, as well as the University of Arkansas' Doctoral Dissertation of the Year Award. In 2001, the Center for Business Ethics, Bentley College, recognized him as an outstanding ethics officer by naming him an Ernest A. Kallman Executive Fellow.

Listed in Who's Who in American Law, Dr. Copeland is a member of the State bars of Texas and Arkansas. Following years of private law practice, he directed the National Center for Agricultural Law Research and Information and was a Research Professor of Law at the University of Arkansas School of Law (1989–1998). He has authored numerous publi cations on business ethics, employer-employee relations, environment law, insurance coverage, product liability, food safety, workers' compensation, and zoning. Since 1989, Dr. Copeland has presented approximately 300 lectures to universities, organizations, and businesses throughout the United States and Scotland.

The Soderquist Center for Leadership and Ethics where Dr. Copeland is affiliated is a not-for-profit organization founded in 1998 in affiliation with John Brown University's Division of Business and Graduate Business Studies. Located in Siloam Springs, Arkansas, the Center is a global resource to equip people in the corporate and non-profit world with the transforming power of ethical leadership. The Center was named for Don Soderquist, Executive in Residence and former COO and Senior Vice Chairman of Wal-Mart Stores, Inc. For more information on The Soderquist Center, visit www.soderquist.org.

Dr. Copeland is truly a thought leader in ethics and compliance as both a renowned practitioner and educator in the field. In this wide-ranging commentary, Dr. Copeland discusses key issues, requirements, case studies, and related best practices and strategies for success in ethical conduct and corporate compliance.

Q: What is your definition of corporate compliance?

A: Corporate compliance is the corporation's willingness to follow external and internal constraints. Externally, the corporation's leadership and employees comply with federal and state statutes and rules. Internally the same people honor the company's corporate code of conduct, policies, and procedures.

To be effective, however, one needs compliance combined with ethics. Employees need to know more than the "dos and do not's" of compliance. They must believe in the corporation's values and judge their conduct and decisions according to those values. Ethical conduct goes beyond mere compliance and deciding between right and wrong. Ethical conduct means choosing the best, or most ethical, course of conduct by applying the company's values.

Q: Why are ethics and compliance so important in a corporate culture?

A: How a corporation acts as an organization reflects corporate culture. What a corporation's leadership says about the corporation is important, but not nearly as important as business conduct. Most corporate policies promise workers respect and dignity. Sometimes, however, there is a difference between the promise and what occurs. Companies treat employees with dignity and respect by following equal employment laws, paying fair wages, providing opportunities for personal growth, and time to be with families. The corporate culture is the result of how employees are treated.

Other corporate declarations are subject to the same analysis. Corporations never publicly state that they pollute the environment. Instead, they produce well-written statements of their commitment to protecting the environment, even if they intentionally or recklessly release harmful contaminants into the environment.

Enron publicly stated its commitment to conducting business with integrity. On paper, Enron had a corporate code of conduct to protect its corporate values of respect, integrity, communication, and excellence. The public statements of Enron's leadership, however, disguised a corrupt culture. The company's ethics and compliance program did not work. The program helped hide from public scrutiny Enron's corrupt culture of dishonest accounting.

In comparison, an effective ethics and compliance program helps develop, sustain, and protect a healthy corporate culture based on values that guide corporate decisions.

Q: In your prior role at Tyson Foods, can you provide some illustrations how ethics and compliance paid off?

A: Tyson's ethics and compliance program started under difficult circumstances. The program began after the company's guilty plea to giving the Secretary of Agriculture illegal gifts. Early in the program, Tyson team members were unsure of the program and had many questions about it. Was the program a form of punishment? How long would it continue? Could you trust the people in charge of the program if you wanted to report a problem?

Eventually, Tyson members believed in the program and effectively used it. They became more trusting of the helpline that they could use to report suspected wrong-doing and do so anonymously if they wanted. Team members became comfortable with directly contacting the ethics office's personnel. They learned to trust the ethics department. Team members' use of the program allowed early intervention to deter problems. Team members reported possible acts of discrimination, misuse of proprietary information, recordkeeping errors, environmental violations, and conflict between employees, product tampering and many other potentially costly issues.

I knew the program was succeeding as the quantity of helpline calls increased and the quality of the calls changed. Team members became more sophisticated in the helpline's use. Team member complaints became more specific. They used the helpline to report real concerns, rather than to complain because they were unhappy with other team members or management decisions. Team members also began using the helpline to get advice before they acted. If they were uncertain about whether Tyson's corporate code of conduct covered a proposed course of action, they would contact the ethics office and seek guidance. Besides using the helpline to get advice, team members also began meeting more often with ethics officers or directly calling the department to get ethics questions answered.

Ethics training sessions became more interactive. My deputy director, Jan Barnsley, and I always made training sessions interactive, but in time team members became more enthusiastic about training sessions. Team members increasingly asked questions during sessions and challenged each other's responses. It also became obvious that team members were more knowledgeable about the corporate code and determined to follow it.

Q: Can ethics be taught to someone or is it a part of their makeup from an early age?

A: This question is often debated and I have asked myself that question. There are some variations on the question. Are some people inherently more ethical than others? Is it impossible to teach ethics to some people? If you can teach ethics, must it happen at an early age so ethical behavior becomes a part of a person's makeup? After years as an ethics officer and professor, I have formed some opinions on the issue.

Ideally, people should learn ethical behavior at an early age. The younger someone is when taught the "Golden Rule" of treating others the way you would want to be treated, the more likely it is to become part of their character. Not everyone, however, gets such early training or, if they do, it does not become a part of their character. Some people refuse to behave ethically, just as some people refuse to follow the law.

Ethical behavior, however, can be taught to most people regardless of a lack of prior ethics training. You teach workers what behavior the company expects from them. You install a program that rewards ethical conduct and penalizes unethical behavior. Employees learn to apply the company's values to business decisions. You cannot always change hearts, but you can affect conduct. Most employees will conform to the company's expectations. Terminate the employment of those that will not behave ethically or legally.

Q: Who are your role models for ethical behavior?

A: In the business world, Don Soderquist is my primary model for ethical behavior. As Wal-Mart's Chief Operating Officer, he set a high standard for corporate and individual integrity and led by example. He continues to do the same today as he works in the United States and throughout the world with business and organizational leaders.

The late J.B. Hunt is another good role model. With a limited education, he built a trucking empire; J.B. Hunt, Inc. Mr. Hunt did so with vision and integrity. He treated his employees and others respectfully.

My father, Howard Copeland, is another role model. He owns a meatpacking plant and he is typical of many small business owners. My father gives his customers good service and keeps his word.

Q: Have you seen changes in ethical conduct since the enactment of the Sarbanes-Oxley Act?

A: Since the passage of Sarbanes-Oxley, many corporate directors are more diligent in fulfilling their fiduciary duties to shareholders. Directors miss fewer board meetings. They put in longer hours in preparing for meetings. Directors demand more timely information on issues before voting on them. Many directors are no longer passive and are more active in corporate governance.

Sarbanes-Oxley improved financial reporting by making financial reports more accurate and reflective of a corporation's income. The requirement that a company's chief executive officer and chief financial officer certify the accuracy of financial filings is reassuring to investors.

All publicly traded corporations now have corporate codes of conduct and at least some ethics and compliance training for executives and employees. I am aware that not every corporation places enough emphasis on ethics and compliance training. Some companies favor form over substance, but it is an improvement and I hope some of those programs will become more meaningful.

The most encouraging thing about Sarbanes-Oxley is how many privately held companies are voluntarily adopting Sarbanes-Oxley-like practices. Some do so because they hope to someday go public. Many adopt Sarbanes-Oxley-like practices because they see the value in those practices and they want to be transparent companies of integrity.

Q: How best can a CEO reinforce compliance requirements within an organization?

A: The CEO is the company's most visible leader. What the CEO does, or does not do, sets the pattern for the behavior of others. The best way for the CEO to reinforce compliance is to be accountable to the same standards of behavior expected of others. A verbally abusive CEO should not be surprised when other company managers behave the same way towards subordinates. A CEO who uses company assets for personal use is by example telling employees it is acceptable for them to do it as well. Of course, when lower level employees get caught doing so they often pay a high price for their misdeeds.

You cannot have two different sets of compliance standards and an effective ethics and compliance program. If executives break company rules without consequences, then other employees will try to break the rules. Corporate hypocrisy is poisonous to any ethics and compliance program.

Q: What best compliance practices can you recommend for public and private companies?

A: Design any compliance program according to the seven requirements outlined in the Federal Sentencing Guidelines for Organizations (FSGO):

1. Establish standards of conduct reasonably capable of reducing the likelihood of criminal conduct;
2. assign overall responsibility for compliance to a specific high-level officer;
3. do not delegate discretionary authority to individuals with a history of illegal conduct or other conduct inconsistent with a compliance program;
4. communicate standards and procedures to employees and agents;
5. establish monitoring, auditing, and reporting systems;
6. enforce standards with discipline and incentives; and
7. take reasonable steps to respond to discovered criminal conduct.

Following the FSGO, however, does not ensure an effective ethics program. It only means you have met the minimum requirements. Best compliance practices require more than a "bare bones" program.

In drafting a corporate code, design a code that fits your organization. Involve the organization's employees in assessing your company's risks. Fit the code to those risks and stress meeting those risks. Do not simply take another company's code and substitute your company's name.

Give your ethics officer and the office as much independence as possible. Some companies place the program and ethics officer in the company's legal department or within human resources. I believe to do so is a mistake. The ethics officer needs the independence and clout to deal with difficult issues. The ethics officer should report directly to the organization's CEO and board of directors.

Also make sure the ethics officer receives the training necessary to do the job. Membership in the Ethics Officer Association (EOA) and attendance at EOA training programs is essential.

Introduce employees to the ethics program and corporate code of conduct when hired. Have employees sign a statement to follow the corporate code. Train employees on the code and repeatedly train them. Communicate the corporate code of conduct and company values to the employees by many means of communication. Use interactive seminars, posters, and newsletters to take the ethics and compliance program to the employees.

Include following the company's ethics and compliance program in employees' annual performance evaluations. Reward employees for ethical conduct.

Design an enforcement procedure for ethics and compliance violations that is fair to employees. Provide employees with some due process. Quickly look into complaints while providing accused employees with an opportunity to respond.

When punishment is necessary, the organization's response should fit the offense. Not all violations should be employment-ending offenses. Minor violations may only need a verbal or written warning. Consistent enforcement and prompt responses are important.

Finally, regularly evaluate your program and adjust it as needed. Even the best programs can be improved. Too many companies never examine, much less reexamine, the effectiveness of their programs.

Q: What, in your opinion, makes a program world-class?

A: Commitment is the difference between mediocre ethics and compliance programs and those that are world-class. The commitment starts with a company's management. A company's leaders committed to a program's success create commitment in others. Commitment produces enthusiasm in the employees to support the program. Even more important, employees learn to trust the company's ethics and compliance program. Commitment, support, and trust result in a world-class program.

Q: How does an organization choose its values?

A: A company chooses its values in two ways. One is a more formal means. A value statement may have been set up early in the company's founding. Companies sometimes use advisers or focus groups to decide values. I teach a course on Mission, Vision, and Values and corporations use many of the same value statements. Commitment to excellence, communication, respect for employees, and respect for the environment are a few examples of what I find in corporate value statements. Too many corporations just look at what other companies have done and select some values that sound good for their own company. Some companies list so many values they become meaningless. There is no focus on what is important in deciding issues.

Ideally, employee representatives from throughout the company help identify company values. Values are effective when decided on and shared by the employees and management. Values go to a company's core and set the boundaries for decisions. Core values remain fixed even as a company's business changes.

A company's values should permeate the company's business and help ensure ethical and legal behavior. What values are important to the company's leaders and employees? More important, what values are followed? Some companies have two sets of values. The first set is for public consumption. The second set is what takes place; or rather how the company works. Employees quickly discover whether a company practices its publicly stated values. Employees conform to those values practiced by the organization, rather than those pronounced to the public.

Q: How do you define tone at the top?

A: Tone at the top of an organization includes values, observations, and experiences with the company. First, what does management say orally and in print about the way the company conducts business? Specifically, what are the company's declared values? Second, what values are seen being practiced when business is conducted? What do employees and others see in the way management leads and does business? Do people see the company's declared values practiced at all management levels?

Finally, what are the personal experiences of employees and others in dealing with a company's management? For example, suppose a company declares honesty to be a core value. Honesty is stressed verbally in business meetings and the company's literature. If employees and others see the company's management being honest in financial reports and in business dealings, the company's core value of honesty becomes more real to them. If in their personal dealings with management they are treated honestly, then honesty is accepted as the business tone. The business leadership is trusted to behave honestly. If someone in the company does something dishonest, the act is treated as a departure from the company's normal conduct. The business tone remains the same, so long as the company quickly addresses the dishonest act.

Q: Why is tone at the top so important in an organization?

A: The tone at the top permeates the entire organization. The Business Roundtable's 2002 Principles of Corporate Governance[1] say that senior management is responsible for setting the tone to establish a culture of integrity and compliance. Employees behave as the company's leadership behaves, especially those in midlevel management positions. Corrupt leaders naturally train followers to be corrupt. Followers who expect more from leaders will leave and go to work for companies whose leaders show integrity and expect it of others.

Q: How do great leaders demonstrate tone at the top?

A: All leaders demonstrate tone at the top through their actions. Leaders are role models. A leader's conduct must consistently align with the company's values. Great leaders uphold the company's values during a crisis. Great leaders refuse to compromise the company's core values, even if the refusal to do so is expensive. It is because those values are shared throughout the organization that great leaders can confidently take such action.

Johnson & Johnson's reaction to the Tylenol crisis of the mid-1980s remains the gold standard for ethical leadership in a crisis. Through no fault of Johnson & Johnson, cyanide was found in some Tylenol bottles. Following its credo of putting patient welfare first, the company withdrew all Tylenol from the shelves. James Burke, Johnson & Johnson's Chief Executive Officer, led discussions on the company's response. Burke reminded everyone of the company's declared commitment to public safety. This is a position shared throughout the organization because of the company's credo.

Q: Can you provide some examples of both good and bad tone at the top that you have studied?

A: I have already described Johnson & Johnson's response to the Tylenol crisis and it is an excellent example of good tone at the top. There is another Johnson & Johnson story, often overlooked, that is also a good example. It shows the consistency of Johnson & Johnson's commitment to its credo.

Baby oil is an important Johnson & Johnson product. Probably most people in the United States use the product at some point. Some people use baby oil as a tanning agent. Aware of the oil's use in tanning, some Johnson & Johnson managers planned a multimillion dollar campaign advertising the tanning benefits of Johnson & Johnson baby oil.

The advertising campaign never happened. It was unveiled to the company's top management about the same time as scientific research began linking skin cancer with sun exposure. Johnson & Johnson's executives requested more information on the skin cancer issue before approving the advertising campaign. After reviewing skin cancer studies, the company's management decided it did not want to encourage people to spend more time in the sun. The company scrapped an advertising campaign because of its credo to protect public health.

Merck & Company remains an example of a visionary company with an excellent tone at the top. With its founding, Merck's leadership stressed the company's vision of helping humanity by destroying disease. The company's cure for "river blindness" is a great example of leaders fulfilling the company's vision and values.

While researching cures for animal diseases, Merck scientists discovered a cure for river blindness. A parasitic worm causes the disease that plagues millions of people in developing countries. Merck's drug, Mectizan, proved effective against the disease, but there was no commercial market for it. The people needing the drug could not afford it and government agencies were not willing to pay for the drug. To relieve human suffering, Merck bore the cost of developing the drug, gave the drug away and paid for much of the drug's distribution.

Unfortunately, examples of bad tone at the top are plentiful after the scandals of Enron, WorldCom, Tyco, Adelphia, and others. Any of those will do as examples of wretched excess and deception by an organization's leaders.

Al Dunlap's career as CEO of Scott Paper and then Sunbeam is an example of how one person can set a negative tone for an entire company. Dunlap earned the nickname "Chainsaw Al" for the cost cutting measures he put into place to turn around troubled companies. Whenever he took leadership of a company, employees rightfully feared for their jobs. Dunlap often quickly raised stock value, but his critics contend he did so by slashing research and development, and by forgoing necessary maintenance.

Another example I use to show bad tone at the top is Armand Hammer and Occidental Petroleum. As CEO, Hammer ran Occidental as his personal kingdom. Using the company's money, he built a museum to house his personal art collection. This was after the Los Angeles County Museum refused certain demands to house his collection.

Arthur Andersen is a good study of tone at the top because of the decay that led to the company's death. Arthur Andersen had a long history of integrity as a top accounting firm. Within the company, stories were told of how company's management turned away business rather than approving questionable financial practices. The company created a public review board made up of outside experts to visit Arthur Andersen facilities to ensure that company's standards of integrity were met.

Gradually, the tone at the top changed as the company competed for profitable consulting contracts. The public review board ceased to exist. The lines became blurred between the company's auditing and consulting activities. Questionable accounting practices were approved to keep clients' consulting business. Arthur Andersen became embroiled in Enron's scandal and shredded Enron financial documents sought by federal investigators. The Enron scandal destroyed Arthur Andersen. The company's collapse shows the need to establish and preserve an ethical tone at the top.

Q: Can you provide some examples of effective tone at the top at Tyson Foods?

A: I can think of several outstanding examples. The first is Tyson's commitment to diversity. Tyson's chairperson, John Tyson, dedicated himself to diversifying Tyson's leadership and to creating management opportunities for women and minorities. The company aggressively recruits women and minorities into management training programs and ensures that all Tyson employees get opportunities for advancement. John Tyson and Tyson Foods have received well-deserved rewards for the company's diversification efforts. Managers at all levels within the company are sensitive to diversity and the company's dedication to diversifying management.

Second, Tyson aids poultry growers in environmental protection. While I was with Tyson, the company approved my idea of a poultry growers' environmental awards program. Each year, Tyson honors its poultry growers that do an outstanding job of complying with environmental laws, are creative in protecting the environment, and improve wildlife habitat. Growers and the Tyson technicians assisting them strive hard each year to win one of the awards.

Besides receiving public recognition and a trophy, a donation in each grower's name is made to a grower selected environmental organization. Tyson management's support of the program ensures its success.

Finally, Tyson's management established a tone of generosity in donating Tyson products to fight hunger in the United States. Tyson supports Share Our Strength (SOS) and that organization's efforts to feed hungry people. Tyson Foods also provides products and Tyson employees to aid in disaster relief. Such efforts are successful because of the tone set by Tyson's management.

Q: How does an organization best exemplify tone at the top?

A: The organization's culture best exemplifies the tone at the top. The culture is a product of the tone at the top. When compliance and ethics become embedded in a company's culture they control business decisions. Neither management nor employees tolerate illegal or unethical conduct. The company's values guide business decisions.

Q: How does an organization measure tone at the top?

A: Others already measure tone at the top for an organization. *Fortune* magazine and other publications yearly evaluate companies on the triple bottom line of economics, social responsibility and environmental sustainability. An entire industry exists to evaluate companies for effective corporate governance. Social research firms such as Kinder, Lydenberg, Domini & Company (KLD) help identify the best corporate citizens. The information provided by such sources at least tells company leaders of the public's opinion of the company's tone at the top.

Self-examination, however, is the best means of measuring tone and it begins with a company's employees. Employees should be surveyed about the company's values and how well those values are met. Let employees answer anonymously without any fear of retribution. Take seriously candid assessments by employees and respond suitably.

Do similar surveys among other corporate stakeholders, such as suppliers and customers. Even if the opinions of others contain some misconceptions, knowing that those exist gives the company an opportunity to correct them.

Eventually, the marketplace measures tone at the top. People invest in, and do business with, ethical companies.

Q: Options backdating is the compliance failure *du jour* with dozens of companies under investigation. Why and how did tone at the top fail in these cases? What could have been done to prevent this from happening?

A: Options backdating represents two leadership frailties. The first is a false sense of entitlement. Executives whose stock option strike prices are "cherry picked" from dates when the company's stock values were low believe themselves entitled to financial rewards without working to increase company value. Backdating does not need any business planning or leadership skills that increase shareholder value.

Second, backdating shows a lack of trust by executives in their management skills. If they use as a strike price the market value of their shares when the options are granted, they implicitly send the message that their management efforts increase the company's value. Executives and shareholders will benefit from the executives' management skills. The message sent is very different when stock options are backdated. Backdating says the company's management is unsure that it can increase shareholder value, but wants to be rewarded as if it has done so. In a sense, backdating is cheating. It is profit without risk.

What to do about backdating is simple. Boards of directors should forbid it. Many financial abuses occur because company boards are passive. Directors fail to fulfill the fiduciary duties owed to shareholders. They approve executive requests for excessive compensation, or, as regards backdating, rewards without performance.

Q: Can you provide any closing thoughts?

A: I fault directors for much of what goes wrong within for-profit and nonprofit organizations. Too many directors enjoy their titles, and the benefits that go with them, and ignore their fiduciary duties. I often lecture and write on the topic "Passive Board Members are *Passé*." I focus on the fiduciary duties of loyalty, due care, and obedience when working with directors and how the courts define those duties. Director training includes presenting directors with situations and asking them to respond given their fiduciary duties.

Another tactic I use to educate directors is to take them through directors and officers (D&O) liability insurance. Few directors are knowledgeable about D&O coverage and are too confident about D&O coverage protecting them from liability claims. When they get a greater understanding of D&O coverage and its limits, directors become very attentive to the need to meet fiduciary duties. It has been my experience that most directors appreciate thorough and challenging training programs.

NOTES

1. The Business Roundtable is an organization of chief executive officers of leading companies in the United States. The Business Roundtable is recognized as an authoritative voice on American business and corporate governance. Their Principles of Corporate Governance is a publication of the Business Roundtable that details their guiding principles for advancing corporate governance. Principles of Corporate Governance, The Business Roundtable, May 2002, available at www.businessroundtable.org/pdf/704.pdf.

CHAPTER 9

Building a World-Class Compliance Program: The Seven Steps in Practice (Part I)

"The time is always right to do what is right."
Martin Luther King, Jr.

For a long time, both Congress and the American public believed that the penalties imposed upon white-collar criminals and organizations were far too lenient as compared to other crimes. The original 1987 version of the Federal Sentencing Guidelines (Guidelines) only covered the sentencing of individuals. A major gap remained concerning how organizations, such as corporations, partnerships, or other legally recognized forms of business would be treated if they committed crimes. Congress then directed the United States Sentencing Commission (USSC) to study this sentencing disparity and promulgate a new set of guidelines specifically addressing organizational offenders. On May 1, 1991, the USSC officially promulgated the Federal Sentencing Guidelines for Organizations (FSGO). They were later amended effective November 1, 2004 to provide even greater protection.

Chapter 8 of the FSGO covering organizational crime has been strengthened over the years, particularly by congressional directives authorizing the USSC to tackle particular issues, such as corporate crime. The amendments in 2004, coming in the wake of repeated instances of corporate scandal and a growing sentiment by the public that the problem must be dealt with, addressed the perceived need for improved compliance by organizations, as well as giving more direct guidance to those organizations that sought to enhance their own compliance efforts to prevent further scandal.

The FSGO were enhanced by emphasizing effective compliance and ethics programs in order to mitigate punishment for a criminal offense. The FSGO requires an organizational culture that encourages ethical conduct and a commitment to compliance with the law. Chief executives and directors are responsible and accountable to ensure compliance. Effective compliance programs must now have adequate resources, appropriate authority, training programs, reporting mechanisms, risk assessments, and periodic evaluations to promote an ongoing culture of compliance.[1]

Of particular note to this book, the 2004 amendments modified the section promulgating the sentencing guidelines for organizations, adding an official definition of an effective compliance program. These revised guidelines specifically elucidated the importance and need for such a compliance program within an organization. Since these are the guidelines that will direct federal prosecutors and judges in evaluating an organization's culpability (or lack thereof), it is imperative that a compliance program, at minimum, directly meet these standards.

As long as the Guidelines have been in effect, they have often been a source of great controversy.[2] Defense attorneys and their clients decried the sometimes draconian sentences handed out and judges lamented their inability to modify the mandatory minimums, particularly in cases involving drugs. This controversy reached the Supreme Court in 2004; many expected the justices to strike down the Guidelines once and for all. To the surprise of many observers, the Guidelines emerged more or less unscathed. In essence, through the trio of *Blakely v. Washington*, *United States v. Booker*, and *United States v. Fanfan*, the Court decided that while the Guidelines are no longer mandatory, judges may still constitutionally follow them in their sentencing decisions. In practice, while judges have the freedom to depart from the recommended sentences, most of them still follow the Guidelines, or at least adhere closely to them. The same goes for federal prosecutors who still use them in charging decisions and sentencing recommendations. At the end of the day, the Guidelines still play an important role in the legal system.

THE SEVEN STEPS TO AN EFFECTIVE COMPLIANCE PROGRAM

The "Seven Steps" to an effective compliance and ethics program as detailed in the FSGO serve as the backbone for building such a program. They provide clear guidance on how to build it, and give great insight into the government's expectations. When evaluating a potential case, prosecutors will be looking for a program that meets the requirements of the seven steps. If a company's compliance program meets those steps, it can hope for a reduced or suspended sentence, and at least provide more ammunition at the bargaining table. However, if the minimum requirements are not met, it is a clear indication to the government that the organization does not place a high value on compliance and ethical conduct. For if an organization cannot even adhere to seven well-known and readily achievable steps, why would the government believe that it would follow more complex and difficult regulatory guidelines?

According to the FSGO, to have an effective compliance and ethics program, "an organization *shall* exercise due diligence to protect and detect criminal conduct; and otherwise promote an organizational culture that encourages ethical conduct and a commitment to compliance with the law (emphasis added)."[3] Note the inclusion of the word shall; this indicates that this requirement is mandatory for those companies with a compliance program and that the government unconditionally expects these requirements to be followed. Even though the government expects strict adherence to the FSGO, it does recognize that not every violation will be prevented. "Such compliance and ethics program shall be reasonably designed, implemented, and enforced so that the program is generally effective in preventing and detecting criminal conduct. The failure to prevent or detect the instant offense does not necessarily mean that the program is not generally effective."[4]

The FSGO allow for the possibility that a rogue employee committed the crime. If this is the case, and if the company had an effective compliance program in place, the organization may be allowed to escape unscathed, provided it cooperates in the prosecution of the employee. The FSGO recognize that even the best compliance programs cannot catch every misdeed, particularly those of an employee operating alone. Of far greater concern are those misdeeds performed by those in power within the company who actively subvert the compliance program for their own ends, or those companies who, upon discovery of the crimes, seek to cover them up rather than respond appropriately. Compliance Insight 9.1 is the story of fraud at the highest levels of a public company and the absence of a compliance program.

SEVEN STEPS OVERVIEW

The Seven Steps of Compliance as mandated by the FSGO require organizations to build and maintain an effective compliance and ethics program based on the following actions:

1. Compliance Standards and Procedures
   - The organization shall establish standards and procedures to prevent and detect criminal conduct and ensure compliance with the law. In

COMPLIANCE INSIGHT 9.1: ADELPHIA COMMUNICATIONS CORPORATION: A CEO'S PERSONAL PIGGY BANK

Thomas F. X. Feeney is a Client Specialist for the global law firm of Dewey & LeBoeuf. Prior to his affiliation with the firm, Mr. Feeney worked for ten years as a U.S. Postal Inspector. For the majority of that time, he investigated complex white-collar crimes including securities fraud, commercial bribery, and mail fraud. He was commended by several United States Attorney's Offices and received the Executive Award of the Chief Postal Inspector for his exceptional work. Among his significant cases was the investigation of the massive corporate fraud at Adelphia Communications Corporation. Feeney's investigation gave him great insight into the compliance failures that allowed the fraud to continue for so long without discovery. Here are his insights from leading the investigation.

When analyzing the corporate fraud at Adelphia[a] using the seven steps of an effective compliance and ethics program as identified in the 2004 Amendments to the Federal Sentencing Guidelines for Organizations, the company's failure to adhere to the Guidelines is readily apparent. Adelphia's most obvious failing was its lack of compliance with the first, and arguably most basic guideline: A firm must have in place standards and procedures to "prevent and detect criminal conduct."[b] Nearly all of Adelphia's problems stemmed from its lack of established standards and procedures. Adelphia did not have any means designed to prevent and deter criminal conduct; let alone deal with the most basic situations. In one case, the lack of written procedures to conduct a simple transaction led to concealment of the theft of some $50 million.

Adelphia's dearth of established procedures can be traced directly to its history. Had the company developed under different circumstances, it might have codified its procedures, enacted internal controls, and prevented criminal conduct. In short, had the company's history been different, the fraud might not have occurred.

Adelphia was not like other companies because of its location and its management. Located in Coudersport, Pennsylvania, a town of 2,600 in rural Potter County, Adelphia's headquarters was a two hour drive from Buffalo, New York, and a four hour drive from Pittsburgh, Pennsylvania. As a young engineer working for an electronics manufacturer, John J. Rigas commute took him through

Coudersport, where he bought the local movie theater. He diversified into providing television programming to a community that could not receive over-the-air broadcast signals, and in so doing, became one of the pioneers of cable television. He founded Adelphia in 1953 and, assisted by his sons Michael and Timothy, he was still running it in the 1990s. For years, Adelphia's employees and management were drawn from the area surrounding Coudersport. It became the largest employer in the area, offering a good job in a place where few existed. Many employees had never worked at any other company and thus did not know how odd the company's business practices were.

In 1999, Adelphia was still operating in rural Coudersport and still run like the mom-and-pop operation it had been. But there was a significant problem; it had become a public company in the intervening years. Things that may be common in a small business—loans taken by the founder, procedures created by management whim—are disastrous and potentially illegal in a public company. When John Rigas decided to take cash withdrawals from the company, he wasn't a small shop owner borrowing money from the till. This "till" was a public company; its contents were owned by its shareholders, not by its management. And though John Rigas may have founded the company, managed its operations, held a lot of its stock, and sat on its board of directors, he did not own the company and thus had no right to its cash.

Adelphia's lack of standards and procedures contributed heavily to the disastrous outcome. The company had no written procedures documenting under what circumstances money could be transferred to John Rigas. He did not sign loan agreements or execute notes. He just picked up the telephone and directed the transfers. After the company went public in 1986, the employees continued transferring money to his accounts whenever he requested it—as they always had done. And they did so, not because it was written in any company procedure that they should transfer the funds, but because it was simply the way things had always been. No formal guidelines existed to counteract the corporate inertia. When one employee finally questioned the loan practice, only because he was not sure if there was a monthly limit, the company's CFO determined that any amount in excess of $1 million per month had to be approved by him. Who was the CFO? John's son, Timothy.

A company's procedures should "at a minimum, be in written form and disseminated throughout an organization with the directive that they be followed".[c] Adelphia had no policy for the cash transfers "in written form," meaning knowledge of such a procedure could not be "disseminated throughout [the] organization" and remained restricted to those few employees who processed the transfers. The lack of written procedures kept many from knowing about, thus being in a position to even question, this self-dealing practice at Adelphia. Those who may have questioned the cash transfers were not aware of them because of the company's lack of transparency.

The unrecorded, unauthorized transfers of cash are the clearest example of the *ad hoc* nature of certain of Adelphia's practices and how such practices were contrary to the most basic corporate compliance guideline. And while such transfers amounted to more than $50 million, they were only a part of John Rigas looting of the company he founded and sold to the public. At his later trial for corporate fraud, witnesses, including his personal accountant, addressed his additional use of the public company's money to fund $1.6 billion of securities purchases and to repay more than $250 million of margin loans.

Codification of Adelphia's procedures, especially the cash transfer procedure, should have been the company's first step in establishing orderly operations and internal controls. Lacking written procedures, the company had no real chance of effectively and systematically reducing the likelihood of criminal conduct.

---

[a]This Compliance Insight addresses the fraud pursuant to which Adelphia officers and employees John Rigas, Timothy Rigas, Michael Rigas, James Brown, and Michael Mulcahey were arrested in July 2002. Many changes have occurred at the company since then and failure to differentiate between the pre-2003 Adelphia and the Adelphia of today would be a disservice to current management and the honest Adelphia employees who worked so hard to right the wrongs of the company's earlier incarnation.
[b]United States Sentencing Commission, *Federal Sentencing Guidelines Manual*, 476, www.ussc.gov/2004guid/CHAP8.pdf.
[c]"U.S. Sentencing Commission Announces Stiffened Organizational Sentencing Guideline in Response to the Sarbanes-Oxley Act," *Thompson Hine*, June 1, 2004, www.thompsonhine.com/publications/publication6.html.

other words, an organization's code of conduct must be robust and embed ethical conduct as an integral component of the ethics and compliance program.

2. Organizational Leadership and a Culture of Compliance
   - The organization's governing authority shall be knowledgeable about the content and operation of the compliance and ethics program. This would normally be the CEO, CFO, and the Board of Directors.

- They shall exercise reasonable oversight with respect to the implementation and effectiveness of the compliance and ethics program.
- Specific individual(s) within the highest levels of the organization shall be assigned overall responsibility for the compliance and ethics program.
- Specific individual(s) within the organization shall be delegated day-to-day operational responsibility for the compliance and ethics program. The individual(s) with operational responsibility shall report periodically to high-level personnel and, as appropriate, to the governing authority on the effectiveness of the compliance and ethics program.
- To carry out such operational responsibility, such individual(s) shall be given adequate resources, appropriate authority, and direct access to the governing authority of the organization.

3. Reasonable Efforts to Exclude Prohibited Persons
   - The organization shall use reasonable efforts not to include within the substantial authority personnel who the organization knew, or should have known through the exercise of due diligence, have engaged in illegal activities or other conduct inconsistent with an effective compliance and ethics program.

4. Training and Communication of Standards and Procedures
   - The organization shall take reasonable steps to communicate periodically and in a practical manner its standards and procedures, and other aspects of the compliance and ethics program by conducting effective training programs and otherwise disseminating information appropriate to such individuals' respective roles and responsibilities.
   - Training shall be provided to members of the governing authority, other high-level leadership, employees, and, as appropriate, the organization's agents.

5. Monitoring, Auditing, and Evaluating Program Effectiveness
   - The organization shall take reasonable steps to ensure that the organization's compliance and ethics program is followed, including monitoring and auditing to detect criminal conduct.
   - The organization shall take reasonable steps to evaluate the effectiveness of the organization's compliance and ethics program.
   - The organization shall take reasonable steps to have and publicize a system, which may include mechanisms that allow for anonymity or confidentiality, where the organization's employees and agents may report or seek guidance regarding potential or actual criminal conduct without fear of retaliation, such as hotlines.

6. Performance Incentives and Disciplinary Actions
   - The organization's compliance and ethics program shall be promoted and enforced consistently within the organization through appropriate incentives to perform in accordance with the compliance and ethics program.
   - The organization's compliance and ethics program shall be promoted and enforced consistently within the organization through appropriate disciplinary measures for engaging in criminal conduct and for failing to take reasonable steps to prevent or detect criminal conduct.
7. Response to Criminal Conduct and Remedial Action
   - After criminal conduct has been detected, the organization shall take reasonable steps to respond appropriately to the criminal conduct and to prevent further similar conduct, including making any necessary modifications to the organization's compliance and ethics program.
   - The organization shall periodically assess the risk of criminal conduct and shall take appropriate steps to design, implement, or modify each compliance requirement to reduce the risk of criminal conduct identified through this process.[5]

In addition to these seven requirements, there are others that must be implemented by an organization. An organization must incorporate and adhere to industry practices and standards of compliance as required by government regulation. Unless this is followed, an organization is not considered as having an effective compliance and ethics program. Courts are required to sentence the company to at least probation if the organization failed to have an effective compliance program in place when one was required and can upwardly depart from the guidelines if a compliance program is not in place. Organizations must remember that the way to avoid or at least lessen the impact of prosecution is through self-reporting, cooperation with the government, acceptance of responsibility, and an effective compliance and ethics program.[6] Appendix A contains a detailed summary of the FSGO as well as recommended action steps to achieve effective compliance.

STEP 1: COMPLIANCE STANDARDS AND PROCEDURES

The FSGO require an organization to "exercise due diligence to prevent and detect criminal conduct; and otherwise promote an organizational culture that encourages ethical conduct and a commitment to compliance with the law."[7] Organizations must therefore "establish standards and procedures to prevent and detect criminal conduct"[8] as well as ensure that organizational policies and procedures are followed. This includes standards of business conduct and internal controls reasonably capable of reducing the likelihood of criminal conduct and other violations of policy. While this is usually embodied in a code of conduct for the organization, something much deeper is needed. That is an ethical culture built into the structure of the organization. This institutionalization of ethics and compliance will transcend any one person and continue far after executive leaders have come and gone. It is hard to find an ethical collapse that would still have happened if the company had strong and ethical people in positions of authority. Questions that organizations need to ask include:

- Does the current ethics and compliance program emphasize ethical conduct or just compliant conduct?
- Does the company's code of conduct encourage individual responsibility or just provide a series of rules to follow?
- Is ethical conduct an embedded component of the compliance program?
- Does the organization's code of conduct make a compelling case for ethics and compliance?[9]

An organization must encourage individual responsibility for compliance with standards and policies in all its employees. This begins at time of hire and continues throughout an employee's career. Every employee, whether the CEO or the receptionist, must make the same commitment to ethics. Obviously, the higher level a person is in the organization, the greater the opportunity to evangelize the importance of ethical conduct to other employees. Executives and managers have a crucial responsibility to continually explain the importance of ethics and compliance. Yet, there is more that must be stated. Enron had a compliance program and a 65-page code of conduct. That very wordy code had absolutely no impact in preventing the massive accounting fraud. The branding of integrity, honesty, and compliance is important for all companies, especially those emerging from scandal.

Code of Conduct

The cornerstone of an effective compliance program and culture of compliance is a strong value system based on integrity. These values can best be reflected in a code of conduct or ethics to ensure that employees, vendors, contractors, and other related parties know what is expected of them so as to make the right decisions.[10] The code should be based on the organization's core values and clearly delineate which behaviors are appropriate and which are not. It should be written in plain language and be easily understandable. Consideration should be given to preparing separate codes specifically focused on finance and procurement employees as well as vendors. While it is important to explain in the code what is right and wrong, it is just as critical to reinforce the need for employees and others to seek advice and help when faced with ethical questions. Whether they are called hotlines, business conduct lines, or helplines, reporting mechanisms must be well-communicated and readily available for anyone seeking help. Codes of conduct are further discussed in Chapter 10 and Appendix B.

Code of Conduct Benchmarking and Evaluation

An ongoing evaluation of an organization's code of conduct is another best practice. In its Q2 2007 issue, *Ethisphere Magazine* benchmarked the codes of conduct for 50 finance and technology companies using eight criteria. The criteria that *Ethisphere* uses are tied directly to the FSGO and excellent ones to consider in evaluating a code of conduct. The following are the criteria that were used in the benchmarking:

- **Public Availability:** A code should readily be available to all stakeholders. What is the availability and ease of access to the code by employees and others outside the company?
- **Tone at the Top:** Extent to which the senior leadership of the organization is visibly committed to the values and subjects covered in the code.
- **Readability and Tone:** What is the style and tone used in the code? Is it easy to read and reflective of the organization's culture?
- **Non-retaliation:** Is the non-retaliation policy stated and explicit? If so, how clearly is it stated?
- **Commitment to Stakeholders:** Does the code identify its stakeholders and what is the level of compliance commitment?
- **Risk Topics:** Does the code cover all appropriate and key risk areas for the company's given industry?
- **Learning Aids:** Does the code provide learning aids such as Q&A, FAQs, checklists, do's and don'ts, examples of behavior, case studies, etc., to assist employees and others in understanding the important elements of the code?
- **Presentation and Style:** Is it a compelling read? Factors include the layout, fonts, pictures, word usage, and structure.[11]

Organizations would do well to use these criteria in evaluating their individual codes and make changes as necessary. Codes of conduct should be living documents that are continuously reviewed and updated.

Being reasonably certain to reduce the likelihood of criminal actions in an organization does not mean that there never will be an instance of fraud or abuse. No program can be 100% effective in stopping all fraud and violations of policy. A test of an effective program is how the organization can detect and respond to an allegation and successfully resolve that issue. Consider this example: A vendor is approached by an employee of a company demanding a kickback. The vendor is shocked at this unethical conduct and decides to report it to the organization. She finds the company's hotline number on the company's Web site. She is initially afraid that her reporting of the incident may impact her relationship with the company, but her reading of the company policy on ethical conduct and non-retaliation convinces her she is well-protected. She provides the company with specific details on the kickback attempt resulting in an official investigation.

The vendor cooperates in the investigation, and subsequently, the allegations are founded. In addition, the company learns that its employee has received kickbacks from numerous other vendors who did not have the ethical makeup of the complainant. The employee is later prosecuted for his criminal activity and the vendor's relationship with the company is stronger than before. This is an example of an effective compliance program where several different elements of the program all worked and worked well.

STEP 2: ORGANIZATIONAL LEADERSHIP AND A CULTURE OF COMPLIANCE

The FSGO require that an organization's "governing authority shall be knowledgeable about the content and operation of the compliance and ethics program and shall exercise reasonable oversight with respect to the implementation and effectiveness"[12] of the program. Questions that organizations need to ask include:

- Is it clearly articulated how senior management is engaged in the compliance process?
- How does the board strategically oversee the compliance and ethics program?
- What are the information-flow processes that senior management and the board use to effectively assess the program?
- How do high-level personnel actively advocate the organization's values?
- Does the chief compliance officer have adequate resources and authority to fully enforce the compliance program?[13]

The Infosys Message

The message that a company sends to the public about its views on corporate governance and compliance can speak volumes about their business and how it is run. Today, the best medium for broadcasting one's message to the widest possible audience is the Internet. Infosys Technologies is a global technology services firm headquartered in Bangalore, India. Infosys uses a compelling approach to corporate governance on their Web site.[14] The company states that they have "been a pioneer in benchmarking its corporate governance practices with the best in the world." They introduce their corporate governance program by reprinting a portion of a speech given by Securities and Exchange Commission Chairman Christopher Cox before the Committee for Economic Development in Washington, DC on March 21, 2006. It reads as follows:

> *Happy companies have robust growth in revenues, strong balance sheets, and healthy profits that reflect genuine business success, not phony bookkeeping.*
> *And they share other important traits as well.*
> *They abide by high ethical standards, which is a key to their solid success. They don't obstruct the flow of information to share-holders, but rather view the shareholder as the ultimate boss.*
> *They choose directors on the strength of their abilities, charac-ter, and capacity for independent judgment.*
> *And their internal controls work well, so that the company's executives can take immediate corrective action when something goes wrong.*

The Role of Executive Leadership

Chief executives, senior leaders, and managers set a very important tone at the top with every word they say and every action they take. They can positively influence an organization with their accountability and integrity. A leader's commitment to all elements of compliance sets an example for everyone else. If an executive does not follow company policies and procedures, it is reasonable to assume that those below will not follow them either. The leaders (and I use that term loosely) at Enron, WorldCom, Tyco, and Adelphia were not true leaders as they led their companies down the road to disaster. They literally broke all the rules and they suffered the consequences. Unfortunately, so did their employees and shareholders.

Leading by example can be done in many ways. Being among the first to complete required compliance training, holding direct reports accountable for also completing the training, quickly responding to business conduct violations, ensuring fair, balanced, and incremental discipline, and living the company values are a few examples of how a leader can set the right tone at the top.

The Role of the Board of Directors

The Board of Directors and especially the Audit Committee of an organization are the overseers of accountability and compliance. They are in many ways the "police officers" of an organization acting in a "checks and balances" role to executive leadership.[15] They must thoroughly understand the compliance and ethics program in place. They must exercise appropriate oversight of the compliance program and ensure that it is truly effective in all aspects. The board is responsible for ensuring that the FSGO requirement that high-level individuals within the organization be assigned responsibility for the compliance program is carried out. Today's fully engaged board members take an active leadership role in promoting ethical conduct in their organization.

Identifying, measuring, and mitigating fraud risks are essential in implementing the Seven Steps. "The audit committee should evaluate management's identification of fraud risks, implementation of antifraud measures, and creation of the appropriate tone at the top. Active oversight by the audit committee can help reinforce management's commitment to creating the proper antifraud culture."[16] The audit committee role in providing oversight to executive leadership must include the potential risk of fraudulent financial reporting and the override of internal controls or collusion.[17]

The Corporate First Responders

The Chief Compliance Officer (CCO) has quickly become one of the most important new roles within an organization today. The CCO is often a company's "first responder," taking action at the first sign of trouble. Like first responders, with swift and decisive action, they can minimize the damage as best as possible. Without them, the injury could potentially be fatal. For an example of how a bad compliance officer can destroy a company, see the discussion of AbTox, Inc. in Compliance Insight 9.4 later in this chapter.

Compliance officers' roles include proactive and reactive efforts, and both must be given emphasis to be fully effective. "Proactive efforts need to emphasize the complimentary goals of crime prevention and corporate ethical behavior. Reactive efforts measure how well a corporation reacts when it learns that questionable and potentially illegal conduct has occurred."[18]

The CCO has primary responsibility, with the strong support of executive leadership, for building a world-class compliance program within their organization and maintaining its effectiveness. In some organizations, the CCO is the general counsel but delegates the day-to-day role to a direct report such as a Director of Compliance. A sample compliance program charter can be found in Appendix B.

Chief Compliance Officer

Compliance officers are critical to the implementation and ongoing success of the compliance program. Identifying and hiring a highly qualified compliance officer is a best practice that cannot be overlooked. Former prosecutors and federal agents have significant experience that can benefit a compliance program. "Adding former government officials to a company's roster brings a certain credential of integrity to the process," states Susan Hackett, Vice President of the Association of Corporate Counsel.[19] For example, the newly created compliance program at CA, Inc. gained instant credibility when they hired Pat Gnazzo, a highly regarded and experienced CCO, in 2005.

COMPLIANCE INSIGHT 9.2: TOP COMPLIANCE AND ETHICS OFFICERS RESPONSIBILITIES IN 2006

Compliance and Ethics Leadership Council Survey, 2006

1. Compliance and Ethics Training Program
2. Development of Compliance and Ethics Policies and Procedures
3. Compliance Risk Identification/Assessment/Monitoring
4. Code of Conduct
5. Helpline Administration
6. Enforcement of Compliance and Ethics Policies and Procedures
7. Monitoring and Interpreting Developments Relating to Compliance with Applicable Laws and Regulations
8. Investigations
9. Managing Relationships with Regulators
10. Records Management

Reprinted with permission from the Corporate Executive Board, Washington, DC © 2006.

Hiring a talented CCO is one best practice but not the only one. The CCO must have a high profile in the organization to be effective. A highly visible CCO can reinforce the importance of the overall compliance program and explain the absolute necessity in always following the letter and spirit of the law as well as company policies and procedures. The best way to accomplish that is for the CCO to be an executive officer with dual reporting lines to both executive leadership and the board. The combination of integrity, reputation, independence, and authority are a potent mix for a CCO. The FSGO also mentions the need for "adequate resources" to build and enforce the compliance program. A company must have at minimum an adequate number of highly skilled people with appropriate authority to successfully carry out the compliance program mandate. This is especially true if the organization has worldwide operations with personnel in many countries. Just imagine a general counsel for a Fortune 500 company that suffered a compliance failure telling a federal prosecutor that the cause was not having enough corporate investigators to detect and prevent the occurrence. That excuse would fall on deaf ears.

Compliance and Ethics Staff Sample Job Description

An effective compliance program includes several different people, responsible for different areas of the compliance function. Oftentimes these responsibilities overlap. The following are sample descriptions of individual positions and their roles and respective responsibilities.

A compliance manager designs the ethics and compliance education programs and compliance systems solutions and ensures their proper implementation. As part of his or her responsibilities, he or she identifies compliance and ethics needs and issues and responds appropriately, as well as reviews and develops record retention policies to serve compliance requirements. The compliance manager works with other departments such as legal, human resources, and internal audit on various issues, such as planning and implementing the rollout of compliance education programs and customizing the included content. A global ethics and compliance associate's duties might include overseeing the company helpline, tracking and oversight of case management, monitoring investigations, and maintaining database and report metrics. He or she would be accountable for driving compliance partnerships with the business unit, line, and functional departments.

A manager of investigations would manage the global investigation process and the overall case management process. He or she would run case reports and provide metrics for management, while helping to develop compliance training tools. A business and ethics training director would oversee compliance investigations, coordinate employee training, perform some training, and oversee employee certification. A records manager oversees company-wide record management policy and execution. Reporting directly to the CCO, the records manager would implement new records management/retention policies, track manual records and the administration of electronic records, and train employees on retention policies, updating them as necessary.[20]

Organizational Structures

Companies have typically housed their compliance programs in the legal department, overseen by an attorney with compliance experience. Newly built or smaller compliance programs tend to be part of the legal department, while the redesigned programs discussed below work with numerous business units. There are four typical designs for compliance programs utilized by companies; the first two place the compliance and ethics program outside the legal department, while the second two place it inside. These organizational models and related research come from the Corporate Executive Board and are used with their permission.

In the first model, the compliance program is part of the risk management office. The CCO reports to the Chief Risk Officer. This usually means that the compliance officer focuses more on risk and minimizing exposure and less formally on ethics. Under the CCO, compliance directors oversee business unit compliance programs. This model is typically adopted by companies in regulated industries with considerable compliance requirements, such as banks and financial services organizations. This structure strengthens the CCO's ability to identify and quickly respond to emerging risks. Compliance is integrated into the operational risk management process that allows for a better understanding of interrelationships between compliance risks and other business risks. The CCO's direct reporting relationship with the Chief Risk Officer facilitates better prevention and detection of compliance risks. However, channeling compliance through a risk framework may lessen the focus on promoting awareness of business ethics, and the lack of direct access to the CEO may have an impact on compliance and ethics priorities.

In the second model, the CCO reports directly to the CEO. This model is prevalent in heavily regulated industries, particularly health care; companies rebuilding after corporate governance crises often use this model to create an independent compliance and ethics program with adequate authority and resources. Here, the compliance office is more autonomous, with a relatively large budget to support companywide compliance initiatives. The CCO has more freedom to design the compliance program's focus and to manage the compliance directors below him or her. The elevated

COMPLIANCE INSIGHT 9.3: TOP FIVE COMPLIANCE STAFF SKILL SETS AND RELATED ROLES AND RESPONSIBILITIES

1. Problem Solving and Communication Skills
   - Recommend and enforce disciplinary actions for compliance and ethics violations
   - Report incidents and breaches to senior management and the Compliance and Ethics Officer
   - Respond to employee questions and concerns regarding business standards policy
2. Program Management (Project Management, Cross-Functional Coordination)
   - Manage new central initiatives and projects driven out to business units, such as designing and implementing a compliance risk-assessment process
   - Work cross-divisionally on planning and implementing the rollout of communications from the compliance and ethics office
3. Business Unit Partnership (Training and Ongoing Support)
   - Ensure compliance and ethics program activities align with business objectives and become integrated into business activities
   - Lead development of compliance and ethics training program and work with business units and functions on program initiatives
   - Meet with business unit executives to report on and ensure adequate visibility of compliance and ethics program initiatives
4. Subject Matter Expertise (Legal Area Expertise)
   - Provide specialist advice and assistance to business units in implementing regulatory initiatives and policies
   - Provide periodic live training and education to business unit executives and management around specific policy issues (e.g., insider trading, anti-money laundering)
5. Industry Knowledge
   - Help formalize process in complying with changing state law compliance requirements
   - Develop specific training plan and course curriculum for key management by function and division

---

Reprinted with permission from the Compliance and Ethics Leadership Council, Corporate Executive Board, Washington, DC © 2005.

and independent position of the CCO and his or her access to the CEO provides instant authority and stature to the compliance program. The direct relationship with business units facilitates compliance participation in business unit decision-making processes. This structure communicates to shareholders that the company strives to go beyond just the minimum legal and regulatory compliance requirements. This prominent position and increased budget also come with increased pressure to achieve compliance goals and to be able to measurably demonstrate to the company that the expenditures are worthwhile.

The third model places a smaller compliance program within the legal department. The CCO reports to the General Counsel, while the program operates with a limited discretionary budget, out of the legal department's overall budget. Rather than dedicated compliance directors, part-time business unit compliance and ethics liaisons provide interface with corporate compliance. This model is found most often in companies with a lower degree of regulatory requirements. Here, small staff levels are typical, befitting the lack of regulatory intensity. The direct relationship with general counsel facilitates clear alignment with legal priorities, and the staff can focus on designing training, coordinating investigations, and promoting company-wide compliance initiatives. However, this structure limits the ability to coordinate activities throughout the company or to respond quickly to emerging issues. Furthermore, the lack of direct access to the CEO means the compliance program does not have substantial credibility with business unit heads and staff.

Finally, the fourth is a decentralized model within the legal department. This model is used by decentralized companies with a low degree of regulatory intensity, such as consumer product or food and beverage organizations. The CCO again reports to the general counsel, but the compliance unit serves mostly as an internal resource to the business units. The individual business units are accountable for their compliance responsibilities, assigning their own personnel to handle any issues. Business unit staff accountability encourages the customization of training and communication to local needs. Holding employees and functional experts accountable promotes local ownership of compliance and ethics initiatives. Nevertheless, this decentralized structure has its drawbacks. As it is not a full-fledged compliance entity, it demands extensive partnering with other functions to manage compliance activities. Reliance upon other departments and their staff to handle compliance efforts means that the compliance efforts may come into conflict with other established departmental interests, and that there may be a lack of consistency across the board, due to the different standards of each unit.[21]

Building an Appropriate Compliance Organizational Model

Companies are shifting away from older compliance models that reported to the general counsel, to a newer model that emphasizes greater compliance autonomy and direct oversight by and a formal relationship with the board of directors. A 2006 survey showed that 46% of compliance and ethics officers planned to or were currently redesigning their function. Only 48% of compliance and ethics officers reported to the general counsel in a 2005 survey, down from 74% in 2002.

Several factors have driven this change. Moving the compliance unit out of the general counsel's office avoids potential conflicts of interests between the compliance function's goal of uncovering risks and violations, and the legal department's role in minimizing the company's legal liability. Compliance officers should be able to investigate and report wrongdoing without interference from another department. The post-Sarbanes-Oxley focus on ethical culture and tone at the top has also led to this shift, as it differs from the legal department's typical mission and may require different skill sets to do so successfully. This priority change has emphasized "non-legal" skills, rather than the typical liability avoidance of the legal department. Additionally, boards of directors want to improve their oversight abilities of compliance and ethics functions, doing so by maintaining reporting relationships with compliance officers.

Compliance and ethics may achieve more influence within the organization by reporting directly to the CEO and the Board of Directors. Business unit executives are less likely to push back on compliance and ethics-related initiatives when they know the compliance program has the support of the CEO.[22]

A chief accounting executive for a public company told a story of how one of the company's executives based in China was faced with an ethical dilemma. This executive was negotiating with a Chinese company to provide services to them. The representative from the Chinese company made it perfectly clear that a kickback would have to be provided in order to secure the business. The executive pulled out of the negotiations and the possibility of a very lucrative contract rather than sacrifice his integrity and ethics. This incident was escalated to senior leadership including the CCO and internal audit. A bulletin was then sent out to all employees describing, in general terms, this potential ethical lapse and how the company did the right thing. This is a great example of effective compliance in action.

COMPLIANCE INSIGHT 9.4: YOU CAN'T SANITIZE DIRTY DEEDS

While one does not normally see corporate compliance officers doing the perp walk along with CEOs and crooked accountants, they are not immune from prosecution for their actions. It is not common, but it has been known to happen; prosecutors will have no trouble taking down a chief compliance officer if the circumstances warrant. Robert Riley, the former Vice-President of Regulatory Affairs and Chief Compliance Officer of AbTox, Inc., which was located in Mundelein, IL, is one of only a few Chief Compliance Officers to be tried and convicted in federal court on federal fraud charges. He received a six-year sentence while Ross Caputo, AbTox's President and Chief Executive Officer got ten years in jail.[a]

AbTox manufactured medical devices, specifically sterilizer equipment, selling them to hospitals to clean medical tools. AbTox had difficulty obtaining the required FDA approval to sell its product, eventually getting the FDA to approve a smaller version for an expressly limited purpose. However, AbTox defrauded hospitals by selling them the larger version for general use, even though it lacked the required FDA approval. AbTox used numerous and continual misrepresentations of material facts to make it appear as though its product was safe and approved for use, even going so far as to use an "independent" outside company to validate its product's uses (the other company was in fact a sister company of AbTox, but that fact was never disclosed).[b] At trial, hospital official after hospital official testified that they would not have bought the product had they known it was not FDA-approved. The defendants proceeded in selling the product despite numerous warning and cease-and-desist letters from the FDA.[c]

Problems mounted further for AbTox when it was discovered that brass instruments sterilized in the equipment developed a blue-green residue on them. AbTox quickly dismissed the concerns of hospitals who inquired about the residue, telling them the instruments were completely safe and the residue appeared because the hospitals did not completely dry the instruments before using the sterilizers. Had AbTox conducted simple tests on the residue—as was recommended by one of AbTox's own scientists—or conducted a cursory search of medical literature, it would have learned that the residue was damaging to the human eye, a fact that was well-documented throughout medical reports.[d]

Many of these concerns from customer hospitals went directly to Riley. Riley distributed to these hospitals a toxicology report that stated the residue was harmless; however, the toxicologist's report was based on limited, selective information provided by Riley himself, and the report itself was edited before distribution. Riley deliberately gave the toxicologist incomplete information to skew the findings. The residue caused injury to over 25 patients during minor eye operations, leaving 18 of them blind in at least one eye. Riley failed to respond to reports of these injuries and did not conduct an investigation or report them to the FDA as he was required to by law.[e] Riley informed others that the injuries were caused by soap, and not by a byproduct of AbTox's sterilization process.

When hospitals stopped using AbTox's product, the injuries stopped as well. In the midst of this, AbTox filed a renewed certification application with the FDA. The FDA again rejected the application, pointing out numerous defects in the product and ordering AbTox not to sell it. Riley gave a copy of this letter to Caputo but otherwise kept it secret and continued to sell the sterilizer. Later, when specifically directed by the FDA to file an incident report, Riley filed a false report, blaming the eye injuries on soap, despite substantial evidence to the contrary. Riley and Caputo continued to falsely assure employees and customers that all problems were being taken care of and FDA clearance was forthcoming.[f]

Overall, "defendants Caputo and Riley effectively carried out a bait and switch scheme on the FDA and its customers, obtaining clearance on one sterilizer but using the clearance to sell another. The defendants continued to sell the large uncleared sterilizer, in defiance of law and FDA directives, through a pattern or falsehoods and deception, until the company shut down operations on April 7, 1998, under pressure from the FDA. In the meantime, AbTox had illegally sold 168 adulterated sterilizers in the United States, causing an intended loss in excess of $16 million."[g]

At trial, a jury convicted both defendants of conspiracy, fraud, mail fraud, wire fraud, and the introduction of an altered or misbranded device into interstate commerce. The "Court and the jury saw overwhelming evidence that the defendants had engaged in a prolonged, massive fraud upon the FDA and relevant hospitals by marketing an illegal sterilizer that ultimately put the general public at risk."[b] Yet despite this evidence, defendants Caputo and Riley never acknowledged their misdeeds or took responsibility. "At sentencing, it was apparent that both defendants still believed they had merely been convicted of technical, regulatory violations. . . Despite repeated admonitions and warning letters from the FDA, the defendants placed themselves above the law, believing they had better scientific and industry knowledge than the FDA. Essentially, both defendants viewed the FDA as a regulatory nuisance that could be neutralized through various misleading and false submissions."[i]

When looking at the facts of this case, one would have to agree with District Court Judge Ruben Castillo's assessment that "[i]t is hard to imagine a more egregious corporate crime. . ."[j] Furthermore, it is hard to imagine a more egregious compliance failure. AbTox's chief compliance officer took part in the crime and helped to keep the fraud covered up. AbTox's compliance program "was a total failure from top to bottom."[k] Caputo chose Riley to serve as compliance officer precisely because he knew Riley would be ineffective. Riley had no compliance training or background prior to being named AbTox's chief compliance officer. Caputo knew he could manipulate and dominate Riley, ensuring his illegal schemes would continue.[l] Despite Caputo's domination of Riley, Riley was nevertheless a willing and active participant in the fraud. He went to jail just as Caputo did. The defendants should have expected a stiff sentence as Judge Castillo is the Vice Chair of the USSC and is intimately familiar with compliance programs and sentencing guidelines. Riley and Caputo should serve as examples of everything not to do in a compliance program and remind others to take compliance seriously, because if one fails to do so, the consequences can be severe.

---

[a] *United States v. Caputo, et al*, Memorandum Opinion and Order, No. 03 CR 0126 (N. Dist. IL 2006), 2.
[b] Ibid., 7-8.
[c] Ibid., 5-6.
[d] Ibid., 10.
[e] Ibid., 11.
[f] Ibid., 13-14.
[g] Ibid., 14.
[h] Ibid., 22.
[i] Ibid.
[j] Ibid., 23.
[k] Ibid., 26.
[l] Ibid.

STEP 3: REASONABLE EFFORTS TO EXCLUDE PROHIBITED PERSONS

The FSGO require that an organization must make reasonable efforts to ensure that personnel with substantial authority have not engaged in illegal activities or conducted themselves in a manner inconsistent with the compliance and ethics program. Questions that organizations need to ask include:

- Does the organization conduct background checks on current and future executive hires?
- Does the organization conduct background checks for all employees?
- Does the organization have a mechanism for determining whether a particular violation is material that might require disclosure under United States securities laws?
- Is the compliance and investigations team prepared to conduct a thorough and professional investigation in a timely manner?
- What are the mechanisms in place for the company to learn about and respond to violations of business conduct in a prompt manner?
- Does the organization perform root cause analysis of the reasons for specific compliance failures?[23]

The best way to exclude prohibited persons is to ensure they never are hired in the first place. The best indicator of future performance is past performance and comprehensive background investigations are needed to determine this. Background checks are a must for all new hires and should include criminal record checks, credit history, civil litigation, education, professional certifications, and reference verifications. The more sensitive the position, the greater the degree of background review that is needed.

Unfortunately, resume padding and deceit are rampant. One executive recruiter estimates that 40% of all resumes contain some falsehoods.[24] Typical false statements include degrees never received, exaggeration of achievements, overstating of titles and salary, lying about skills and abilities, and inflating college GPAs. The former CEO of RadioShack resigned in February 2006 after questions surfaced about college degrees he claimed to have received.[25] Although there were many media reports about this and other executives' padded resume claims, some executives failed to learn from this sad experience. In June 2007, the chief executive in Asia Pacific for InterContinental Hotels, the world's largest hotel chain, lied in his resume when he falsely claimed to have degrees from Cornell University and Australia's Victoria University.[26] "He attended classes at Victoria and Cornell, but we understand that he did not graduate from either," said a company spokesperson speaking on a condition of anonymity.[27] Great compliance includes thorough background checks to include a full resume review.

This background check process must also be conducted for employees brought in through mergers and acquisitions. Knowing the potential background issues with these employees is important in compliance with this program element. In many acquisitions, a larger, well-established company is buying a smaller, privately held company that may not have a compliance program in place. As an example, I was once told of a company that turned a blind eye to expense reporting abuses by its employees. The company was very small and without adequate safeguards and controls. Employees considered falsely claiming personal expenses as business expenses, a perk that no one did anything about. When this small company was later acquired by a larger company, would the employees readily give up their "perk" or continue their fraudulent ways?

While most companies will have some form of background check at hire, very few conduct subsequent background checks. Even the best employees can have changes in their lives that companies should know about because these events can impact the employers. A domestic violence arrest and conviction can portend serious consequences at work, especially if the employee and spouse work at the same company. An arrest for embezzlement might be very relevant if the subject employee works in a finance role. Any number of related issues should be known to an employer. Not all criminal offenses are job-threatening or even relevant but an organization should at least be aware of them when making employment decisions, such as whether to retain or to promote the employee. Those offenses that reflect a person's character or a pattern of criminal behavior should be red flags for a company. Thus, a recommended best practice is to have periodic updates to criminal, credit, and litigation checks. Consideration should be given to having a policy requiring employees to self-report any relevant incidents. In addition, there should be new background investigations when people are promoted into senior leadership roles where the financial and reputational risks are greater.

The Investigative Response

Every company that wants to be serious about compliance needs a fraud-fighting unit. A robust fraud prevention program will include fraud risk assessment, detection, education, awareness of fraud issues and prevention, and responsive investigations. However, preventative programs, no matter how good they are, will not stop all fraud. "Therefore, an investigative response component through which company investigators can quickly respond to allegations of fraud is needed for all prevention programs. The fraud investigative unit must be responsible for the detection, investigation, and prevention of fraud and must have the strong support of senior management and the Audit Committee."[28]

Any unit created by a company needs to be staffed with experienced fraud investigators. Due to the complexities of fraud schemes and their myriad forms, it takes many years for someone to gain the experience and skills to be an expert in fraud detection and investigation. Consideration should be given to hiring former law enforcement professionals, corporate investigators, forensic accountants, and others with extensive investigative experience as well as those certified in related disciplines. Certified Fraud Examiners (CFE), Certified Protection Professionals (CPP), Professional Certified Investigators (PCI), Certified Compliance and Ethics Professionals (CCEP), Certified Public Accountants and other highly skilled investigative and forensic experts should be part of every organization's compliance function. Beyond just their investigative skills, these investigators must also be agents of change and the voice of compliance convincing upper management (and then all levels below) of the importance of fraud prevention.[29]

The hiring of these fraud professionals demonstrates the company's commitment to high integrity, and with their assistance, will help the company embrace a robust fraud prevention and investigation program. The investigators' skills should also be supplemented with high-tech tools and resources to further their investigative efforts. Ongoing training of the investigative staff is also required. A sound recommendation is that each investigator should receive a minimum of 40 hours of training each year with emphasis on investigative procedures, employment law, and other legal aspects. "The message that needs to be conveyed is that the company is ready, willing, and able to respond quickly and appropriately to the allegations of fraud."[30]

Consideration should also be given to developing an investigative framework for all investigations conducted. This framework would provide a detailed step by step process for investigative excellence and oversight. There should be an intake process for how compliance issues are routed for review and an investigative determination. An assignment process must also be included to decide who actually conducts the investigation and under what oversight. Prior to the start of an investigation, a detailed investigative plan should be created that identifies the scope of the investigation and all related elements. Included in the plan should be what documents will be analyzed, what tools will be needed in the investigative process, who will be interviewed, who will lead the investigation, what investigative assistance will be needed from human resources, legal, investigative vendors, and others, the timeline for completion of the investigation, and other key elements of an investigation.

Investigator's Code of Conduct

Another best practice to consider is the creation of a specific investigator's code of conduct. The role of corporate investigators and the internal investigative process has been the focus of media reporting over the last few years involving Fortune 500 companies. There were a number of issues raised regarding the behavior of their investigators including spying on employees and journalists, surveillance techniques, using pretexting and subterfuge to obtain personal information, and other questionable investigative techniques. The result has been a greater oversight of the investigative role in business organizations. Above all else, investigators must not permit any bias, prejudice, or preconceived opinions to impede an investigation and always report facts accurately and completely. Thus, the creation of an investigator's code of conduct that embodies professional conduct, best practices, compliance with laws and polices, and prohibits inappropriate and unethical conduct is another process that can further protect an organization from reputational and financial risk.

NOTES

1. Martin T. Biegelman and Joel T. Bartow, *Executive Roadmap to Fraud Prevention and Internal Control: Creating a Culture of Compliance*, (Hoboken, NJ: John Wiley & Sons, Inc, 2006), 98–99.
2. While the Guidelines have been tremendously controversial, the FSGO have not been for the most part. Criticism of the Guidelines focused heavily on mandatory minimum sentencing and sentencing disparity. Application of the Guidelines often led to absurd and inequitable results, where first-time drug offenders received longer sentences than murderers. Criticism also focused on the sentencing disparity between cocaine possession and crack-cocaine possession. However, the FSGO have not engendered anything close to the level of outrage created by the Guidelines. This may be due in part to fairer application of the provisions, or less public sympathy for corporations. For better or for worse, the plight of corporate executives going to jail or of corporations paying stiff fines for criminal conduct does not stir public outrage. In fact, corporate offenders have historically been perceived as getting off easy in comparison to their blue-collar brethren.
3. United States Sentencing Commission, *Federal Sentencing Guidelines Manual*, www.ussc.gov/2004guid/CHAP8.pdf, 476.
4. Ibid.
5. *Federal Sentencing Guidelines Manual*, 476–81.
6. Biegelman and Bartow, *Executive Roadmap*, 101.
7. *Federal Sentencing Guidelines Manual*, 476.
8. Ibid.
9. "Summary of the 2004 Federal Sentencing Guidelines Amendments and Recommended Action Steps," *General Counsel Roundtable*, June 2004.

10. Biegelman and Bartow, *Executive Roadmap*, 71.
11. Douglas Allen, "50 Codes of Conduct Benchmarked: How Does Your Organization Stack Up?," *Ethisphere Magazine*, Q2 2007, www .ethisphere.com/Ethisphere_Magazine_0207/50-codes-Q2.
12. *Federal Sentencing Guidelines Manual*, 476.
13. "Summary of the 2004 Federal Sentencing Guidelines."
14. Infosys Corporate Governance page, www.infosys.com/investor/ corporategovernance.asp.
15. Biegelman and Bartow, *Executive Roadmap*, 368.
16. Statement on Auditing Standards 99, "Consideration of Fraud in a Financial Statement Audit," Management Antifraud Program and Controls Exhibit, American Institute of Certified Public Accountants, 2002.
17. Ibid.
18. *United States v. Caputo*, Memorandum Opinion and Order, No. 03 CR 0126 (N. Dist. IL 2006), 26.
19. Connie Guglielmo, "Hewlett-Packard Ethics Chief Tackles Spying Aftermath," Bloomberg.com, April 24, 2007, www.bloomberg.com/ apps/news?pid=20601109&refer=home&sid=awZRPpHPAxH4.
20. "Establishing a Compliance and Ethics Program: Defining Staff Skills and Responsibilities," *Compliance and Ethics Leadership Council*, October 2005.
21. "Establishing a Compliance and Ethics Program: Building an Appropriate Organizational Structure," *Compliance and Ethics Leadership Council*, October 2005.
22. "The State of the Compliance and Ethics Function," *Compliance and Ethics Leadership Council*, December 2006.
23. "Summary of the 2004 Federal Sentencing Guidelines."
24. Karen DuBose Tomassi, "Most Common Resume Lies," Forbes.com, May 23, 2006, www.forbes.com/2006/05/20/resume-lies-work_cx_ kdt_06work_0523lies.html.
25. Ibid.
26. "InterContinental Hotels Executive Resigns After Resume Lies Exposed," *International Herald Tribune*, June 14, 2007, www.iht.com/ articles/ap/2007/06/14/business/EU-FIN-Britain-False-Resume.php.
27. Ibid.
28. Martin T. Biegelman and Joel T. Bartow, *Executive Roadmap to Fraud Prevention and Internal Control: Creating a Culture of Compliance*, (Hoboken, NJ: John Wiley & Sons, Inc, 2006), 239.
29. Ibid., 240.
30. Ibid., 239.

CHAPTER 10

Building a World-Class Compliance Program: The Seven Steps in Practice (Part II)

"The only thing a man can take beyond his lifetime is his ethics."
Thomas Jefferson

STEP 4: TRAINING AND COMMUNICATION OF STANDARDS AND PROCEDURES

The FSGO require that organizations "shall take reasonable steps to communicate periodically, and in a practical manner, its standards and procedures, and other aspects of the compliance and ethics program.... and [conduct] effective training programs and otherwise disseminate information"[1] about the compliance program. Questions that organizations need to ask include:

- Does the organization assess its risks in order to identify an appropriate training curriculum for its employees?
- Does the company communicate to employees the consequences for compliance failures?
- Are company values and standards communicated to vendors and other business associates?
- Does the company have an adequate reporting mechanism for employees and others to communicate incidents and issues?
- How does the company identify and reach all employees for training purposes?
- Has the company determined who in the organization are considered "agents"?

- How frequently is training provided within the organization and how often is it updated?
- Are corporate values and issues of law properly communicated as rules that must be obeyed as drivers of the corporate culture?
- Are members of the board provided relevant training at board meetings or in other sessions?
- Is the compliance program budget adequate and is there a periodic reassessment?
- Does the organization establish methods for measuring effectiveness of their training program?
- Has the organization identified any history of ethics and compliance failures experienced by competitors, as well as any best practices that can be applied to the compliance program?[2]

One of the most important elements of an effective compliance program is training for all employees from the CEO down. Appropriate training reinforces an organization's commitment to ethical conduct and compliance with policies, procedures, and laws. Training must include the organization's code of conduct and all its various components. Key areas that need to be covered include conflict of interest policy, antiharassment and antidiscrimination policy, antitrust, protection of intellectual property, fraud risk, FCPA risk and compliance, whistleblowing and reporting of compliance issues and concerns, and protection against retaliation. The importance of training and need for universal training should come from the highest reaches of a company. Leading by example is another best practice. Thus, as mentioned earlier, an organization's leadership should be among the first employees to complete training courses. When training is conducted in a classroom setting, executives should consider taking required training with the rank and file employees and sitting among them. This can do much to reinforce the importance of training as well as tone at the top.

Both traditional in-person and online training should be employed. In-person training allows for greater interaction and provides the opportunity for the instructor to answer specific questions as they arise. In-person training fosters discussion of key issues to reinforce their importance. A group setting can also include role-playing exercises and gauge the understanding of issues important to employees. Online training is growing in popularity and can reach large audiences in a very cost-effective manner. Online training allows for customization by location, language, employee function, and subject matter. Employees can decide when they want to complete training and how much they want to complete at one time. Tracking of employee attendance and course completion can be easily accomplished with online training. Whether in-person or online, tracking of employee training hours must be recorded. Consideration should also be given to a minimum requirement of training hours completed per year.

Designing and Distributing the Code of Conduct

A well-written and compelling code of conduct is a key component of a successful ethics and compliance program. It both establishes expectations of conduct and communicates these expectations to employees. "A code of ethics provides a moral compass for employees by defining the company's position on ethical issues and promoting integrity. To be effective, management has to embody the code of ethics, and all employees have to be informed and committed."[3] Code of conduct certification programs ensure that all employees have read and understand what the code requires of them.

Disseminating the code through a variety of channels helps to further awareness of it. By making the code available in print, through e-mail, and on the company's Web and intranet sites, as well as other available avenues, the company provides employees with multiple ways to access the code should the need arise, as well as clearly illustrating its commitment to what's in the code. A company that creates a code of conduct but does not make it widely available demonstrates the depth of its ethical commitment, which is to say, none at all. Beyond making it widely available, a company can take steps to make the code more accessible. They can make the code short and use concise and easily understood language. While the code should be lengthy enough to thoroughly cover the necessary issues, it should not be so long that people will not read it. To make it easy to understand, a company can break down a policy into "what it means" and "what to avoid" to aid understanding and retention. Providing a question and answer section for guidance, along with real company examples or scenarios, helps employees better navigate the gray areas they face. Integrating employee code certification into performance reviews ensures greater employee participation.[4]

Publicizing Ethical Lapses

All organizations, no matter how good their compliance programs, will have ethical lapses by their employees. It is human nature, but these personal failures can be turned into learning opportunities for the betterment of the entire organization. Thus, communicate the impact of non-compliance. This communication is especially important when a significant compliance lapse or public event occurs such as the arrest of an employee for a criminal offense involving company assets. Senior leaders need to inform the organization about the event, how it happened, the compliance failures involved, and what to do to ensure it does not happen again. These events, while painful, can be used as learning opportunities from which to grow and improve.

Use an ongoing communication such as an "Integrity Corner" in internal communications to employees where ethics lapses and disciplinary actions are publicized. While specific information about the employees and others who were disciplined is not recommended to be disclosed, the facts of the case can be used for learning and prevention. Some companies actually list on their Web sites the number of investigations conducted into compliance failures, the number of related employee terminations, hotline referrals, and other related information. One company uses a well-publicized reward system offering up to $25,000 to employees who report violations of their code of conduct. While very few companies offer cash rewards, it has proven very effective for this particular company. Of course, as with any hotline or reporting mechanism, due care must be given to protect against the receipt of false allegations.

Gift Policy and Cultural Differences

Most United States companies have policies restricting the gifts that their employees can receive so as to limit potential conflicts of interest. These policies are necessary in protecting the organization but there must be an understanding of cultural differences elsewhere in the world. American policies restricting the giving and receipt of gifts in the course of business sometimes are at odds with cultural traditions, particularly in Asia where the tradition of gift-giving is deeply ingrained. Companies must be sensitive to these traditions but also ensure that no one is pressured into participating.

In China, "red envelopes" or "red packets" are given on social and family occasions or holidays such as Chinese New Year. The gifts, money presented in a red envelope, symbolize good luck, and the amount of money given is usually a lucky number itself. These *Lai See* gifts are an important social tradition, because they allow the recipient to measure the strength of the relationship with the gift-giver, based on the amount of money received. Japan has something analogous called *otoshidama*, though Japan and also Korea use white envelopes. Similar traditions exist throughout Southeast Asia.[5]

Companies doing business in Asia wish to respect native traditions but also recognize the pitfalls with this practice. In China, for instance, the red envelope is also the standard form in which political bribes are given.[6] Typical company policies do not encourage the acceptance of these gifts and expressly prohibit solicitation of them, but allow for the gifts as a friendly courtesy gesture. These policies limit the amount of money given to a nominal sum. Training and communication is necessary to provide understanding and compliance with gift policies while limiting the risk.

Other Training and Communication Best Practices

- Training should be scenario-based using a variation of real-life events and compliance failures that the particular organization previously encountered. Web-based training is especially suited for this mode of teaching.

- Managers are role model and mentors. When employees see their managers following the code of conduct and leading by example, greater compliance occurs. Thus, the training of managers, both new and long-term ones, is necessary in implementing a world-class compliance program.

- Senior leadership should communicate to all employees their ongoing commitment to integrity and compliance. This can be done via e-mail and can periodically focus on a particular area of risk such as fraud prevention or protection of intellectual property.

- Address third party risk by requiring the training of the vendors and contract employees that an organization uses. Educating vendors about fraud and prevention activities will yield important benefits. If vendors do not have their own internal compliance programs, encourage them to develop such programs. Doing this will add great value to their organizations and strengthen business opportunities.

- Continually reinforce the importance of reporting of compliance issues by employees and those outside the organization. This mode of communication is often the best way that an organization learns about compliance problems.

- Send e-mail reminders prior to the start of the holiday season reminding employees of the company's policy and restrictions about accepting gifts from vendors. In addition, remind vendors of the organization's policies about the receipt of gifts and require them to comply with these policies.

- Make it easy for anyone accessing the organization's Web site to find the section on corporate compliance. Have the link prominently displayed on the home page.

- Include a requirement in all mid-year and annual employee reviews to discuss the importance of integrity, compliance requirements, the existence of the organization's hotline, and the need to report all compliance issues.

- Ensure that all employees know the name and contact information of the organization's Chief Compliance Officer. Have regular meet and greets with the CCO and his or her staff to hear firsthand about the importance of compliance.

- Use newsletters, table top tents, posters, home mailings as well as e-mails to constantly communicate the existence of the organization's compliance program. One company prints their code of conduct on paper placemats in their company cafeterias so they are easily and constantly viewed.
- There are always innovative approaches to compliance and ethics training. It just takes imagination and a commitment. One Fortune 500 company held an ethics contest where employees could make and submit home videos on the subject. The videos were used in ethics training. They were well-received as they carried important messages in addition to being entertaining.[7]
- The Board of Directors must also receive ongoing communication on all aspects of an organization's compliance program. These communications should include updates on risk assessments, internal control weaknesses, significant internal investigations, compliance training, and other commonly reported topics. Compliance Insight 10.1 details the key components of a comprehensive board report.

STEP 5: MONITORING, AUDITING, AND EVALUATING PROGRAM EFFECTIVENESS

The FSGO require that organizations periodically evaluate the effectiveness of their compliance program and include monitoring and auditing systems designed to detect criminal conduct. The program must "have and publicize a system, which may include mechanisms that allow anonymity or confidentiality, whereby the organization's employees and agents may report or seek guidance regarding potential or actual criminal conduct without fear of retaliation."[8] Questions that organizations need to ask include:

- Does the organization have an anonymous and confidential reporting mechanism to respond to people seeking guidance about compliance and ethics?
- Are the current policies and procedures adequate for a robust ethics and compliance program?
- Has the company identified policies and procedures to encourage employees to report incidents?
- Has the company identified and created tools and data to assess the effectiveness of the compliance program?
- Are employees empowered by education and training to resolve ethical and legal dilemmas?[9]

COMPLIANCE INSIGHT 10.1: KEY COMPONENTS OF A COMPREHENSIVE BOARD REPORT: HALLMARKS OF OUTSTANDING COMMUNICATION, COMPLIANCE AND ETHICS LEADERSHIP COUNCIL RESEARCH, 2006

Commonly Reported Categories	Typical Reporting Frequency	Standard Practice	Emerging Practice
Risk Assessment	Quarterly	▪ List of key risks and associated mitigation plans ▪ Update on major incidents	▪ Reporting of future risks ▪ Changes in policies, procedures, and controls in response to risks ▪ Overview of risk-assessment method and process ▪ Periodic review of mitigation plans
Training	Quarterly	▪ Percentage of employee base that has completed specific training modules	▪ Percentage of target audiences in high-risk functions that has completed specific modules ▪ Outline of planned training modules
Allegations and Investigations	Quarterly	▪ Trends in volume and types of allegations ▪ Data on case cycle time	▪ Breakdown of issues by category, business unit, geography, and severity ▪ Focus on status of complaints and open investigations

(*Continued*)

COMPLIANCE INSIGHT 10.1: (Continued)

Commonly Reported Categories	Typical Reporting Frequency	Standard Practice	Emerging Practice
Regulatory	Quarterly	■ Update on key regulatory events that affect industry ■ Update on ongoing regulatory investigations and legal cases	■ Focus on regulatory developments that pose highest risk and impact company strategy ■ Focus on business changes that affect compliance obligations
Program Effectiveness	Annually/ Quarterly	■ Discussion of key program elements and important implementation milestones ■ Review of periodic audit results	■ Present overview of framework that drives program improvement ■ Benchmark program elements against external standards ■ Report key trends (compare data over time to identify systemic problems in the company) ■ Provide powerful examples of tone at the top and positive behaviors (specifically management)

COMPLIANCE INSIGHT 10.1: (Continued)

Commonly Reported Categories	Typical Reporting Frequency	Standard Practice	Emerging Practice
Resources and Personnel	Annually	• Annual budget allocation • Relevant staff developments	• Benchmark of budget against industry peers • Analysis of available resources against program needs (gap analysis)
Annual Plan	Annually	• Overview of next year's compliance and ethics departmental plan	• Plan links departmental initiatives and key risk areas • Plan clearly details interim milestones and owners across the company
Ethics Awareness	Annually	• Presentation of ethics survey results • Update on ethics communication initiatives	• Analysis of survey results by business unit and managerial versus non-managerial responses • Benchmarking of responses against other companies • Demonstration/visuals of communication tools and compliance intranet

Reprinted with permission from the Corporate Executive Board, Washington, DC © 2006.

COMPLIANCE INSIGHT 10.2: EMBEDDING COMPLIANCE IN THE BUSINESS, COMPLIANCE AND ETHICS LEADERSHIP COUNCIL RESEARCH, 2006

Recent scandals, coupled with the breadth of ongoing regulatory requirements, are driving interest in embedding accountability for compliance activities in the line and focusing employee attention not only on financial results but also on how these results are achieved. Council research suggests that efforts to cascade compliance expectations and reinforce ethical behavior are often frustrated by three challenges: 1) insufficient or misaligned compliance incentives, 2) lack of emphasis on the consequences of noncompliance, and 3) standardized training that fails to influence employee behavior. A Compliance and Ethics Leadership Council study illustrates how companies align performance objectives and compliance expectations and drive employee awareness of compliance and ethics. The Council's study found the six most significant research findings are as follows:

Finding #1—Focus Performance Evaluations on Both Desired Results and Desired Behaviors. Companies are incorporating compliance behaviors and ethical conduct into employee performance scorecards to emphasize to all employees that the means by which business outcomes and results are achieved are as important as the results themselves.

Finding #2—Outline Clear Guidelines for Consequences of Noncompliance. To articulate the consequences of noncompliance and ensure the consistent enforcement of disciplinary policies and processes across the corporation, compliance and ethics officers are providing business units with guidelines for disciplinary action and outlining escalation paths for compliance violations.

Finding #3—Direct Compliance Messages Toward Teaching and Not Just Communication. Focusing compliance communications on real ethical dilemmas and publishing the real consequences of noncompliance through case examples and scenarios offer guidance to employees on how to both apply these policies in day-to-day situations and preempt potential violations.

Finding #4—Cascade Examples of Noncompliance Through the Entire Organization. Leading companies are disseminating examples of communication using a variety of methods to maximize their organizational reach and provide a larger audience visibility into the real consequences of noncompliance.

Finding #5—Develop a Targeted Compliance Training Strategy. A training approach customized to employees' preexisting knowledge and job requirements frees compliance training resources (in terms of both employee time and company expense) and reduces the training burden on employees.

Finding #6—Engage Business Managers in Compliance Training. Requiring business managers (rather than third party consultants) to deliver compliance and ethics training allows managers to more effectively tailor training to the context of employees' particular jobs and initiates real, honest, and relevant discussion of hypothetical ethical issues between managers and their direct reports.

Reprinted with permission from the Corporate Executive Board, Washington, DC © 2006.

Hotlines

Hotlines are an excellent way to receive allegations of fraud and other wrongdoing. "Hotlines allow employees and others outside the company to communicate compliance concerns to the company for appropriate action... If a company does not already have a hotline in place, it is putting itself at risk."[10] Tips from employees are the most common way of detecting frauds, and hotlines are the best way to collect this information. With hotlines, "build it right and they will call." If a hotline is built properly and its existence is publicized to employees, it insures that they will feel comfortable coming forward with critical information.[11]

With hotlines, several basic rules apply. The hotline must be easily accessible to callers in every country where the business operates and be available in multiple languages. It should be staffed 24 hours a day, seven days a week by live operators trained to handle these calls. Rather than handling the calls in-house, they should be outsourced to a third-party provider to ensure transparency and most importantly, confidentiality and anonymity.[12] Confidentiality and anonymity are the most important features of a hotline. Confidentiality means that the information revealed in the call is transmitted only to people who need to hear it. Anonymity means that the caller's identity will be kept secret, if desired by the caller. This goes beyond just the caller's name; potentially identifying details should also be kept secret. An employee's sense of trust and faith in the hotline is a vital part of its success.[13] In my first book, I devoted a full chapter to hotlines and whistleblowers as this is a crucial element of compliance. For more information on this topic please refer to that book.[14]

Non-Retaliation Policy

In 2007, the Compliance and Ethics Leadership Council of the Corporate Executive Board studied the leading indicators of potential misconduct. Their study found that the fear of retaliation was the single greatest concern among employees. This should be no surprise to an organization. Studies by the Association of Certified Fraud Examiners continually find that employee tips are the most common way to discover fraud and abuse. Every company needs a strong policy against retaliation, to encourage employees to come forward and to protect them from any reprisals. This policy should be put into the code of conduct distributed to all employees and be incorporated into training programs. Anonymous reporting, if the employee so desires, should be available for the reporting of complaints regarding accounting, internal control, auditing, or any other policy or code of conduct matter. All complaints should be handled in a confidential manner, even if the reportee did not request anonymity. Disclosure of the matter should be made only to those persons necessary to conduct a full investigation of the alleged violation or to carry out appropriate discipline.[15]

Evaluating Compliance Programs

The effectiveness of compliance programs can be measured in a number of ways. These include having adequate resources to ensure the compliance mandate is successfully fulfilled. Each organization needs to determine the appropriate number of resources needed for the various components. For example, the number of professionally trained and experienced people assigned compliance and investigation responsibilities is one determination. Other metrics to consider are the number of employees trained and certified each year and whether this comprises all employees worldwide; employees' scores on ethics surveys; how many issues and questions are escalated to the compliance department each year; how many different reporting mechanisms are available to employees to report issues; how timely is the response to allegations of misconduct and other compliance issues; how long it takes to complete investigations and impose possible disciplinary action; and how violations of business conduct are reported to employees. This evaluation process also goes to the tone at the top of an organization.

A great tool to use in evaluating the effectiveness of an organization's compliance program is the Compliance and Ethics Program Assessment Wizard™ created by the Corporate Executive Board's Compliance and Ethics Leadership Council (CELC). The Wizard is a comprehensive measurement and benchmarking system for compliance and ethics program performance. It is a Web-based, self-assessment of program maturity that assesses an organization's compliance program across eight key elements and 28 sub-elements. The elements and sub-elements align closely with the revised Federal Sentencing Guidelines and incorporate expectations of the SEC and European regulators. The Wizard is further discussed in Appendix C.

Other Best Practices for Evaluating Program Effectiveness

- Periodically review company policies and procedures to ensure they are updated as necessary to reflect changes in laws and regulations both domestically and internationally.
- Identify and review the tools and data the organization uses to assess compliance effectiveness.
- Ensure that every employee has completed required training and, more importantly, understands the implications of that training especially in reporting compliance concerns and violations of business conduct.
- In evaluating hotline effectiveness, consider the following:
  - How well communicated is the existence of the hotline?
  - How many calls does the hotline receive each year?
  - How many actual escalations of compliance concerns or other questions about the program or the company were received?
  - For allegations received, how long did it take from the time of the receipt of the allegation until the investigation is commenced and then concluded?
  - How many issues were founded versus unfounded?
  - How many terminations and other lesser disciplinary actions resulted from hotline calls?
  - How are the hotline calls and related organizational responses tracked and reported to the board of directors?
  - Are Sarbanes-Oxley, financial accounting, and other key issues and risks also escalated to the board of directors?
  - Is the hotline periodically tested by making calls from various worldwide locations to check effectiveness and efficiency of reporting and escalation?

- Does the organization's internal audit function conduct an annual review of the hotline program?
- While many of the calls to a hotline will be anonymous with no further communication, do not forget that the caller will be watching for the outcome. Let's use as an example an anonymous employee escalating a legitimate allegation of fraud by another employee. If the subsequent investigation corroborates the allegation and results in the termination of the subject employee, the anonymous caller/employee will gain great confidence that the compliance program does work and works well.
- It is a good rule to always remember that some of the allegations reported through the hotline may be false and simply made to harm the subject for one reason or another. All allegations, especially those made anonymously, must be thoroughly and professionally investigated to determine if there is any basis for the complaint. Finding an allegation to be unfounded is just as important as proving an allegation is true.
- Establish a compliance and ethics advisory group of external industry professionals that regularly reviews the organization's compliance program and makes recommendations for improvement. Consider experts from top law firms, academia, compliance and ethics professional organizations, and other corporations as members of this advisory group. As with any use of external professionals, the organization's legal department must be contacted for appropriate review and approval of this possible approach.
- Retain accounting and consulting professionals from the major consulting firms to periodically conduct the compliance program assessment. They have significant experience in the design and implementation of compliance programs and have much valuable experience to share.

STEP 6: PERFORMANCE INCENTIVES AND DISCIPLINARY ACTION

The FSGO require that the "organization's compliance and ethics program shall be promoted and enforced consistently throughout the organization through (A) appropriate incentives to perform in accordance with the compliance and ethics program; and (B) appropriate disciplinary measures for engaging in criminal conduct and for failing to take reasonable steps to prevent or detect criminal conduct."[16] Questions that organizations need to ask include:

- Does the company celebrate ethics success as strongly as it condemns unethical or criminal conduct?

- Does the performance management and compensation system reinforce and reward ethical behavior?[17]

Discipline

It is an unfortunate fact of life that some individuals will violate an organization's standards of business conduct. Depending on whether the offense is a fraud or other abuse of policy and the severity of the offense, the company may face a serious risk. When that happens, organizations must be prepared to act appropriately to administer fair, balanced, and incremental discipline. How an entity responds to incidents of alleged or suspected fraud will send a strong deterrent message to all employees and will help reduce the number of future occurrences. The following actions should be considered in response to compliance violations:

- Conduct a thorough and professional investigation of the incident.
- Administer appropriate and consistent disciplinary actions against violators.
- Assess, redesign, and improve relevant internal controls to mitigate future occurrences.
- Communication and training about the consequences of committing fraud or other violations should be used to reinforce the entity's values, code of conduct, and expectations.

Knowing that violators have been disciplined for wrongdoing can be an effective deterrent, increasing the perceived likelihood that those who commit crimes and other violations of policy will be caught and punished. This also reaffirms an organization's commitment to high ethical standards and integrity.[18]

Zero tolerance for fraud and other serious crimes must be the standard in every organization. Whether a person steals one dollar or one million dollars, fraud in any amount cannot be tolerated. A person lacking integrity must be removed from the organization. Once removed, action must be taken to ensure that the person is not allowed to return in another employment capacity. Human resources must ensure that employees terminated for compliance violations are not rehired by placing that person on an "ineligible for rehire" list and always referring to it before hiring new employees.

Organizations should always consider referring criminal violations by employees and others to law enforcement for possible prosecution. Not only is this appropriate as a good corporate citizen, but there is a definite deterrence factor to consider. Knowing that they face possible prosecution and incarceration will deter some people from committing crimes. In addition, holding people accountable for their actions sends a strong message that the organization is intent on protecting their interests in a high-integrity environment and will hold accountable those who break the law. The general counsel or outside counsel should be the focal point for final decisions as to criminal referrals. Companies should also consider publicizing prosecutions of employee fraudsters to reinforce a culture of compliance and a zero tolerance for fraud.[19] Compliance Insight 10.3 provides suggestions for deterring management misconduct.

COMPLIANCE INSIGHT 10.3: KEY OBJECTIVES AND PRINCIPLES IN DETERRING MANAGEMENT MISCONDUCT, COMPLIANCE AND ETHICS LEADERSHIP COUNCIL RESEARCH, 2006

Four key objectives and the related ten principles in deterring management misconduct are as follows:

- Objective #1: Educate Managers
  - Principle #1: Train Managers on the Economic Consequences of Misconduct
  - Principle #2: Educate Managers About Communicating Ethical Messages
  - Principle #3: Provide Regular Updates on Performance Against Compliance Goals
- Objective #2: Hold Managers Accountable
  - Principle #4: Test Managers on Desired Behaviors
  - Principle #5: Embed Ethics and Compliance into Performance Objectives
  - Principle #6: Establish Ethics Checks as Condition of Promotion
- Objective #3: Improve Detective Capabilities
  - Principle #7: Encourage Employees to Speak Up
  - Principle #8: Implement Controls to Prevent Retaliation
- Objective #4: Develop Leading Indicators
  - Principle #9: Review Existing Internal Data to Anticipate Fraud
  - Principle #10: Use Multiple Date Sources to Anticipate Ethical Breakdowns

---

Reprinted with permission from the Corporate Executive Board, Washington, DC © 2006.

Awards and Recognition for Ethical Behavior

Appropriate incentives are key to ensuring proper employee behavior. The recent bestseller *Freakonomics* describes the great power that incentives have in shaping human behavior, be they economic, social, or moral incentives. A small tweak in incentives can produce dramatic changes in behavior; given a big enough incentive, people will change their behavior, no matter what.[20] Thus, a company can take advantage of this, making sure that it provides proper incentives for its employees to act ethically, as well as making sure that it is not, either inadvertently or otherwise, giving employees incentives to act unethically.

Companies need to provide incentives to encourage good behavior, and to reward those who act ethically. Just as a company punishes bad behavior, it should reward appropriate behavior, to further encourage it. This recognition should be both external and internal: advertising to the public the company's ethical achievements and recognizing employees' individual achievements. A company that consistently acts ethically will be recognized. Ethical achievements should be publicized, whether on the company's Web site or in the media. Considering all of the publicity corporate malfeasance receives, good behavior should also receive some coverage. Ethical companies can be nominated for special awards, as was the case with Premier, Inc., which won the Malcolm Baldrige National Quality Award, discussed at length in Chapter 11.

Companies should also focus on rewarding their own employees. There are several different ways to give employees the proper incentives to act ethically. Some companies give awards to employees who have demonstrated high ethical standards, particularly in trying circumstances. Using awards and recognition for employees who embrace integrity and honesty does much to reinforce the commitment to compliance. People can be recognized for a variety of compliance and ethics successes. These may be for escalations of compliance issues, improvements to internal controls to mitigate risk, writing articles on compliance that were published internally, preparing training programs to promote the culture of compliance, or other such examples. Recognition in the form of compensation, plaques, and certificates of appreciation can go a long way in promoting ethical behavior

Employees with high integrity should be praised in front of the entire company, as exemplars of what the company strives to achieve. An example of this can be found again in Chapter 11. Sometimes a company will not be able to publicize the actions of a whistleblower, but the company should still recognize this person confidentially, through a private ceremony with the CEO, CFO, CCO, or other appropriate executives. Some other companies provide financial incentives for reporting allegations of wrongdoing, fraud, and policy abuses. This is a unique approach. One company that has adopted this policy, a Midwest manufacturing company, receives numerous reports of misconduct while false or vindictive reporting is almost nonexistent. The reason for this company's success is that employees must identify themselves to claim the reward. This greatly reduces the possibility of deception and false reporting.

STEP 7: RESPONSE TO CRIMINAL CONDUCT AND REMEDIAL ACTION

The FSGO require that organizations "periodically assess the risk of criminal conduct including making any necessary modifications to the organization's compliance and ethics program."[21] Questions that organizations need to ask include:

- Does the organization create tools to monitor and assess the compliance program, as well as make continuous improvements to the program?
- Does the company identify and create processes to track changes in the business, products, services, and organizational structure that could lead to compliance risks?
- Does the company embed ethics and compliance messages into other company communications?
- Does the company quickly create internal control enhancements as appropriate to prevent compliance failures?
- Does the company treat ethics as an integral part of how the company does business?
- Who is (are) the person or persons responsible for making disclosures to outside parties in case of a violation?
- Does the company have a "compliance resume" so that if a criminal violation occurs, the company can demonstrate that it took every reasonable step to comply with the highest standards of corporate compliance?[22]

It is hoped that by implementing the Seven Steps of effective compliance, organizations can protect against criminal conduct by its employees. Unfortunately, that is not always the case as even good companies can have bad days. Fraud and unethical conduct can occur in any company. The determining factor will be how an organization responds when non-compliance issues arise. Depending on the severity of the issues such as financial accounting fraud, other Sarbanes-Oxley issues, FCPA violations, and other matters requiring disclosure, the organization may need to self-report to the SEC, the Department of Justice, and/or other oversight organizations.

Entities must have a documented process on how to respond and disclose compliance failures. This should include the potential issues that are in scope for disclosure and who will make the disclosure. In most cases, the disclosure of compliance issues should be handled by the general counsel or his designee such as the CCO. The use of outside counsel experienced in such matters is a common and highly recommended practice. Of course, a professional and highly managed internal investigation should be conducted to determine the validity of the issues. Once the allegations have been corroborated, appropriate disclosure is needed. Compliance Insight 10.4 provides strategies for improving compliance risk assessment capabilities.

Reasonable Response After the Discovery of a Business Conduct Violation

The FSGO require that an organization take reasonable steps to respond to the discovery of a violation. However, the question may arise, what constitutes "reasonable" steps? The FSGO recognize that not all organizations are alike and that they will need to respond to violations differently. There are three factors that will determine what is reasonable and what precise actions are necessary for a program to prevent and detect violations and be considered effective. They are: the size of the organization; the likelihood that certain offenses will occur; and the history of the organization.

The requisite degree of formality of a program to prevent and detect violations of law will vary with the size of the organization. The larger the organization, the more formal the program should be. A larger organization should generally have established written policies defining the standards and procedures to be followed by its employees and other agents.

The likelihood that certain violations will occur because of the nature of an organization's business also factors into the decision-making process. If because of the nature of the business there is a substantial risk that certain types of offenses may occur, management must take steps to prevent and detect those types of offenses. For example, if a company deals with toxic substances, it must be prepared for spills and take steps to prevent them.

An organization's prior history may indicate types of offenses that it should take actions to prevent. Recurrence of misconduct similar to that which an organization has previously committed casts doubt on whether it took all reasonable steps to prevent such misconduct. An organization's failure to incorporate and follow applicable industry practice or the standards called for by any applicable government regulation weighs against a finding of an effective program to prevent and detect violations of law.[23]

COMPLIANCE INSIGHT 10.4: UPGRADING COMPLIANCE RISK ASSESSMENT CAPABILITIES

A Compliance and Ethics Leadership Council study highlights companies' strategies to enhance their ability for better assessing exposure to compliance risks. The six most significant research findings are presented below:

Finding #1—Consider a Mixture of External and Internal Indicators. Leading companies are sensing potential compliance risks by closely examining the size and root causes of incidents in their industry, evaluating past audit results, and assessing macrotrends inside their organization such as leadership changes and staff turnover. Other leading indicators include 1) performance surprises (i.e., extraordinary financial performance of a specific business unit) and 2) information gleaned from exit interviews and survey results.

Finding #2—Promote Forward Thinking in Risk Assessments. Leading companies emphasize the importance of anticipating future compliance risks (occurring in a one- to three-year time frame) that could jeopardize business plans, including the recognition of consumer responses that fuel regulatory activity or situations in which a competitor was penalized for conduct that was perceived to be in line with regulations or societal expectations.

Finding #3—Firmly Engage Business Unit Leadership in the Risk Assessment Process. Leading companies engage business unit leadership to emphasize their stake in the assessment process to leverage their awareness of key risk areas, and to prevent complacency by requiring selected business unit managers to present risk findings to senior management-led compliance committees.

Finding #4—Create Greater Business Unit Accountability by Integrating Compliance Risk Assessment in the Strategic Planning and Budgeting Process. Leading companies increasingly make compliance risk assessment a required part of the annual business-planning and budgeting process at the business unit level, driving local management to consider and respond to compliance risks that pose the greatest threat to the achievement of their financial goals and strategic priorities.

Finding #5—Collaborate Extensively with Other Functions That Have Distinct Subject-Matter Expertise. In evaluating the effectiveness of internal controls that would help mitigate inherent compliance risks, compliance and ethics teams begin to leverage the institutional knowledge and organizational reach of the finance function, including internal audit, the controller's office, and, if applicable, the Section 404 office that oversees the documentation and testing of all internal controls supporting the accuracy and integrity of financial reporting.

Finding #6—Reduce Bias in Risk Prioritization Ranking. Leading companies and ethics functions reduce the risk of bias and quick judgment by rating the impact of a risk across multiple dimensions (including financial, legal, and reputational) and designing a rating scale that clearly defines the meaning of risk scores and forces respondents to make hard decisions about the criticality of the risk.

Reprinted with permission from the Corporate Executive Board, Washington, DC © 2005.

Compliance Emergency Preparedness Kit

All companies should have a Compliance Emergency Preparedness Kit (CEPK) when serious compliance failures are discovered. These failures may include FCPA violations, financial accounting fraud perpetrated by senior officers, other criminal violations that require reporting to government authorities, as well as any issue that could reasonably find its way to page one of the *Wall Street Journal*. Unlike a regular emergency kit, which contains water, food, and medical supplies, this kit covers in detail what to do in case of a compliance emergency. Companies should be prepared for it, because it could happen at any time. And just like a natural disaster, it can't be avoided but with proper preparedness the damage can be minimized.

Advance preparation is an element of Enterprise Risk Management (ERM). ERM involves risks and opportunities and according to the Committee of Sponsoring Organizations of the Treadway Commission (COSO) is defined as "a process, effected by an entity's board of directors, management, and other personnel, applied in strategy setting and across the

COMPLIANCE INSIGHT 10.5: A CORPORATE COUNSEL'S VIEW ON RISK ASSESSMENT AND FLEXIBILITY IN FOREIGN OPERATIONS

Steven A. Lauer is Corporate Counsel for Global Compliance Services, a renowned worldwide provider of third party hotline services based in Charlotte, North Carolina. Lauer's wealth of experience includes serving as a general counsel, attorney in private practice, consultant, and Executive Vice President of *The Metropolitan Corporate Counsel*, a monthly journal for in-house attorneys. He has authored numerous articles on compliance as well as speaking at conferences and seminars on the subject. Lauer is Vice Chair for Programs of the Corporate Counsel Committee of the American Bar Association Section of Business Law and a member of the Corporate Compliance Committee of the ABA's Section of Business Law. Here he provides his view on risk assessments and operations in foreign countries.

The best compliance programs rest upon disciplined, rigorous analyses of the business-, ethics- and compliance-related risks attendant to their business operations. Moreover, a periodic review of the assumptions on which the program is based—in essence, a variant of the risk assessment completed at the program-design stage—should take place as well in order to address two basic answers: have the risks changed by virtue of new or modified business activities, new or amended laws or regulations or the identification of previously unappreciated risks associated with existing activities? Has the ability of the organization to monitor and/or to minimize the potential impact on its business of those risks changed, whether because the organization's financial condition has changed (for the better or worse), its capabilities have changed (e.g., the departure of internal experts who understood and led the firm's response to those risks), or some other changed dynamic indicates the need to re-assess the compliance and ethics program's capabilities? Such an assessment—at the beginning of an organization's compliance and ethics program or during its lifetime, should also tie into its business and other operations in multiple ways. Do the results of those assessments provide information with which to analyze the organizational excellence or quality program of the business? Does the firm's dispute-management process take advantage of its compliance and ethics program and does the compliance and ethics program learn from its dispute-management history?

An organization's compliance and ethics program must be flexible. For example, a whistle-blowing hotline for a multinational organization with operations in the European Union must take into account the varying scopes for permissible allegations that the nations that belong to that Union allow. France's interpretation of the permissible scope of a hotline is less permissive than that of Belgium or Germany. Country-specific telephone lines and allegation-intake measures, and particularly awareness campaigns that publicize the hotline in conformity with those distinct requirements, are among the useful, even necessary, mechanisms in such a situation. Clients use those tools to implement as consistent a hotline protocol as possible while meeting the varying expectations and demands of countries' laws and regulations. Likewise, the training for an organization's employees must also take into account jurisdiction-specific compliance expectations, like the supervisor-training needs regarding harassment that are mandated in California, Connecticut, and several other states.

enterprise, designed to identify potential events that may affect the entity, and manage risk to be within its risk appetite, to provide reasonable assurance regarding the achievement of entity objectives."[24] A well conceived CEPK addresses the ERM requirement to identity potential events that can significantly impact an organization.

A CEPK contains a checklist of things to do in case the company discovers a compliance failure. The types of issues and events that would trigger an emergency response must be fully discussed and documented as needing such a response. Once defined, the kit will document the roles and responsibilities of the CEO, CFO, General Counsel, Chief Compliance Officer, other senior executives, Board of Directors, and other key personnel. The kit will include staff responsibilities, which personnel will be involved in any investigative response, the role of outside counsel, and even name the official spokesperson who will be responsible for disclosing the violation to outside parties. The names and contact information for outside counsel and other specialists who may be called upon to assist in case of such an emergency should also be readily available. The kit should also include contingency plans for action if the violator(s) is found to be the CEO, CFO or other key person. With these step-by-step instructions, a company will not be shocked into inaction and will know exactly how to proceed and handle whatever happens.

It is also highly recommended that the organization create a "compliance resume" and include it in the CEPK. This resume would include a detailed description of prior compliance issues that the company discovered and mitigated including remedial action. A compliance resume is also one of the many recommended steps for compliance with the Seven Steps of the FSGO. In the event a compliance issue or criminal violation occurs, the organization can demonstrate to the independent auditors, SEC, DOJ, FBI, and others that it took every reasonable step to comply with the highest standards of corporate governance.[25] A summary of the FSGO amendments and related action steps to achieve effective compliance is included in Appendix A.

This kit will help to demonstrate that the company took strong remedial action after the discovery of the violation. The FSGO require the company to take reasonable steps to respond appropriately. The reasonableness and appropriateness of the response will, of course, depend on the type of violation, the type of company, the industry that it is in, and the regulations with which it must comply. A major violation in a heavily regulated industry will demand much swifter and decisive action than a minor violation in a less heavily regulated one. These considerations should go into the kit, with different checklists depending on the type of violation uncovered. With appropriate action and preparedness, the company can prove that it took every reasonable measure to comply with the highest standards of corporate governance.

AVOIDING ACCIDENTS ON THE ROAD TO COMPLIANCE

A mistake that a compliance program can make is focusing too much on the "easy" things and too little on the "hard." It's easy to do the training, prepare and rollout a code of conduct, institute a hotline, talk up the culture and tone at the top. It's much harder to tackle areas such as discipline, audits, monitoring, incentive compensation, and being the corporate cop. Compliance expert Joe Murphy says that there is an "overemphasis on the soft side of compliance such as training, a code of conduct, and the new buzz word of culture, because they are easier to tackle than the tougher issues."[26] Yet, it's the tougher issues that can get an organization into trouble.

Consistent, fair, and incremental discipline is often one of the hardest areas for an organization. While each case of discipline involving violation of business conduct must be evaluated separately, there must be a predictable and balanced approach when fraud and policy abuse occur. There must not be different standards of disciplinary action for executives and other employees. If a salesperson is terminated for falsifying an expense report, then an executive who does the same offense must also be terminated. Sending mixed messages, especially in disciplinary actions, can be very damaging. All organizations and their employees must be responsible for both the spirit and the letter of the law with a zero tolerance for fraud violations.[27] Discipline and how it is appropriately administered can do much to reinforce the ethical tone and culture of an organization.

It's no different with audits, monitoring, incentive compensation, and other tough issues. These are critical areas for compliance and they must be strongly addressed. As Murphy further states, "Don't just talk, do." There must be a program in place that responds to all compliance elements. Murphy adds that "an organization can't design its compliance system based on a Pat Gnazzo, it must design it based on an Andy Fastow."[28] That makes great sense. Gnazzo, the longtime CCO at United Technologies and currently the CCO at CA, Inc. is a highly experienced compliance professional with great integrity and accountability. At both companies, he has built excellent compliance programs. Gnazzo and his compelling compliance program at CA were profiled in Chapter 5.

People with integrity who always do the right thing are not the ones to worry about. Companies need to have compliance programs for the potential Fastows who might not always do the right thing. Fastow, the former Enron CFO who pleaded guilty for his part in the massive accounting fraud and who subsequently testified against Jeffrey Skilling and Ken Lay, is who the compliance program should be built for.

It's a given that Gnazzo will oversee a strong compliance framework wherever he is but what happens when he leaves? What if in the future, the CCO is inexperienced or an ineffective leader and fails to continue the prior program or succumbs to pressure to weaken it? What if the CEO is an overpowering personality who is also corrupt? Will the compliance system be able to provide true checks and balances against the abuse of power? Build the program to ensure the behavior of a weak person and not just the strong. Murphy argues that compliance can be imbedded in the structure of an organization to overcome this. Having a strong and independent board of directors is another important element for effective compliance.

The Sarbanes-Oxley Act requires that each audit committee have at least one member who is a "financial expert." This person must have an understanding of generally accepted accounting principles and financial statements; experience in the preparation of auditing of financial statements for comparable companies; experience with internal accounting controls; and an understanding of audit committee functions. The reasoning for this expertise is sound and further protects a public company. Boards have as their members CFOs and others with notable financial experience and reputations. So, why isn't there a similar requirement for boards to have chief compliance officers as members? Just because this requirement isn't mandated in Sarbanes-Oxley, doesn't mean it shouldn't be followed. The justification is as strong as the requirement for a financial expert.

Very few companies today have chief compliance officers sitting on their boards. That should change and change soon. A compliance officer adds compliance literacy and backbone to a board of directors who must provide that strong corporate oversight role. The role of corporate cop and gatekeeper is an absolute necessity on a board. If Adelphia Communications Corporation had an independent board with a compliance officer as a member, one can argue that the corporate fraud that brought down the company and resulted in prison terms for their CEO, CFO, and other executives, may not have occurred.

The FSGO's Seven Steps are great tools to use in implementing an effective compliance program but they only provide the foundation and framework to build upon. Great organizations know that much more needs to be done to build world-class compliance programs. "It is up to the organization to tailor a program to meet its organization's challenges and to provide flesh, blood, muscle, and life to the program. The Sentencing Guidelines' seven elements of an effective program are simply minimum requirements."[29]

NOTES

1. 2005 Federal Sentencing Guidelines Manual, Ch 8, Sentencing of Organizations, November 1, 2004, §8B2.1(b)(4)(A).
2. "Summary of the 2004 Federal Sentencing Guidelines Amendments and Recommended Action Steps," *General Counsel Roundtable*, June 2004.
3. Martin T. Biegelman and Joel T. Bartow, *Executive Roadmap to Fraud Prevention and Internal Control: Creating a Culture of Compliance*, (Hoboken, NJ: John Wiley & Sons, Inc., 2006), 112.
4. Establishing a Compliance and Ethics Program: Designing and Distributing the Code of Conduct," *Corporate Executive Board*, October 2005.
5. "Chinese New Year," *ReligionFacts.com*, www.religionfacts.com/chinese_religion/holidays/chinese_new_year.htm; The GAP, Inc. Code of Business Conduct, Jan. 1, 2005, 6, www.gapinc.com/public/documents/Code_English.pdf.
6. "Chinese New Year," *ReligionFacts.com*, www.religionfacts.com/chinese_religion/holidays/chinese_new_year.htm.
7. The Defense Industry Initiative on Business Ethics and Conduct, 2003 Annual Report to the Public, 5, www.dii.org/annual/2003/AnnualReport2003.doc.
8. Ibid.
9. "Summary of the 2004 Federal Sentencing Guidelines."

10. Biegelman and Bartow, *Executive Roadmap*, 264.
11. Ibid.
12. Ibid., 269–71.
13. Ibid., 268.
14. Ibid., 254–81.
15. "Establishing a Compliance and Ethics Program: Developing a Program Charter," *Compliance and Ethics Leadership Council*, October 2005.
16. 2005 Federal Sentencing Guidelines Manual, Ch 8, Sentencing of Organizations, November 1, 2004, §8B2.1(b)(6).
17. Ibid.
18. Management Antifraud Programs and Controls, Statement on Auditing Standard 99, "Consideration of Fraud in a Financial Statement Audit," American Institute of Certified Public Accountants, 2002.
19. Biegelman and Bartow, *Executive Roadmap*, 247–48, 356.
20. Steven D. Levitt and Stephen J. Dubner, *Freakonomics: A Rogue Economist Explores the Hidden Side of Everything*, (New York: William Morrow, 2005), 23.
21. 2005 Federal Sentencing Guidelines Manual, Ch 8, Sentencing of Organizations, November 1, 2004, §8B2.1(c).
22. "Summary of the 2004 Federal Sentencing Guidelines."
23. "Supplement to Appendix C—Amendments to the Guidelines Manual," *United States Sentencing Commission*, November 1, 2004, 102, www.ussc.gov/2004guid/APPC-2004SUPP.pdf.
24. *Enterprise Risk Management—Integrated Framework*, Committee of Sponsoring Organizations of the Treadway Commission, (2004), www.coso.org/Publications/ERM/COSO_ERM_ExecutiveSummary.pdf.
25. "Summary of the 2004 Federal Sentencing Guidelines."
26. Joseph E. Murphy, telephone interview with author, April 27, 2007.
27. Biegelman and Bartow, *Executive Roadmap*, 355–56.
28. Murphy, interview.
29. Dr. John D. Copeland, "The Tyson Story: Building an Effective Ethics and Compliance Program," *Drake Journal of Agricultural Law*, Winter 2000, 348.

CHAPTER 11

Recognizing Compliance Excellence: Premier, Inc. and Winning the Baldrige Award*

"Compliance isn't something done by the external auditors who come in periodically and review progress. It should be done daily by everyone in the enterprise whose job responsibilities touch any of the defined internal controls."
Sumner Blount, Director of Security Solutions, CA, Inc.

A s the compliance and ethics profession evolves, the need to demonstrate how such efforts improve the performance of the organization becomes more important. Like any other component of a company's operation, a compliance department's contribution to that company's quality and continuing success likely will determine—or at least affect—that department's effectiveness and stature internally and externally.

Some have tried to establish the inherent value of an ethics and compliance program by focusing on the prevention of illegal activity and ethical lapses. While this is an important component of a compliance and ethics program, this is only part of the equation. This approach also presents

---

*Much of this chapter's content was provided by Steven Lauer with permission from Premier, Inc. The Premier Code of Conduct and the Premier Group Purchasing Code of Conduct are copyrighted material of Premier, Inc. and reprinted and referenced in this chapter with their permission. In addition, Premier, Inc. graciously gave Steven and me access to the specific tools and elements of their excellent Ethics and Compliance Program so it could be profiled here. For that I am most grateful and appreciative to both Premier, Inc. and Steven.

considerable difficulty, as it requires the proof of a negative. Accumulating proof that a company would have violated a law or suffered a lapse in adherence to its ethical standards represents a difficult challenge at best. Even if one can demonstrate that the company avoided violating a law or other standard, demonstrating that the company's ethics and compliance program was the reason that the violation was avoided represents a significant additional hurdle. Evidence of the causal relationship between an ethics and compliance program and the avoidance of a violation is extremely rare.

Can an ethics and compliance program provide "positive" benefits to a company that is more demonstrable than the absence of problems? How can such value be shown and what types of metrics would be of assistance in that effort?

The National Institute of Standards and Technology (NIST) annually selects winners of the Malcolm Baldrige National Quality Award, which it credits with "making quality a national priority and disseminating best practices across the United States."[1] That award recognizes "businesses—manufacturing and service, small and large—and ... education, health care and nonprofit organizations that apply and are judged to be outstanding in seven areas: leadership; strategic planning; customer and market focus; measurement, analysis, and knowledge management; human resource focus; process management; and results."[2] As NIST has noted, "the Baldrige criteria for performance excellence have played a valuable role in helping U.S. organizations improve. The criteria are designed to help organizations improve their performance by focusing on two goals: delivering ever improving value to customers and improving the organization's overall performance."[3]

In 2006, NIST selected Premier, Inc. as the winner in the service category. While the focus of the Baldrige Award is on an organization's excellence across the board, in announcing that award to Premier, NIST noted, among other things, that "Premier has taken a leadership role in promoting best practices in ethical conduct, transparency, and accountability within its industry."[4] Since NIST determined that Premier's ethics and compliance program (ECP) deserved mention as part of the basis for that award, that program also might serve as a valuable model for how a corporate ethics and compliance program can—and can be seen to—add value to a business enterprise. Let's examine Premier's ECP and how it contributes to organizational excellence at that company.

PREMIER, INC.

Premier, Inc. occupies a strategic position in the health-care industry. Not-for-profit hospitals and health system organizations are its owners and it is the second largest health care strategic alliance in the United States. Premier has 1,000 employees in corporate offices in Charlotte, North Carolina and other locations in California and Washington, DC. The company was created in 1996 and now includes three business units to deliver services to its owners: group purchasing and supply chain management; insurance and risk management; and information and performance improvement. Its group purchasing activities represent the largest such operation in the country measured on the basis of the annual volume of goods purchased on behalf of its hospital owners.

Premier describes a group purchasing organization as "any entity that as all or part of its business activities is authorized to act as the agent of a provider of health care services to enter into contracts with vendors, pursuant to which vendors agree to sell or furnish goods or services consistent with the terms set forth in the vendor contracts."[5] Premier's Web site states that its core purpose is "to improve the health of communities." They have an annual revenue of $433 million.

Premier's group purchasing business must comply with federal laws and regulations relating to contract administrative fees and satisfy the "safe harbor" provisions in federal anti-kickback laws. As a group purchasing organization (GPO) Premier satisfies the standards expressed in the Code of Conduct for GPOs developed in 2002. Many other parts of its businesses also face regulatory constraints at the state level, like its insurance activities. The hospitals that own Premier face their own host of regulatory mandates and Premier's operations must be consistent with the regulatory constraints that they face.

Within this overall regulatory and market environment, Premier applied for and received the prestigious Baldrige Award. How did Premier's ECP contribute to that success?

A CALL TO ACTION

Oftentimes, improvements in compliance are spurred by questionable conduct, public disclosures, government inquiries, and a subsequent move to an ethical culture. Premier went that route to a heightened state of compliance. In 2002, Premier was at the center of a government investigation into anti-competitive business practices and conflicts of interest related to their buying practices. Premier was not the only organization named in media reports and Senate hearings but Premier's executive leadership decided "that even the appearance of a conflict of interest was unacceptable."[6] Premier's leadership decided that they wanted to be a role model for the industry for best practices in ethics and compliance.

PREMIER'S RESPONSE

In March 2002, Premier's Audit Committee commissioned a study of Premier and the GPO industry to recommend best practices and procedures that Premier could consider for improvements in ethical conduct. Premier retained Kirk O. Hanson, a highly regarded university professor and business ethicist, to conduct the study. Hanson was just the person to undertake such a project. He is the Executive Director of the Markkula Center for Applied Ethics at Santa Clara University in Santa Clara, California. The Markkula Center is one of the preeminent ethics centers in the United States with extensive experience working in business, government, and health care ethics.

The Audit Committee "wanted an independent assessment of the ethical issues facing the industry and an independent set of best practice recommendations."[7] The study would focus on business practices within the GPO industry, the current ethical climate within the industry, identification of best practices in compliance, a determination of the state of Premier's compliance program, as well as opportunities for improvement.[8] Hanson had complete independence in the study and required that his report be made public upon completion. He believed that a public release of the report not only demonstrated his independence but spoke volumes about the intent of Premier to truly improve both the industry and its company.

In conducting his research for the study, Hanson interviewed almost 100 company executives, directors, employees, consultants, partners, vendors, journalists who had written on GPO issues, and Congressional staff involved in the related government inquiry. Hanson visited every Premier location in the United States and requested and reviewed countless company documents. After completing the first draft of his report, he assembled a blue-ribbon committee of experts in the field of ethics and organizational management to review his findings. He then presented his draft recommendations to groups including Premier executives, employees, board members, and health care executives from partner organizations and requested their feedback. After this extensive review, Hanson then met again with Premier's executive leadership to present his findings and recommendations.[9]

Hanson's study was entitled "Best Ethical Practices for the Group Purchasing Industry: A Report to the Audit Committee of the Board of Directors of Premier, Inc." (GPO Report) and was released in October 2002. Hanson's report detailed 50 recommendations involving "ethical policies and practices... to cover most ethical questions specifically faced by GPOs. They address a number of practices that are not now, and some that have never been, practices of Premier, Inc."[10]

The GPO Report covered general ethical standards and guidelines, conflict of interest issues, contracting practices, disclosures and related reporting, and governance reform. Key among the many recommendations was the need to institute the following compliance elements:

- Comprehensive code of conduct as a cornerstone for an ethical culture
- Gift policy that forbids GPO employees from receiving gifts from vendors
- Vendor code of conduct
- Disclosures by employees of equity interests in vendors
- Recusal for conflicts of interest
- Prohibition on insider trading
- Limitation on sole source contracts
- Annual financial reporting
- Appointment of an ethics and compliance officer
- Creation of a hotline
- Ongoing audit committee review and oversight
- Annual report to the audit committee on ethics performance and compliance[11]

In the GPO Report, Hanson commented that he received full cooperation from Premier's management throughout the period of study. In addition, many of his recommendations were already being acted on even before his final report was issued. For all the 50 comprehensive recommendations, please refer to the GPO report.

PREMIER'S FIRST COMPLIANCE OFFICER

In January 2003, Megan Barry was hired as Premier's first Ethics and Compliance Officer and is still at the company in this important role. Barry has extensive experience with multinational corporations in issues involving business ethics and corporate responsibility. She also has a track record for innovation in compliance. While at Nortel Networks in the 1990s, as their Director of Corporate Social Responsibility and Business Ethics, she posted their code of conduct on the Internet making them one of the first companies to do so publicly.

Barry knew that she needed to convince Premier employees of this major change in how the company did business and obtain their buy-in. She did this by telling them that the government was watching closely to see how Premier was responding to the issues raised in the Senate hearings. She also told employees that instituting an effective compliance program would ensure the viability of Premier and help the organization grow. Barry instituted education for all of Premier's employees so they completely understood all the changes in policy as she reworked their ethics and compliance program. "All" employees meant all employees, whether a member of the maintenance staff or the leadership team.

Barry's "experience at Premier suggests that a multi-pronged approach strengthens employees' efforts to act responsibly. This approach includes enhancing employees' decision making, fostering an overall ethical culture, and identifying and providing sufficient resources to effectively address ethical issues."[12]

PREMIER'S ETHICS AND COMPLIANCE PROGRAM

To understand the role of Premier's ECP in its application for and receipt of the Baldrige Award, we must first understand the ECP. What does it include and how does it operate? How does it contribute to organizational excellence at Premier?

Premier's ECP includes the following elements:

1. *Code of conduct.* In 2002, the Healthcare Industry Group Purchasing Association (HIGPA), at the suggestion of a Senate committee, began to develop a voluntary code of conduct. Premier, as a member of that association, participated in that effort, but Premier had previously retained an independent ethicist (as described above) to analyze the group purchasing industry and to provide to Premier recommendations to improve its policies and practices. The ethicist's report and recommendations as detailed above and released in October 2002, served as the foundation for Premier's "Group Purchasing Code of Conduct." That code covers all the issues identified in the code adopted by HIGPA but exceeds the standards contained in the industry-wide program in several respects. For example, unlike the HIGPA code, Premier prohibits insider trading by its employees and those of any Premier-affiliated entity "based on knowledge of [Premier's] vendors or their prospects gained through [the employees'] employment" at Premier.[13] In another example of the more inclusive nature of Premier's code, "[n]o advisor who is in a position to influence Premier GPO contracting decisions shall serve as advisor in an area in which they hold extensive equity interests," whereas the HIGPA code does not address this possible conflict at all.[14] The HIGPA code does call for advisors to disclose such interests and to recuse themselves from decisions by the GPO but to not recuse themselves as advisors on such issues. Premier's Business Conduct Guidelines apply to activities

of the company outside the scope of its group purchasing (to which the HIGPA code would apply) and contains many provisions and ethical standards that are similarly outside the scope of the group purchasing activities. Premier's Group Purchasing Code of Conduct is available at www.premierinc.com/about/mission/ethics-compliance/code-of-conduct-read-friendly/code-of-conduct_table-of-contents.htm and the HIGPA code can be accessed at www.higpa.org/about/code/.

2. *Employee training.* Premier's employees receive training on a variety of subjects and in a variety of ways. In addition to training on substantive job tasks and responsibilities, Premier's ethics and compliance officer provides to Premier's employees the following types of education on ethical business practices: annual code of conduct training (in person, by video teleconference, and through Web-based courses); orientation for new employees that includes one hour of ethics training; and training within the company's business units that includes ethics responsibilities and practices, and the application of Premier's code of business ethics and conduct to employees' day-to-day job-related activities. Premier's employees also receive training on topics such as process management and improvement, employee, workplace and environmental safety, disaster recovery, and other subjects.

3. *Ethics and compliance officer.* Premier's ethics and compliance officer reports directly to the Audit Committee of the company's Board of Directors and prepares an annual Code of Conduct Compliance Report. The Ethics and Compliance Office provides central oversight and support for Premier's ECP and works with senior management, Premier's hospital owners, suppliers, and employees to monitor adherence to the company's Group Purchasing Code of Conduct and Business Conduct Guidelines.

4. *Hotline.* Premier established a third-party-provided mechanism by which employees can report, anonymously if they so choose, violations of the company's Group Purchasing Code of Conduct, its Business Conduct Guidelines, and other policies.

5. *Ethics-related communication.* Premier conducts a comprehensive communication campaign targeted to employees regarding the operation of its ECP and the various means by which they can raise concerns and issues. Those communications take a variety of forms. Employees receive e-mails informing them of upcoming compliance and ethics training courses. Premier posts on its intranet short video clips for the same purpose; those clips include a series of screen shots highlighting ethics-related messages that reinforce the purpose of the training. Employees who fail to attend the mandated ethics and compliance training receive follow-up e-mail reminders. Answers to ethics-related

questions that employees submit through the annual Values Conference channel are communicated back to employees by means of a weekly newsletter that is distributed to all employees. The Ethics and Compliance Office publishes a monthly "topics" column that appears in several newsletters.

6. *Case and issue management.* Premier created a system that enables the Ethics and Compliance Office to track reports of inquiries, allegations, resource requests and the submission of conflict-of-interest disclosure forms. Employees can access the disclosure form, for example, through the company's intranet. When doing so, they follow online instructions and guidelines for its completion and submission. The Ethics and Compliance Office sends reminder e-mails to employees who fail to complete the form in a timely fashion.

7. *Competency assessment tool.* Premier measures employees' adherence to Premier's purchasing code of conduct through its VERIFY Self-Monitoring Group Purchasing Code of Conduct Compliance Program. Certain employees (called Attesters) attest to the compliance of their business processes and practices with the company's Code of Conduct. They identify the procedures that they follow to verify compliance, the documentation of those procedures and the underlying level of compliance, along with any exceptions or other comments. They submit the results of those analyses to the Ethics and Compliance Office. The supervisors of the attesters review their attestations. The Ethics and Compliance Office reports on the aggregate results of those annual attestations in its Annual Group Purchasing Code of Conduct Compliance Report.

8. *Survey of ethical reputation.* A third-party firm measures adherence to the purchasing code of conduct annually through a survey of Premier's employees. That firm conducts the survey confidentially and reports the data to Premier in an aggregated fashion so that individual responses are blind. Senior management and Premier's Board of Directors review the survey results.

9. *Audit Committee.* The Audit Committee of Premier's Board of Directors receives quarterly reports on progress against the initiatives of the Ethics and Compliance Office and compliance with the purchasing code of conduct. Those reports identify ethics-oriented key performance indicators for the company.

How does the ECP support Premier's organizational excellence? Can we identify any concrete ways in which the ECP furthers Premier's goals of "be[ing] a major influence in reshaping health care" and assisting its owners/customers to "be the leading health care systems in their markets"?[15]

Those components of the ECP—or comparable components—appear in many companies' programs. What distinguishes Premier's ECP from its counterparts at other organizations? Can Premier's ECP serve as a model for how a corporate ethics and compliance program can serve business goals distinct from those related directly to ethics and compliance issues? Can a compliance professional build a more positive business case for such a program?

COMPLIANCE AND ETHICS TOOLS AND ORGANIZATIONAL EXCELLENCE

Premier utilizes the various elements of the ECP to improve its business operations and lessen the chance of noncompliance and ethical lapses. For example, the various communications channels in the ECP constitute ways in which the company can learn about the need for changes to those operations. When the company's third-party vendor for the hotline receives a call—whether a complaint, concern or inquiry—or another communication arrives that identifies a failure to follow company procedures or suggests a way in which the company might operate more efficiently or effectively, Premier can review the report in order to learn if that failure offers an opportunity to design or to implement a business improvement. Some employees use the various communications channels in the ECP to submit suggestions for operational improvements directly. Examples include the following:

- Premier sponsored a "Lunch and Learn" program for employees whose job changes at the company would involve relocation. An employee who had relocated noted that information regarding tax-related impacts of relocation would enable employees moving for Premier's benefit to be more productive by reducing some of the stress associated with that process.
- An employee submitted to Premier's employee suggestion box (called "Premier Ideas") a suggestion to make available to employees for purchase, items such as shirts, pants, and office products bearing the Premier logo in order to promote corporate spirit. In response, Premier appointed an employee as the point of contact through whom employees can purchase such items. Premier communicated that decision and appointment by means of a company newsletter called "Monday Minutes."
- The office floors in Premier's Charlotte, North Carolina, facility contain many cubicles. An employee noted that finding one individual among

the cubicles was a confusing process. The company prepared maps of the floors, identifying cubicles and the employees who occupy them, that are now posted by the elevators in that facility.

When three organizations merged in 1996 to form Premier, Inc., management identified a need to forge a single set of values for the combined organization. Accordingly, as part of a "values initiative," each of those pre-existing organizations nominated 4–5 individuals to determine and validate the combined organization's values. Premier held its first "Values Conference" in 1998, where employees discussed the company's values and how to integrate them into operations. That conference led to the creation of teams to identify the underlying behaviors that would operationalize those values. The Values Conference has become an annual event attended by all employees. "Premier's Values Team and sub-teams are examples of how Premier gathers employee input and diverse opinions to guide organizational improvements. The processes facilitate a systematic collection of social responsibility, customer and employee input through an annual conference, a Values Team, cross-location sub-teams, and a values e-mail box."[16]

Premier provides its employees multiple avenues by which to raise ethical and operational concerns. The company's "Vendor Grievance process gives suppliers an avenue to report concerns, providing for any grievances to be reviewed, responded to, and used in improvement."[17] Premier's vendors can access that grievance process through Premier's website at www .premierinc.com/about/suppliers/vendor-grievance-policy.jsp. Whether a vendor has a contract-specific grievance or a generalized one, it can submit that grievance by e-mail, receive a confirmation electronically, and receive a decision within thirty days of Premier's receipt of the matter. Vendors' rights under those procedures appear at www.premierinc.com/ about/suppliers/bidders-rights-responsibilities.jsp.

Premier treats its employees as a valuable resource, in terms of both its ongoing operations and its business improvement efforts. The annual training that constitutes an important element of the ECP, much of which is conducted in face-to-face format, enables the ethics and compliance officer to measure the effectiveness of that training and to solicit feedback from those employees who experience that training. That feedback can include information and ideas relative to necessary or advisable organizational or process improvements.

Training employees and reinforcing a culture of compliance improves Premier's operation and its ECP in other ways—ways that dovetail nicely with the 2004 changes to the Federal Sentencing Guidelines for Organizational Crime. In those changes, the United States Sentencing Commission provided much more detailed guidance on how a corporate compliance and ethics program could qualify as an "effective" program and the benefits that might accompany that label. One of the changes made by the Sentencing Commission in 2004 directs that a "compliance and ethics program shall be promoted and enforced consistently throughout the organization through (A) appropriate incentives to perform in accordance with the compliance and ethics program; and (B) appropriate disciplinary measures for engaging in criminal conduct and for failing to take reasonable steps to prevent or detect criminal conduct."[18]

Several elements of Premier's ECP bring that admonition to life. "Senior Leaders use [Premier's] values-based rewards and recognition program to personally support and reward individual and team-based behavior through use of [its] Employee Choice Awards, unit rewards and Premier awards programs."[19] Premier's chief executive officer "personally presents Premier Awards recognizing values-based behaviors in work, Team Awards, and the Turtle Award during the Values Conference; Senior Leaders are first to congratulate winners. The Premier Team Award (based on [Premier's] Core Values and American Society for Quality team award criteria) recognizes project teams obtaining significant results while embodying Core Values."[20] Employees nominate their associates for those awards and review the nominations. The winners receive publicity on Premier's Web site and in employee gatherings. The CEO personally selects the winner of the Turtle Award, which "celebrates an employee's 'sticking its neck out' at some risk to pursue a desired outcome, regardless of ultimate success."[21] Employee Choice Awards over the course of a year "recognize values-based behaviors of both individuals and teams."[22] Other awards at the business-unit level also provide opportunities to recognize positive ethics behavior on the part of employees. All of these recognition programs "are strong performance motivators."[23] Clearly then, Premier implemented several well-thought-out employee recognition mechanisms that reinforce its ethics and values. Those mechanisms exemplify the Sentencing Commission's goal that organizations develop "appropriate incentives to perform in accordance with the compliance and ethics program."[24]

Premier has determined how to advance its interest in business excellence through the careful design and use of elements of its ECP. In doing so and in winning the Baldrige Award, Premier has outlined a means by which other companies can build a more positive argument to support their ethics and compliance goals.

In a related and reinforcing postscript, Premier was a recipient of the 2007 Charlotte Ethics in Business Award. The award is presented annually by the Charlotte (North Carolina) chapter of the Society of Financial Services Professionals. The award honors "companies that demonstrate a commitment to ethical business practices in their operations, management, philosophies, and responses to crises or challenges."[25] A commitment to ethics and compliance always pays off.

NOTES

1. "Frequently Asked Questions about the Malcolm Baldrige National Quality Award," National Institute of Standards and Technology, available at: www.nist.gov/public_affairs/factsheet/baldfaqs.htm.
2. Ibid.
3. Ibid.
4. From NIST Press Release announcing award to Premier.
5. Premier, Inc. Group Purchasing Code of Conduct, Definitions, www.premierinc.com/about/mission/ethics-compliance/code-of-conduct-read-friendly/code-of-conduct_definitions.htm.
6. Andrew W. Singer, "Spattered and Scorched, Premier Seeks the 'High Road,'" *Ethikos and Corporate Conduct Quarterly*, May/June 2004, www.singerpubs.com/ethikos/premier.html.
7. Kirk O. Hanson, "Best Ethical Practices For the Group Purchasing Industry: A Report to the Audit Committee of the Board of Directors of Premier, Inc.," October 18, 2002, www.premierinc.com/about/mission/ethics-compliance/attachments/Appx-A_%20Kirk%20Hanson.doc.
8. Ibid.
9. Ibid.
10. Ibid.
11. Ibid.
12. Jason Lunday and Megan Barry, "Connecting the Dots Between Intentions, Action and Results: A Comprehensive Approach to Ethical Decision Making," *Ivey Business Journal*, March/April 2004, p. 1, www.iveybusinessjournal.com/article.asp?intArticle_ID=470.
13. Premier Code of Conduct.
14. Ibid.
15. These quotes are from the "Big Hairy Audacious Goal" (to be reached in ten to thirty years) that Premier hopes to achieve.
16. North Carolina Awards for Excellence: Malcolm Baldrige – Business Application for Premier, March 8, 2006, 27 ("Baldrige Application").
17. Ibid., 7.
18. 2005 Federal Sentencing Guidelines Manual, Ch 8, Sentencing of Organizations, November 1, 2004, §8B2.1(b)(6).
19. Baldrige Application, 1.
20. Ibid., 3–4.
21. Ibid., 4.

22. Ibid., 3.
23. Ibid.
24. 2005 Federal Sentencing Guidelines Manual, Ch 8, Sentencing of Organizations, November 1, 2004, §8B2.1(b)(6).
25. "Local Companies Honored for Ethics in Business," *Charlotte Business Journal*, April 27, 2007.

CHAPTER 12

Designing Robust Fraud Prevention Policies: The Airservices Australia Fraud Control Plan

"If a man defrauds you one time, he is a rascal; if he does it twice, you are a fool."

Author Unknown

I was a presenter at an internal fraud prevention conference in Sydney in November 2005, and had a chance to listen to some of the other speakers. One of them was a security officer from Airservices Australia, a government-owned corporation based in Australia. He presented a fascinating session on how his company strengthened its internal fraud control through communicating an antifraud policy throughout the organization. I was very impressed with the Airservices Australia program that included linking internal fraud control with governance strategies, engaging senior management to deliver the antifraud policy, and monitoring the effectiveness of the program through key performance indicators.

I immediately knew this was a best practice in compliance that I would want to include in my book. Very few companies in the United States actually publish a fraud control plan and yet this is something that needs to be communicated internally and externally. I approached Airservices Australia for access to their Fraud Control Plan and related information on their program. They were extremely gracious in providing me all the information that I needed and I deeply appreciate their assistance. Airservices Australia (Airservices) has an excellent compliance program that they have developed over the years. Later in this chapter, I am reprinting with their permission selected content from their Fraud Control Plan 2005–2007 and their Managers' Guide for Fraud and Corruption Control. Organizations worldwide would benefit from the best practices developed by this innovative company.

Airservices prepares a Fraud Control Plan to meet the requirements of the Australia Commonwealth Fraud Control Guidelines. The Guidelines require a revised fraud risk assessment and plan every two years. Airservices first developed its fraud control plan in 1996. As Airservices' Security Manager Michael Howard explained, "The simplified format of the current fraud control plan arose out of our experience with a number of frauds where established controls were not implemented and employees failed to recognise and report fraud. Maintaining the control environment through auditing, fraud awareness, and confidential reporting are vital."

The Australian Government Attorney General's Department is responsible for coordinating fraud control policy in Australia. This includes the implementation of the Commonwealth Fraud Control Guidelines, promoting best practices in fraud control, and effective risk management techniques.[1] The Guidelines define fraud as "dishonestly obtaining a benefit by deception or other means."[2] The Guidelines apply to government agencies and other organizations that receive significant funding from the Commonwealth. While not required, it is highly recommended that organizations not covered by the Guidelines implement them as a compliance best practice. Chief Executive Officers are responsible for instituting a fraud control plan in their respective organizations and the required reporting of fraud control activities.[3]

The Guidelines define what an effective fraud control plan must have. Included are a fraud control strategy that encompasses detection, investigation, and prevention; a risk assessment process; prosecution of all offenders as appropriate; fair and balanced disciplinary actions; recovery of the proceeds of fraudulent conduct; training of employees in fraud awareness and ethics; specialized training of fraud investigators; fostering a culture of compliance; publicizing the fraud control plan to employees; and reporting on fraud control actions and results.[4]

For reporting purposes, agencies need to collect various data related to their investigation and fraud prevention efforts. Included are the number of cases investigated; the number of cases referred to law enforcement for potential prosecution; the outcome of prosecutions; fraud losses suffered; recoveries; number of employees, contractors, and others involved in fraud and other violations; number of employees involved in fraud investigation and prevention efforts; the training and certifications for those involved in fraud investigation and prevention activities; and the kind and amount of fraud prevention and ethics training provided to employees.

AIRSERVICES AUSTRALIA

Airservices Australia is a government-owned corporation providing safe and environmentally sound air traffic control management and related airside services to the aviation industry. The Australian Flight Information region covers 11% of the earth's surface including Australian airspace and international airspace over the Pacific and Indian Oceans. Each year, Airservices manages air traffic operations for more than three million domestic and international flights carrying some 47 million passengers. The aviation industry also relies on Airservices for aeronautical data, telecommunications, and navigation services.

Airservices Australia's corporate headquarters is located in Canberra, Australia. The corporation has a fixed asset base of $493 million across 600 sites and about 3,000 employees, including 1,000 air traffic controllers working from two major centers in Melbourne and Brisbane and 26 towers at international and regional airports. Airservices also provides aviation rescue and fire fighting services at 19 of the nation's busiest airports where there are more than 350,000 passenger movements a year. As Airservices Australia says, "Airspace and airside, we do it all–from the ground up."

Airservices includes in its annual report its commitment to fraud prevention. In the section entitled "Fraud Control" in the 2005–2006 Annual Report, it reads, "Airservices Australia has fraud prevention, detection, investigation, and data collection procedures and processes that meet its needs and, where required, those of the Commonwealth Fraud Control Guidelines. During the year, the corporation undertook a number of minor fraud investigations that led to disciplinary action against a small number of staff."[5]

There are numerous compliance best practices contained within their Fraud Control Plan. The Plan provides a definition of fraud that is clear and unmistakable as well as various examples of fraudulent behavior that have been observed. Information is provided on the disciplinary ramifications for misconduct as reinforcement that the company takes appropriate action in such cases. The Plan discusses the importance of fraud awareness as a deterrent and the need for all employees to quickly escalate suspicions of misconduct and violations of business conduct. The importance of a formally documented risk assessment and continuous monitoring are also reinforced to identify mitigating controls and a response to the fraud risk. Finally, the Plan defines the key measures of success to determine the effectiveness of the overall fraud prevention program.

COMPLIANCE INSIGHT 12.1: AIRSERVICES AUSTRALIA: HOW WE OPERATE

Airservices Australia's Aspiration, Mission, and Values

Our Aspiration	Empowering people to lead through excellence and innovation
Our Mission	To be the preferred global partner for air traffic and related aviation services. We will achieve this through: ■ Keeping safety first ■ Being an employer and service provider of choice ■ World best operations ■ Profitable growth of commercial activities ■ Responsible environmental management
Our Values	In achieving our ambitious goals, we recognize the need for honesty, accountability and strong leadership to engender a spirit of unity and trust.

Reprinted with permission from Airservices Australia, © 2005.

The following are selected sections of the Airservices Australia Fraud Control Plan and they are reprinted with their permission (© Airservices Australia 2005).

Airservices Australia Fraud Control Plan 2005–2007
A message from the Chief Executive Officer
　　Government policy and good governance requires Airservices Australia to manage fraud risks, and the Board approved Fraud Control Plan, 2005–2007 addresses this objective.
　　Honesty, integrity and accountability are valued because they are the foundation for continued business growth and profitability. However, regrettably, it is a fact of life that a small number of

people in many organizations do not always share these principles, and organizations such as ours need to be prepared.

This Plan builds on our existing values and governance framework, and aims to increase the deterrence and detection of fraud by further developing the following key fraud control strategies:

- *Increased awareness*
- *Identification and reporting*
- *Maintaining confidentiality*
- *Investigating and applying corrective action*
- *Continually monitoring and improving performance*

I commend the Plan to every member of the Airservices team in ensuring we stamp out fraud.
Greg Russell[6]

General

Introduction

Fraud is defined in the Commonwealth Fraud Control Guidelines dated May 2002 as "dishonestly obtaining a benefit by deception or other means." *This definition includes monetary gain and any benefit that is gained from the Government, including intangibles, such as information. Fraud may be committed internally by an employee or externally by a member of the public.*

A proven case of internal fraud constitutes misconduct and breaches the Code of Conduct and provisions contained in certified agreements or contracts of employment. Fraud is also a crime under the provisions of the Criminal Code Act of 1995, *and the proceeds of fraud may be recovered under criminal and civil court orders.*

Airservices Australia acknowledges its corporate governance obligations under the Commonwealth Authorities and Companies Act 1997 *and the* Commonwealth Fraud Control Guidelines 2002 *to implement sound financial, legal, and ethical controls. This includes having a fraud control plan (FCP) that is based on a current fraud risk assessment.*

Fraud Incidents 2003–2005

Airservices Australia has been exposed to the following fraudulent activity in the past two years:

- *Use of Airservices Australia credit cards to purchase items for personal use*
- *Theft of computer equipment*

- *Use of false medical certificates to justify leave*
- *Submission of false petty cash claims*
- *Use of Airservices Australia credit card numbers by unauthorized third parties to purchase services*
- *Submission of false invoices by third parties for services never received*
- *Use of Airservices Australia time and resources (internet, telephones and sick leave) to conduct personal businesses and secondary employment*
- *Overstating of mandatory qualifications to obtain employment*
- *Use of misleading documents to maintain mandatory qualifications*
- *Submission of false documents in respect to salary sacrificing*

Most frauds involved Airservices Australia employees or contractors and were multiple incidents of low value conducted over a period of time. Investigations of the above frauds resulted in two former employees receiving custodial sentences and others being dismissed or disciplined. Airservices Australia recovered monies, where possible, through negation, court orders, and termination payments.

Fraud Control Policy

Airservices Australia Fraud Control Policy

The Board of Airservices Australia has established the following policy:
Airservices Australia is committed to minimizing the risk of fraud to our reputation, assets, and profitability. To achieve this we will:

- *Maintain and publish a fraud control plan in accordance with the Commonwealth Fraud Control Guidelines*
- *Maintain and improve awareness of fraud*
- *Document fraud control procedures*
- *Encourage professional and ethical conduct by our employees and service providers*
- *Encourage the reporting of suspected or actual instances of fraud*
- *Maintain, support, and fully respect the confidentiality of any person making a report and any person named in a report, in accordance with the Commonwealth Information Privacy Principles*

- *Apply best practice fraud investigation standards contained in the Crimes Act of 1914 and the Australian Government Investigation Standards*
- *Take firm disciplinary action against proven offenders*
- *Monitor, review, and continually improve our performance*

All managers are accountable for the implementation and management of fraud control measures in their areas of responsibility.

Implementation Strategies
The requirements of the Fraud Control Policy can be grouped into the following five implementation strategies;

- *Increasing awareness*
- *Identifying and reporting*
- *Maintaining confidentiality*
- *Investigating and applying corrective action*
- *Continually monitoring and improving performance*

Increasing Awareness
High ethical standards and professional conduct are the best form of fraud control. The primary purpose of fraud awareness is to build on the inherently high ethical standards of our employees, encourage them to be alert for fraud, to report suspicious activity, and to deter fraud. Fraud awareness highlights our experience with fraud and the controls that are in place to deter and detect fraud. An employee who commits fraud may be disciplined for misconduct, dismissed, and possibly charged for criminal offences in a court of law. When sentencing, judges take a serious view of Commonwealth employees who engage in fraudulent conduct while in positions of trust.

Our experience is that employees who engage in fraudulent behavior tend to be in positions of trust, and understand and can exploit weaknesses in the control environment.

We will increase fraud awareness by:

- *Continuing to educate managers and employees to make them aware of fraud and the consequences of committing fraud as an active deterrence*
- *Encouraging professional and ethical conduct by employees and service providers and support people who make reports or identify fraud*

- *Promoting the benefits of maintaining a positive control environment*
- *Publishing the results of fraud prosecutions*

Identifying and Reporting

A suspected fraud reported promptly may prevent a person from actually committing a fraud or engaging in further misconduct. Very small amounts of money taken over a long period of time, known as grazing, can lead to large amounts of money being stolen which may lead to a criminal conviction and/or a gaol[7] sentence.

Early reporting of a possible fraud can minimize damage to our reputation and provide greater confidence to management and employees that we have a culture that does not condone dishonesty.

Controls are also designed to identify fraud. Systematic data analysis and modern software tools will be used to assist the early identification and detection of fraud. We will do this using a combination of the following measures:

- *Maintaining a fraud audit and compliance program, including data matching to target areas of high risks*
- *Continuing self assessment programs for managers and the identification of localized fraud risks*
- *Integrating fraud control checks into Audit Assurance programs*
- *Further developing efficient and cost effective controls*
- *Reporting all suspected or actual cases of fraud to the Office of Security Risk Management (OSRM)*

Maintaining Confidentiality

The confidentiality of persons involved in an investigation will be maintained and respected to the extent Airservices Australia is able to do so. This will help to avoid rumours, the possibility of the willful destruction of evidence, prevent an alleged offender from interfering with witnesses and enhance our commitment to natural justice. Reporting of fraud is a sensitive issue, especially when an employee's initial report implicates a supervisor or coworker. We will do this by:

- *Supporting to the maximum possible extent, the confidentiality of any person making a report and any person named in a report, in accordance with the Commonwealth Information Privacy Principles.*

- *Using and disclosing information about suspected or actual fraudulent activity only to those employees who need to know or when authorized by law.*
- *Providing support to any person who makes a report of suspected or actual fraud.*
- *Reporting incidents of fraud to immediate supervisory/managers or, where that is not considered a realistic option and confidentiality is required, reporting the matter directly to the OSRM either verbally or in writing.*

Investigating and Applying Corrective Action

Airservices Australia will investigate all suspected instances of fraud. When a report of fraud is received, all available evidence will be preserved and controls will be implemented to reduce the risk of further losses. We will conduct internal investigations by:

- *Obtaining terms of reference for the investigation from the relevant business centre*
- *Applying the principles of natural justice[8]*
- *Considering the requirements of any certified agreements*
- *Applying best practice fraud investigation case management, including the standards contained in the Australian Government Investigations Standards and the requirements of the Crimes Act of 1914*
- *Completing preliminary internal investigations within 45 days*
- *Providing detailed reports to management on the outcomes and recommendations of all internal investigations*
- *Assisting law enforcement agencies with investigations relating to fraud committed against, or by any person acting on behalf of, Airservices Australia, including acts committed overseas that may breach Australian law*

Where an allegation of fraud has been substantiated, we will take corrective action by:

- *Considering disciplinary action*
- *Referring serious matters to the AFP[9] for further investigation*
- *Submitting briefs of evidence to the Commonwealth Director of Public Prosecutions (CDPP)*
- *Fully supporting any prosecution being conducted by the AFP/CDPP on behalf of Airservices Australia by providing documents and personnel to assist prosecutions*

Where an employee has been found to have committed fraud, we will initiate loss recovery action. We will do this by considering the following actions:

- *Recovering losses from monies owed to employees, such as termination payments*
- *Applying for compensation orders during criminal proceedings*
- *Seeking civil court orders for the recovery of the debt*
- *Placing restraining orders on personal assets to recover the debt*

Where offences involve official corruption, the Commonwealth may also recover monies from superannuation[10] accounts.

Continually Monitoring and Improving Performance

Fraud control strategies and controls are of little practical benefit unless they are monitored and improved along with business practices. Fraud controls must be integrated into published policies and procedures. Developing an integrated approach at all levels deepens the awareness of fraud and acts as a deterrent by displaying to employees and contractors that fraud can be quickly identified and is not tolerated. By building fraud controls into business processes, employees find them easier to understand and apply.

We will continue to monitor and improve our fraud control measures by:

- *Regularly reviewing the fraud risk assessment*
- *Assessing whether current controls are adequate*
- *Identifying and implementing cost effective and relevant controls*
- *Maintaining currency in fraud control strategies by liaising with other agencies and private sector organizations, such as the Australian Government Fraud Liaison Forum*
- *Providing quarterly exception reporting on the implementation of the FCP to the Board Audit Committee (BAC)*
- *Providing a fraud summary in the Annual Report*

Risk Assessment

As part of the development of this FCP, and with a view to the corporate policy on fraud control, OSRM conducted a fraud risk assessment using:

- *Business Risk Management Interim Guidance*
- *Australian Standard AZ/NZS 4360:2004, Risk Management*

- *Australian Standard AS 8001–2003, Fraud and Corruption Control*
- *Attorney-General's Department, Commonwealth Fraud Control Guidelines 2002*

This process involved consultation with Audit Assurance, Melbourne and Brisbane Centres, Airport Services, Directorate of Safety, Environment and Assurance (DSEA), Information Management Services (IMS) Managers, Facilities Management Services (FMS) Managers, Sales and Marketing, Corporate Services (Accounts Payable, Remuneration, Payroll, Accounts Receivable, Procurement, Salary Sacrifice, Treasury), Office of Legal Counsel (OOLC).
The process involved a review of the following:

- *Ernst and Young Fraud Risk Assessment 2003*
- *Fraud exposure as identified by cases between 2003–05 and historical cases*
- *Current policies, management instructions and/or procedures*
- *The effectiveness of current controls*
- *The development of new controls*

This process will be conducted every two years in accordance with the Commonwealth Fraud Control Guidelines.
A copy of the fraud risk assessment can be obtained from OSRM. The fraud risk assessment identified 32 specific fraud risks that required controls or treatment. After controls were applied, there were no HIGH risks, 19 risks were rated as MODERATE, and 13 as LOW. After reviewing the risk assessment and the requirements of the fraud control policy, a number of specific fraud control action items were identified as the focus of this FCP.[11]

Key Measures of Success
The effectiveness of the FCP will be established by using the following key measures of success:

- *Failures to implement established fraud controls*
- *Losses attributed to fraud.*

Failures to Implement Documented Fraud Control and Treatments
Fraud controls and treatments are the established tools through which fraud is managed in the corporation. A failure to implement

documented fraud controls and treatments indicates a potential breakdown of the control environment. This failure may be due to a number of factors, but they include inadequate:

- *awareness;*
- *training;*
- *supervision; or*
- *documented procedures.*

Audit Assurance and the Office of Security Risk Management will report on failures to implement established fraud controls and treatments.

Losses Attributed to Fraud
The success of the FCP can also be measured by losses attributable to fraud over the life of the Plan. Whilst the corporation could be subjected to fraud without its knowledge, reported losses provide a useful measure of the extent and seriousness of fraud across the corporation.[12]

Reprinted with permission from Airservices Australia, © 2005.

THE KEY ROLE OF MANAGERS IN FRAUD PREVENTION

Airservices Australia understands that managers are the first line of defense against fraud and abuse. As such, they train their managers and provide them guidance on how to respond to and prevent fraud within the organization. This is another best practice. The importance of tone at the top is a key theme of this book but that tone must extend throughout an organization. "Good managers are role models to their employees. They provide guidance and mentoring. They show employees how to succeed, and they instill honesty and integrity by their actions. Managers who provide great oversight and lead by example can have a major impact in preventing fraud."[13] My experience has been that when managers are engaged, understand the company's policies and procedures and lead by example, their organizations have far fewer issues with misconduct.

It is exceptional that Airservices Australia specifically focuses on the importance of managers in fraud and corruption control. Similar to their Fraud Control Plan, the Managers' Guide for Fraud and Corruption Control explains the importance of fraud prevention and the impact fraud can have on Airservices Australia. Also included is the important role of managers in achieving that goal as well as providing examples of misconduct. The following are selected sections of the Airservices Australia Managers'

Guide for Fraud and Corruption Control reprinted with their permission (© Airservices Australia 2005).

Managers' Guide for Fraud and Corruption Control Within Airservices Australia

Airservices Australia is committed to the awareness of fraud and corruption control within our organization. Staff and managers need to be suitably empowered not only to understand the effects of fraud and corruption but to feel confident in reporting it knowing that they have the full support of the organization.

The Managers' Fraud Control Tool Kit

The Managers' Fraud Control Tool Kit has been developed to assist managers in:

- *Identifying the likelihood of fraud and dishonest behavior within your areas of responsibility*
- *Developing local strategies to deal with fraud and dishonest behaviour*
- *Knowing what to do when these activities have been identified*
- *Increasing the awareness of fraud amongst your staff by delivering fraud control briefings.*

These strategies coupled with monitoring and supervision of expenditure at appropriate levels set by you will assist in reducing the opportunity of fraud or dishonest behaviour within our workplace.

Contained with this package are the:

- *Fraud Control Plan (FCP)*
- *Personal Guide for Fraud and Corruption Control within Airservices Australia*
- *Managers' Guide for Fraud and Corruption Control within Airservices Australia*
- *Code of Conduct*

Please read the tool kit, become familiar with it, and note the following:

- *The impact of fraud and dishonest activities*
- *The definitions of fraud and corruption*
- *Why fraud and dishonest activity occur*

- *Confidentiality*
- *How to deal with reports of fraud or corrupt behaviour*
- *Presenting the FCP to staff*
- *Briefing new staff*
- *Frequently asked questions*
- *The Fraud Control Plan*
- *Code of Conduct*

Examples of fraud include:

- *Theft of plant/computer equipment*
- *False invoicing*
- *Theft of petty cash*
- *Credit card fraud (inappropriate expenditure)*
- *Theft of intellectual property*
- *False accounting*
- *Release or use of misleading information for deceiving or covering up wrongdoing*
- *Payment of secret commissions*
- *Release of confidential information*
- *Collusive tendering*
- *Serious conflicts of interest*

Specific examples that highlight some of the above categories are:

- *A manager gets an employee to pay for entertaining friends and associates on his business credit card and subsequently uses his authority to sign off on the inappropriate expenditure.*
- *An employee reports in sick for work and arranges for another employee to cover his shift on overtime while working another job or private business.*
- *Employees using business credit cards to buy products clearly not for company use, such as toys.*
- *Employees using business credit cards while on leave.*
- *Cash advances while not on approved travel.*
- *Contracts being awarded to relatives in a closed tendering process.*
- *Petty cash claims for stock items never seen or obviously plentiful.*
- *Submission of false and or altered documents claiming to be originals, such as salary sacrificing invoices or sick leave certificates.*

Such activities have far reaching effects and are not purely measured in dollars.

These activities can damage trust between staff and Airservices Australia clients alike. They also affect:

- *Services*
- *Expectations*
- *Morale*
- *Reputation*
- *Profitability, and therefore job security.*

What are Fraud and Corruption?

Fraud: Is defined in the Fraud Control Plan (FCP) as "dishonestly obtaining a benefit by deception or other means."

Corruption: Is defined in the Australian Standard AS8001-2003 Fraud and Corruption Control as "Dishonest activity in which a director, executive, manager, employee, or contractor of an entity acts contrary to the interests of the entity and abuses his/her position of trust in order to achieve some personal gain or advantage for him or herself or for another person or entity."

The impact of fraud and dishonest activities on Airservices Australia:

- *A number of studies in Australia in recent years indicate that fraud within the workplace can cost at least 3 billion dollars a year.*
- *Airservices Australia is a target for fraud and dishonest activities due to the size and diversity of our business activities.*

Why Does Fraud or Dishonesty Occur?

The most obvious reason for fraud or dishonesty is greed; however there may be numerous other underlying reasons for such activity. These may include:

- *Dissatisfaction within the workplace*
- *Personal problems*
- *Everyone else is getting away with it*
- *Addictions (gambling, drugs, and alcohol)*
- *Attitudes (it goes with my position/entitlements).*

In these instances, the early identification of the fraud or dishonest activity can go a long way to addressing the individual problem rather than allowing a situation to develop to the point where serious action needs to be taken or the safety of our organization is put at risk.

COMPLIANCE INSIGHT 12.2: DEFINING FRAUD IN AN ORGANIZATION

Every organization must define the specific impact of fraud and dishonest activities that it faces. Linking this definition of fraud to the organization's risk assessment is critical. Included will be such factors as the particular industry they are in, size and diversity of business activities, locations of the world in which they operate, government regulatory requirements, and other key considerations. The resulting definition must be clearly communicated to all employees, vendors, and other stakeholders. Creating a detailed and regularly updated fraud control plan such as the one used by Airservices Australia is highly recommended.

A Fraud Control Plan that Targets the Whole Organisation

We are committed to minimizing the incidence of fraud through the identification of fraud risks and the implementation of fraud prevention and detection strategies. Control strategies contained in the FCP are designed to minimize risks to our reputation and profitability. We will do this in four ways:

- *Awareness*
- *Identification and reporting*
- *Investigation*
- *Corrective action.*

Through these core activities we will minimize loss as a result of fraud and develop a workplace environment based on ethical standards, trust, honesty, and accountability.

We will continually identify risks and implement measures to prevent and deter fraudulent or corrupt activities.

Our management guidelines and investigative standards will constantly be reviewed to ensure we are prepared to deal with fraud and dishonest behavior.

High Ethical Standards are the Best Form of Fraud Control

- *It is everyone's responsibility to maintain a high standard of ethical behaviour within the workplace.*

- *It is up to you to report any suspected cases of fraud or dishonest behaviour or areas where procedures are being circumvented.*
- *Very simple levels of supervision and querying can have a very high deterrent effect as staff will be aware that expenditure is being checked at every level.*
- *Training staff in the awareness of fraud and how it affects their own local area is very important in developing a workplace based on ethical standards, trust, honesty, and accountability. Crucial to this awareness training is the positive reinforcement or reporting and the fact that the organization will support staff making legitimate reports.*
- *If you are not sure what constitutes fraud or dishonest behaviour, please discuss the matter with the Office of Security Risk Management.*

Experience has shown that one of the most common ways in which fraud and corruption is detected is by observation, investigations, and reporting by fellow workers of the perpetrators (AS8001–2003 2.2.5).

How to Deal with Reports of Suspected Fraud or Corrupt Behaviour

The timely reporting of suspected fraud or corrupt behaviour has two benefits. Firstly, it prevents the loss or destruction of evidence and secondly, it may stop the suspected individual from committing more serious criminal offences over a longer period of time.

I knew something was wrong, but I didn't want to get involved or know who to tell

Managers who suspect fraud either directly or from a report from one of their staff should immediately prepare a written report to the Office of Security Risk Management detailing:

- *The allegations*
- *Reasons for the suspected activity*
- *Time the activity has taken place*
- *Any documents that support the allegation.*

Comments and observations of all the persons involved in the allegation are essential to supply investigators with important background information.

Importantly, if a report is received from outside the organization about a staff member currently employed by Airservices

Australia the matter should be reported in the same manner as soon as possible.
It is further incumbent on managers to:

- *Secure evidence in respect to the allegation from destruction or interference as soon as possible. This is crucially important for original documents.*
- *Reinforce to the employee making a report the confidentiality policy and that the organization will support them.*
- *Be aware that the employee subject to the report may have to explain their actions at a later time depending on the outcome of the investigation.*
- *Develop a strategy to inform other employees if a staff member is subsequently suspended with a view to protecting the employee who made the original complaint and reduce the likelihood of rumours.*
- *Keep the person who made the report informed of the progress of the matter.*
- *Support and protect employees from harassment or victimization and report any instances of this nature to the Office of Security Risk Management.*
- *Develop a support mechanism equally for those who are subject to the allegation and those who reported it. These matters are often taken very seriously by individuals and our duty of care extends to those people during any reporting or investigative process.*

Malicious reports will not be tolerated and may be dealt with under the Airservices Australia Code of Conduct or other jurisdictions such as civil litigation or even criminal proceedings.
Remember: it will often be the case that your report will direct someone where to look in the identification phase, rather than your employee being crucial in any investigation, such as a key witness.

Presenting the Fraud Control Plan to Employees

It is a supervisors/managers' responsibility to clearly explain the Airservices Australia FCP to their employees under their control and ensure that employees are fully aware of their responsibilities and reporting lines.
When managers discuss fraud control with their employees, it should be done in an open and frank manner to remove any confusion on the part of the employees.

If you are unsure of how to deliver a briefing session please feel free to contact your local Fraud Liaison Officer or the Office of Security Risk Management and we will be pleased to help and deliver a sample package.

Included in any briefing package will be:

- *Personal guide for staff in Fraud and Corruption within Airservices Australia*
- *Managers' Guide for Fraud and Corruption Control within Airservices Australia*
- *Fraud Control Plan*
- *Code of Conduct*

Maintaining Records

It is important for audit purposes that each business centre's Fraud Liaison Officer keeps a record of all staff attending fraud control briefing sessions and report to the Office of Security Risk Management annually on the number of sessions delivered and employees that attended.

Briefing New Employees

New staff to Airservices Australia at all levels should be involved in either a group or individual briefing session as soon as possible upon commencement of employment. They should be provided with a copy of the Personal Guide for Staff in Fraud and Corruption Control within Airservices Australia.

Regular Reinforcement

It is crucial that fraud control briefing sessions are not done on a one-off occasion and that fraud should be openly discussed at staff meetings and other occasions throughout the year. The high level of awareness of the FCP and fraud in general will see a more effective implementation of the plan and a less vulnerable workplace.

Frequently Asked Questions

What steps has Airservices Australia taken to ensure employees who report allegations are protected against discrimination and retaliation?

- *The identity of the person making the report will be kept confidential.*
- *Employees will not be allowed to harass or victimize any staff member making, or involved in the making, of a report. People*

found to be involved in such behaviour will face disciplinary action or serious criminal charges such as attempting to pervert the course of justice or intimidating witnesses. Both of these offences are viewed very seriously by the courts.

- *Where appropriate, ongoing counseling and other management support mechanisms will be provided to staff members who report allegations of fraudulent or dishonest behaviour.*
- *What should be communicated to staff about making a report?*
- *It is important that staff report the matter to people they can trust. If someone feels they may be compromised by reporting matters to people within their own work area then contact the Office of Security Risk Management and we will assist you and the staff member.*
- *Encourage staff not to openly discuss the issues they have raised with other employees especially if they feel the information they are supplying may be compromised.*

What are employees' responsibilities under the Fraud Control Plan?

- *Employees of Airservices Australia should be aware of the FCP and its contents, and comply with its requirements.*
- *Employees are encouraged to develop a workplace environment based on ethical standards, trust, honesty, and accountability.*
- *In pursuit of these goals, employees are accountable for their actions and fraudulent and/or dishonest behaviour will not be tolerated by Airservices Australia.*

What will happen to people who make a malicious report?

- *Any staff member found to have made a false and/or malicious report may face disciplinary action under the Code of Conduct. In some circumstances they may be liable to civil litigation by the person affected by the false or malicious report. Criminal charges such as creating a public mischief may also follow, depending on the specific circumstances.*

What will happen to an employee implicated in dishonest activity?

- *Once a report has been received an initial inquiry will assess the validity of the report.*

- *Upon confirmation of the initial report, an investigation will begin under specific terms of reference and will be conducted discretely.*
- *All investigations will be conducted in accordance with Commonwealth Law Enforcement Board (CLEB) standards and the application of the principle of natural justice.*
- *Fraudulent and/or dishonest behaviour will not be tolerated by Airservices Australia and employees found to have committed such acts will be subject to disciplinary action under the Code of Conduct, which may include dismissal. Those individuals may also be subject to criminal prosecution, including recovery action under the Proceeds of Crime Act 1987.*

Do we have employees who commit fraud?

- *Yes. It is unfortunate, but there have been employees who have committed fraud on our organisation and have been dismissed and subjected to criminal prosecution.*

Why do we bother having a Fraud Control Plan?

- *Airservices Australia aims to be a fraud-free organization.*
- *It will improve our profitability and job security.*
- *It contributes to a workplace environment based on ethical standards, trust, honesty, and accountability.*
- *It's what our clients expect of us.*
- *It enhances our good reputation and increases morale.*
- *It is a requirement of all Commonwealth Government statutory authorities to implement a FCP in accordance with standards, guidelines and procedures.*[14]

Reprinted with permission from Airservices Australia, © 2005.

THE COMMONALITY BETWEEN FRAUD PREVENTION AND COMPLIANCE

One can argue that fraud prevention is actually a synonym for compliance. Their definitions are interchangeable and one cannot have a successful fraud prevention program without corporate compliance. The Association of Certified Fraud Examiners' Fraud Examiners Manual states "Fraud prevention requires a system of rules, which, in their aggregate, minimize the likelihood of fraud occurring while maximizing the possibility of detecting any fraudulent activity that may transpire. The potential of being caught most often persuades likely perpetrators not to commit the fraud. Because of this principle, the existence of a thorough control system is essential to fraud prevention."[15] Compliance is all about strict adherence to organizational polices and guidelines as well as all relevant laws and regulations. Fraud prevention requires compliance and compliance requires fraud prevention

Airservices Australia has embraced this concept and successfully integrated a world-class fraud prevention program in their compliance program. Their Fraud Control Plan and Managers' Guide for Fraud and Corruption Control are best practices that should be held up as example for other organizations worldwide to incorporate into their compliance programs.

NOTES

1. Australian Government Attorney General's Department Fraud Control Policy, www.ag.gov.au/www/agd/agd.nsf/Page/Fraud_control.
2. Commonwealth Fraud Control Guidelines Fact Sheet, www.ag.gov.au/ www/agd/rwpattach.nsf/VAP/(4341200FE1255EFC59DB7A1770C1D 0A5)~Commonwealth-Fraud-Contro-Guidelines-Fact-sheet.DOC/ $file/Commonwealth-Fraud-Contro-Guidelines-Fact-sheet.DOC
3. Ibid.
4. Ibid.
5. Airservices Australia Annual Report, July 2005—June 2006, 116.
6. Aviation expert Greg Russell was appointed Airservices Australia Chief Executive Officer on July 19, 2005. Mr. Russell was the Chief Operating Officer at Athens International Airport until June 2005, before which he held the position of Director, Aviation at Sydney Airport Corporation, Ltd. for four years. He has been an executive and General Manager of the New South Wales regional operator Hazelton Airlines and has held a range of management positions in private companies and government organizations.
7. Gaol is a prison or detention facility for those charged or convicted of crimes. "The word is sometimes written as jail and is said to be derived from the Spanish word jaula meaning cage." Source: Bouviers Law Dictionary at LegalLawTerms.com, www.legallawterms .com/legal-definition-GAOL.html.
8. "The terms 'natural justice' and 'procedural fairness' are used interchangeably. There are three principles of natural justice: the right to be heard and have a fair hearing, the right to have a decision made

by an unbiased decision-maker, and the right to have the decision based on evidence." Source: The University of Newcastle, Australia, www.newcastle.edu.au/service/legal/faq/justice-fairness.html.

9. Australian Federal Police.

10. Pension or retirement accounts.

11. For the sake of brevity, I did not include all the fraud control action items. Suffice it to say, they included specific action items, target dates for completion, and the applicable policy requirements.

12. Reprinted with permission from Airservices Australia, © 2005.

13. Martin T. Biegelman and Joel T. Bartow, *Executive Roadmap to Fraud Prevention and Internal Control: Creating a Culture of Compliance,* (Hoboken, NJ: John Wiley & Sons, Inc., 2006), 301.

14. Reprinted with permission from Airservices Australia, © 2005.

15. Association of Certified Fraud Examiners, *Fraud Examiners Manual,* (Austin, 2006).

CHAPTER 13

The Skunk in the Room

"Powerful men and beautiful women never get to hear the truth."
Dutch proverb

Imagine this nightmare scenario: three college students wrongly accused of heinous crimes they did not commit, a rogue prosecutor operating with no limitations, the news media reporting every detail of the case, prejudicial comments made by the district attorney that violate the students' constitutional rights and stoke the community's racial tensions, and key pieces of exculpatory evidence withheld. In the end, it was a complete disaster of a case leaving the district attorney's office humiliated and universally scorned, and a long-standing public servant disbarred and leaving office in disgrace.

What does the disturbing 2006–07 saga of former Durham County, North Carolina District Attorney Mike Nifong and the Duke Lacrosse case have to do with compliance? Of course, no CEOs would ever want to see themselves and their companies embroiled in such an embarrassing and damaging scenario. This debacle could have been prevented had the person in charge not been reckless and proceeding without using good judgment. But these facts alone do not link it to compliance. While on the surface this case and corporate compliance are completely separate, there is a lesson in the actions of Nifong and this tragedy that every company would be well served to learn. The case proceeded with outrageous allegations, unfounded and unsupported by the evidence. Every aspect of this case from the very beginning screamed that it would be high-profile. As any career prosecutor would advise, a case like this demands thoroughness, extreme due diligence, and patience. A reasonable person in the same situation would have seen that the evidence would not support an indictment, much less the convictions that Nifong publicly declared with absolute certainty he would get.

In the rush to judgment, what apparently happened was that no one stood up and said, "This isn't right." No one took a step back and saw that what was going on was not justice. No one stood up to Nifong and the other assistant district attorneys on the case and took issue with what they were doing. No one asked why they were moving so fast in such a serious case. Why wasn't the story of the alleged victim thoroughly corroborated? Why didn't anyone from Nifong's office agree to meet with the defendants to hear their stories and evidence of innocence? What the Durham County District Attorney's Office needed was a "skunk in the room."

Just what is a skunk in the room and why is it so important to compliance? Skunks are generally highly avoided due to the offensive odor they can emit when alarmed or attacked. They can be extremely unpleasant. No one wants to confront a skunk, let alone have one nearby. They definitely stand out from other animals. A skunk in the room also stands out, as they too are different and often avoided. A skunk in the room is that contrary person who says no when everyone else is saying yes—the person who is not afraid to ask the tough questions, especially when others do not even want to hear them. It's the person who is willing to jar people back to reality. It's not a fun person to be but it's critical for compliance. One cannot ignore the skunk in the room. This is very much like the Henry Fonda character in the classic movie *12 Angry Men*. The movie is about twelve jurors deliberating the fate of a murder suspect. Eleven jurors are ready to pronounce the suspect guilty but one juror decides to speak up in defense of the suspect. The contrary juror is not advocating the innocence of the suspect but just that the situation demands greater scrutiny before the ultimate decision can be made. He will not be bullied or ignored and through sheer force of will makes the other jurors deeply examine their underlying beliefs motivating their decision. He is the ideal skunk in the room.

Why does this matter in compliance? Compliance requires following laws, regulations, and corporate policies. Individuals and companies that fail to follow compliance requirements end up in trouble. Compliance requires vigilance and commitment. To ensure compliance, strong people are needed to carry it out. These are the kind of people who would have told Nifong he was wrong in what he was doing. These are the kind of people who would have protested vehemently if they could not persuade Nifong to see the error of his ways. They would have stopped this travesty of justice. What was missing in the Durham D.A.'s Office, besides the protection of constitutional rights, was the lack of accountability and someone speaking up publicly. In both compliance situations and in Durham, an ethical person, having seen serious mistakes go uncorrected and having the foresight to know the outcome, would have noisily withdrawn to avoid being part of the injustice.

The noisy withdrawal sends a loud and clear message to others about this compliance failure, and this person's lack of tolerance for it.

THE SKUNK IN KING DAVID'S COURT

The idea of a skunk in the room is not a new one, nor is the belief that leaders need to hear contrary opinions in order to command effectively. For instance, it can be seen in the Old Testament of the Bible, in the story of King David and Bathsheba. David, who famously defeated the Philistine Goliath in battle with nothing more than a slingshot, was the powerful king of Israel. One day he saw a beautiful woman bathing, and was immediately smitten. Her name was Bathsheba and he had to have her. Even though King David knew that Bathsheba already had a husband, he had an affair with her and she became pregnant.

Trying to hide his misdeeds, David sent for her husband, Uriah, a soldier serving in the army, in the hope that he would return home to his wife. In his clouded thinking, David thought that with the husband back living with his wife, David's wrong would be covered up. Returning from the middle of battle, Uriah appeared before David. He answered David's questions, but refused to return to his house because his men were still fighting and sleeping in tents, and it would have been unfair for him alone to return to his family. Fed up with his steadfast refusals to abandon his fellow soldiers, David sent Uriah to the battlefront, to a dangerous battle where he knew Uriah would likely die. Uriah fought valiantly, but died in combat. David then took Bathsheba as one of his wives and she soon gave birth to a son.

Sending a man to his death and stealing his wife was inexcusable behavior, even for a king. No one from King David's court or any of his advisors said anything or objected to what he had done. Only the prophet Nathan appeared before David to confront him. Nathan told the king a parable of a rich man who had many sheep but chose to feed a traveler with the lone sheep of a poor man, rather than one of his own. Through this story, Nathan forced David to accept the evilness of his actions and his greed, how he had many riches and many wives of his own, but still saw fit to take from those who had less. Furthermore, the child Bathsheba bore grew very sick and soon died. David finally atoned for his sins and accepted the error of his ways.[1]

King David's sins and an unending lust for what was not his are still unfortunately all too common among some of today's corporate executives. However, even after compliance failures occur, there are still opportunities for a skunk in the room to step up and force leaders to confront their mistakes. As is well-known, the cover-up is often far worse than the crime itself. Here, King David had an affair with a married woman, and to cover it up had her husband killed. He was punished for his misdeeds, just as any corporate executive who ignores compliance responsibilities and engages in wrongdoing should ultimately be.

JOHN F. KENNEDY, THE BAY OF PIGS, AND GROUPTHINK

Great leaders recognize that to reach the best possible decisions, they need a diversity of opinion in the decision-making process. Leaders who are surrounded by sycophants or those unable to voice contrary opinions are in a very precarious position. They are at risk of operating in a bubble, divorced from reality and unable to confront serious problems. If they do not take extra steps to make sure people feel comfortable expressing contrary opinions, their organizations could suffer devastating consequences.

An excellent example of this is the disastrous Bay of Pigs invasion of Cuba in 1961. After the Cuban exile-led invasion turned into a colossal embarrassment for the Kennedy Administration, much of the blame rested on the inadequate discussion and planning that took place beforehand. When President John F. Kennedy discussed the plans for the invasion with his advisors, many of whom where considered the best and brightest minds of their era, the group was unified with little dissenting opinion, and those who dissented were quickly silenced. As the group was in agreement, their assumptions and beliefs went unchallenged and soon calcified into "fact." What was going on in those meetings is what is called "groupthink," when members of a group form unified conclusions without testing them, with the goal of avoiding conflict. The result is decision borne out of conformity, not from rigorous examination or critical and rational thinking.[2]

Individual members are afraid of appearing to go against the group by challenging their opinions, or by bringing in outside ideas that do not conform to what has already been discussed. Members are afraid of looking foolish for bringing up questions or of angering superiors who want a quick decision made. To minimize conflict, whether consciously or unconsciously, the members reach a consensus. Since everyone basically agrees with one another, the similar opinions and agreement by the members convince them that their ideas are correct, even though those ideas have not been critically examined or verified.

The plan for the invasion was deeply flawed and riddled with false assumptions. However, Kennedy's top advisors did not speak out against the plan, partly because the plan's assumptions meshed with their own underlying assumptions and also because they did not want to upset the president. Any advisor who dissented faced harsh criticism from the others.

For instance, noted historian Arthur Schlesinger Jr., then a Kennedy advisor, met privately with the president to express his reservations. He was later firmly rebuked by then-Attorney General Robert Kennedy and was told the President had already made up his mind and his decision had to be supported.[3]

In the wake of this disastrous failure, President Kennedy set out to find a way to prevent a reoccurrence of this problem. Taking full responsibility, he even asked reporters, "How could I have been so stupid as to let them go ahead?"[4] Both Kennedys saw this failure as an opportunity to improve and strove to never repeat their mistakes.

Looking back on it, President Kennedy became convinced that the lack of open debate and criticism, and the failure to consider contrary opinions lay at the heart of the problem. He realized he needed a skunk in the room to facilitate the necessary debate. Unlike leaders who surround themselves with yes men and women, Kennedy wanted people who he could trust but who would disagree with him and voice contrary opinions. He set about achieving this in several ways. He would often leave the room during policy discussions, so as not to influence his advisors. Just his very presence and reactions during the discussion could unconsciously influence the direction of the debate. Additionally, Robert Kennedy served as an official "intellectual watchdog," a sort of "devil's advocate" position. He challenged others' ideas, even if the idea voiced was sound, just to make sure that people were able to explain why they supported something, that they could defend it, and that the idea stood up to critical scrutiny.[5]

With this new system, President Kennedy achieved one of the great victories of the Cold War during the subsequent Cuban Missile Crisis, winning a nuclear showdown with Russia. By putting his reforms into action, he was able to achieve this victory and perfectly balance individual leadership and unfettered policy discussion. "Unquestionably, President Kennedy ultimately guided [his advisors] in the direction of the final recommendation, but only after considerable open debate. Never, however, did he achieve a consensus, an indication that participants felt free to speak throughout the crisis."[6]

THE PERFECT STORM OF CORPORATE AND PERSONAL FAILURE

Sometimes there is that skunk in the room who provides that dissenting, yet ultimately correct opinion, but no one else will listen. That was the case in the Hewlett-Packard (HP) spying and pretexting scandal that made headlines in 2006. Had anyone listened to the skunk in the room, this story would not need telling. The HP scandal began as a clash of personalities among board members that resulted in an internal investigation to root out a boardroom leak. In its zeal to identify the member of the board of directors who was the source of confidential information to the news media, HP employed questionable investigative techniques including impersonations of journalists, board members, and HP employees, spying and pretexting,[7] and covertly installing a "web bug" tracer program in a reporter's computer. This was an investigation out of control with little oversight. It resulted in state and federal probes as well as Congressional hearings and overall reputational harm to HP. The daily tribulations of HP were front-page stories in papers across the United States. HP forgot that old but still relevant saying that one should "never pick a fight with someone who buys paper by the roll and ink by the barrel."

The skunk in the room at HP that no one listened to was a senior investigator named Vince Nye.[8] He quickly realized that what the other investigators and company officials were doing was a one-way ticket to disaster. "I have serious reservations about what we are doing," Nye said in a February 2006 e-mail to superiors. "I am requesting that we cease this phone-number gathering method immediately and discount any of its information."[9] In a follow-up e-mail to another HP investigator in March 2006, Nye questioned whether the tactics were ethical and potentially illegal. He said "[i]f one has to hold his nose and then conduct a task, it is logical to step back and consider if the task or activity is the right thing to do."[10] Nye said he had spent more than 20 years in law enforcement and would not use these tactics.

As a result of the debacle, several high-level HP employees including the chairwoman of the board of directors, general counsel, chief ethics officer, and manager of global investigations lost their jobs. To settle the investigation by the California Attorney General, HP paid $14.5 million and agreed to a number of corporate reforms, especially involving how it conducts internal investigations. The sad thing is that HP is a great company with a long history of ethical conduct. This was an aberration and one that HP took steps to fix and put behind them. HP understood the importance of having an effective compliance program and took dramatic steps to reinforce their program.

In October 2006, HP hired John Hoak for the newly created position of Chief Ethics and Compliance officer. Hoak is experienced both as an attorney and business leader. This position provides oversight of the ethics and compliance program. Hoak reports directly to the CEO as well as to the independent director of the board responsible for compliance, investigative procedure, and conduct. "What began as a well-intentioned exercise in risk management—an investigation into leaks of confidential information by members of our board—grew into something that no one wanted or anticipated," said Hoak.[11] He added, "HP has a long legacy of ethical business leadership but the pretexting issue the company faced in 2006 signaled that some policies and processes weren't strong enough."[12]

This scandal caused HP to look closely at its compliance program and as a result, took a number of significant actions including the following:

- Accepting responsibility as a company for their compliance and ethical lapses;
- apologizing to the victims of the spying and pretexting;
- severing all ties to the private investigation and consulting firms who carried out the pretexting;
- accepting the resignation of the chairwoman of the board, general counsel, and chief ethics officer who should have provided greater oversight of the investigation;
- hiring a former federal prosecutor to conduct an independent assessment of systems and practices related to investigations;
- establishing a new senior executive post to address and improve ethics and compliance issues worldwide;
- launching an internal communications campaign to keep HP employees updated on the compliance issues involved in this matter and reinforcement of HP's Standards of Business Conduct; and
- developing specific training programs for employees engaged in investigations to reinforce ethics and compliance.[13]

As is the case in so many compliance failures, the lessons are learned after the impact has been felt. HP learned those lessons and made major changes and improvements in their compliance program as a result. That's a very good thing but it would have been even better if their program had caught these compliance failures before they occurred. A world-class compliance program learns from the mistakes of others and does not repeat them. They also listen to those who speak up and say what no one else is saying. Had anyone listened to the skunk in the room at HP, and fully heard and truly understood the ramifications, none of this would have happened.

THE NEW CA WAY

This book opened with a nightmare scenario of a situation out of control and on a path of potential ruin. Unfortunately, the nightmare was all too real for Computer Associates. The huge accounting fraud at this company resulted in prison terms for its senior executives, a deferred prosecution agreement for the company that required major changes in how it does business, and the implementation of a strong compliance and ethics program. The new CA and its world-class compliance program were profiled earlier in this book. So, a fitting way to end is a look back on the many compliance failures that contributed to the fraud at Computer Associates resulting in its rebirth as CA, Inc.

There was a failure of leadership at the company. Executive leadership created a "culture of fear" and "shunned written policies and procedures." There was a "preference for promoting from within" the company and the result was a management team "too young, too inexperienced, and too dependent on senior leaders."

There were numerous organizational weaknesses. Computer Associates had a "horizontal organizational structure that discouraged open communication" between different company departments. They were "devoid of mid-level managers" as senior leaders controlled decision-making, and meetings were almost unheard of. Almost as hard to believe, "at quarter end, the CFO manually reviewed contracts for revenue recognition issues and then created handwritten lists of contracts to be booked."

Training was non-existent. While there was a code of conduct, no one received training about its importance. Not only was there an "absence of written policies and procedures," but employees were forced to learn of accounting and other important policies through "word-of-mouth."

Internal audit was under-staffed, randomized, and had no authority to conduct critical audits. The head of the internal audit department for the majority of Computer Associate's existence was not a CPA. Just as important, the CFO at the time was not a CPA. Add to this the culture of corruption involving senior executives who eventually pleaded guilty for their criminal actions, a board of directors apparently in the dark, and the lack of a compliance department. The result is the unfortunate story of what happened at Computer Associates.[14]

There was no skunk in the room at Computer Associates. Even if there had been someone to speak up, he or she would not have been heard. There was a culture of intimidation that suppressed dissenting opinion. And if someone did speak up to report a business conduct violation, the company hotline rang on the desk of the general counsel. This was the same general counsel who pleaded guilty to participating in the "35-day month" accounting fraud. There was no one who would have listened and done anything. Thanks to the changes made by CA's new executive team, this should not happen today.

WORLD-CLASS COMPLIANCE MEANS SPEAKING UP

A company may have the best-designed compliance program, following the Seven Steps of the Federal Sentencing Guidelines for Organizations and all of the advice and best practices laid out in this book, but it won't work unless the people work too. People must be willing to speak up when something is not right, and be willing to come forward and report violations. An "effectively" designed compliance program needs these people. Hotlines, for instance, are useless unless people feel comfortable and empowered coming forward with information. As mentioned above, Computer Associates had a hotline but people were fearful to use it.

Some of the biggest corporate scandals of recent years came to light when whistleblowers called attention to the crimes going on around them. It takes a great deal of courage and conviction to be a whistleblower: a person puts their job, and sometimes even their life, on the line to stand up for what they believe in and do their ethical duty. Cynthia Cooper from WorldCom, who exposed to the board the accounting fraud her internal audit team discovered, is but one example. These corporate sentinels are an important part not only of corporate America but worldwide organizations, keeping companies honest and bringing compliance failures to light.

But, many times it does not need to go that far. Employees and others should have many opportunities to speak up, long before a problem reaches scandal proportions. Furthermore, most problems are on a much smaller scale—most of the time, compliance problems relate to day-to-day types of activities, rather than large-scale accounting fraud violations. A business doesn't have to let it get to the point where a major investigation is necessary. In short, what is needed is a skunk in the room. Be that skunk. When something isn't right, say so. Start a dialogue, discuss the issue with others, make your point known. Even if you're just playing devil's advocate and want some more discussion before a final decision is made, do something.

Be the skunk at the party not afraid to speak up. Be the Henry Fonda character in *12 Angry Men* asking the tough questions others cannot. Don't forget that bad things happen when good people stay silent. A company that suffered catastrophic compliance failure, like Computer Associates, also had a culture of silence where people were afraid to speak up and speak out. This is not a coincidence. Yet, Computer Associates went from defiance to compliance and emerged as the new CA, Inc., a far stronger and compliant company.

ACHIEVING WORLD-CLASS COMPLIANCE

Compliance will always begin and end with people. That includes everyone from the CEO to the newest intern. That means people who are willing to speak up and be heard, even when it is not popular to do so. That means ensuring a corporate culture where employees are not afraid to report wrongdoing and other potential violations of business conduct. As the Compliance and Ethics Leadership Council of the Corporate Executive Board found in their landmark 2007 study of the leading indicators of potential misconduct, the fear of retaliation was the single greatest concern among employees. Great companies encourage reporting and protect those that do. No one wants to hear bad news but organizations must. Build your program with trust and confidence, and with continuous reinforcement, and people will call and people will comply.

There are other important caveats to remember. Just meeting the minimum requirements of the Federal Sentencing Guidelines for Organizations is not enough. World-class compliance programs go beyond the Seven Steps to ensure both a reactive and proactive approach but with a far greater emphasis on the proactive. It means stopping the risk from ever happening in the first place but when it does, take the appropriate steps and do the right things to mitigate whatever issue arises. It means protecting the organization, employees, shareholders, customers, and others from potential harm. In short, it is detecting, correcting, and preventing compliance failures.

Ethics, integrity, accountability, and strong leadership are all elements of a culture of compliance. These traits are a constant for any successful company. When a business talks about increasing shareholder value, return on investment, and driving revenue, the best investment is building and maintaining a world-class compliance program. Best in class compliance is a competitive advantage. Compliance, not defiance, is the solution.

NOTES

1. The Bible, King James Version, 2 Samuel 10–12.
2. See, *e.g.*, Irving L. Janis, *Victims of Groupthink*, (New York: Houghton Mifflin, 1972). This book defines groupthink as "a tendency towards premature and extreme consensus-seeking within a cohesive policy-making group under stress."
3. Arthur Schlesinger, Jr., *One Thousand Days*, (Boston: Houghton Mifflin, 1965), 252–56, 259.
4. Janis, *Victims of Groupthink*, 154.
5. James N. Giglio, *The Presidency of John F. Kennedy*, 2 d ed., (Lawrence: Univ. of Kansas Press, 2006), 208.

6. Ibid., 209.
7. Pretexting as defined by the Federal Trade Commission is the practice of obtaining personal information under false pretenses. Individuals involved in pretexting will sell the personal information they covertly obtain to others who may use it to commit identity theft and other crimes. Pretexting is against the law.
8. It should be noted that media accounts have identified another HP investigator named Fred Adler who also recognized the possible illegality of HP's tactics and sent a warning e-mail to his superiors in early 2006. Unfortunately, his warning was also not heeded.
9. Marcy Gordon, "E-mail Warned Bosses HP Probe Should Stop," *Seattle Times*, September 29, 2006, C1.
10. Ina Fried, "HP Investigator Twice Raised Objections," CNET News. com, October 3, 2006, http://news.com.com/HP+investigator+twice+ raised+objections/2100-1014_3-6122362.html.
11. Jon Hoak, "Building Ethics from the Ground Up," Ethisphere.com, Quarter 2, 2007 issue, http://ethisphere.com/building-ethics-from-the-ground-up/.
12. Ibid.
13. Ibid.
14. William McCracken, Renato Zambonini, Douglas H. Flaum, David B. Hennes and Carmen J. Lawrence, "CA, Inc. Special Litigation Report," April 13, 2007, online.wsj.com/public/resources/documents/20070413 _CA.pdf.

Summary of the 2004 Federal Sentencing Guidelines Amendments and Recommended Action Steps

General Counsel Roundtable
Research, 2004

T o underscore the importance of compliance programs, the U.S. Sentencing Commission proposed to Congress on April 30, 2004 a number of amendments to its sentencing guidelines that extensively define and expand the standards, structures, and procedures of an "effective" compliance program. The amendments were approved and went into effect beginning November 1, 2004 and require companies to evaluate and modify, if necessary, their existing compliance and ethics programs to meet the specifications of the new criteria.

The following table, prepared by the General Counsel Roundtable, summarizes the actions mandated by the seven amendments to the U.S. Sentencing Commission's sentencing guidelines. The table also includes some, though certainly not all, steps companies may take when assessing strengths and weaknesses of their compliance programs.

MANDATED ACTIONS OF THE AMENDMENTS TO SENTENCING GUIDELINES FOR ORGANIZATIONS

Area Under Amendment	Mandated Actions	Recommended Steps
Standards and Procedures	The organization must establish standards and procedures to prevent and detect criminal conduct. This includes standards of conduct and internal controls reasonably capable of reducing the likelihood of criminal conduct.	■ Determine whether the current ethics and compliance program emphasizes critical ethical conduct or just compliant conduct ■ Ensure that the company's code of conduct encourages individual responsibility instead of simply laying out a series of rules to follow ■ Recognize "ethical conduct" as an integral component of any compliance program ■ Review and ensure that the company code of conduct makes a compelling case for ethics and compliance
Organizational Leadership and Culture	The board of directors or the highest level of governing body of the organization must be responsible for the following: ■ Understand the content and operation of the compliance and ethics program	■ Clearly articulate how the senior management team is engaged in the compliance process ■ Determine how the board strategically oversees ethics and compliance

(Continued)

MANDATED ACTIONS OF THE AMENDMENTS TO SENTENCING GUIDELINES FOR ORGANIZATIONS

Area Under Amendment	Mandated Actions	Recommended Steps
	▪ Exercise reasonable oversight over the program's implementation and effectiveness ▪ Assign specific individuals among the highest level of governing body overall responsibility for the program ▪ Assign an individual(s) responsibility for the "day-to-day" operations of the program. This individual(s) shall have direct access to the governing authority, report periodically to the governing authority, and should be provided with adequate resources	▪ Develop information-flow processes for board and senior executives to effectively assess the program ▪ Ensure that high-level personnel actively espouse the organization's values ▪ Establish appropriate authority and resources for the chief compliance officer ▪ Identify the best focal point to champion the compliance program
Reasonable Efforts to Exclude Prohibited Persons	The organization must make reasonable efforts to ensure that personnel with substantial authority have not engaged in illegal activities or conducted themselves in a manner inconsistent with the compliance and ethics program. If an organization delays reporting an offense or if high-level personnel participated in, condoned, or were willfully ignorant of an	▪ Conduct background checks on current and future executive hires ▪ Create a mechanism for determining whether the violation is material information that might require disclosure under the securities laws

(*Continued*)

MANDATED ACTIONS OF THE AMENDMENTS TO SENTENCING GUIDELINES FOR ORGANIZATIONS

Area Under Amendment	Mandated Actions	Recommended Steps
	offense, the organization will not receive credit for the existence of a compliance and ethics program.	▪ Ensure that the compliance and ethics team is prepared to conduct a thorough investigation in a timely manner ▪ Identify and/or create the mechanisms that the company has in place to learn about and respond to incidents promptly ▪ Prepare to perform root cause analysis of the reasons for the specific compliance violations
Training and Communication	The organization must provide training and disseminate information relevant to the compliance and ethics program and its objectives. Individuals within the organization that need to be trained include members of the following: ▪ The governing authority (board of directors or the highest level governing body) ▪ The organizational leadership ▪ The organization's employees	▪ Assess the company's risks in order to identify an appropriate training curriculum for employees ▪ Communicate company values and standards to vendors and other business associates ▪ Communicate with employees the consequences for failures to self-govern properly

(Continued)

MANDATED ACTIONS OF THE AMENDMENTS TO SENTENCING GUIDELINES FOR ORGANIZATIONS

Area Under Amendment	Mandated Actions	Recommended Steps
	▪ The organization's agents, as appropriate	▪ Create adequate systems to communicate incidents to the compliance and ethics team ▪ Decide how the company will identify and reach all of its workers for purposes of training ▪ Decide which people the organization works with meets the definition of "agents" ▪ Determine the frequency with which training curricula will be updated ▪ Determine whether issues of law and corporate values are being communicated as rules that must be obeyed or as drivers of the corporate culture ▪ Determine whether members of the board will be educated during board meetings, at other timed, and/or through means other than in-person sessions ▪ Determine/reassess the budget for the new ethics and compliance program ▪ Establish methods for measuring the effectiveness of the training program

(Continued)

MANDATED ACTIONS OF THE AMENDMENTS TO SENTENCING GUIDELINES FOR ORGANIZATIONS

Area Under Amendment	Mandated Actions	Recommended Steps
		■ Identify any history of ethics and compliance failures experienced by competitors, as well as those best practices that can be used to respond to these risks
Monitoring, Auditing, and Evaluating Program Effectiveness	Organizations must periodically evaluate the effectiveness of the compliance program. The compliance program must include monitoring and auditing systems that are designed to detect criminal conduct. ■ The program must include a reporting system that will provide a means for employees and agents to report or seek guidance about potential or actual criminal conduct. ■ The reporting system must incorporate a non-retaliation policy and should allow for anonymous or confidential reporting.	■ Create mechanisms that respond to people seeking guidance about compliance an ethics ■ Determine the period reporting that will be required during the course of assessing the effectiveness of the compliance program ■ Identify the existing policies and procedures to encourage employee reporting of incidents. Determine whether these policies and procedures can be applied to a broader ethics and compliance program ■ Identify/create the tools and data the company has in place to assess the effectiveness of the compliance program ■ Ensure that employees are empowered by education to resolve ethical and legal dilemmas

(Continued)

MANDATED ACTIONS OF THE AMENDMENTS TO SENTENCING GUIDELINES FOR ORGANIZATIONS

Area Under Amendment	Mandated Actions	Recommended Steps
Performance Incentives and Disciplinary Actions	The organization shall consistently enforce the compliance program through the use of incentives for compliance and disciplinary measures for engaging in or failing to take reasonable steps to prevent and detect criminal conduct.	■ Ensure that the company celebrates ethics successes as strongly as it condemns unethical or illegal conduct ■ Ensure that the performance management and compensation systems reinforce ethical behavior
Remedial Action	The organization must conduct periodic risk assessments of criminal conduct within their operations and take the appropriate steps to design, implement, or modify each element of the program to reduce the risk of criminal behavior. Upon detection of criminal conduct, the organization must take reasonable steps to respond appropriately, as well as prevent further criminal conduct.	■ Create tools to monitor and assess the compliance program, as well as to make continuous improvements to the program ■ Identify/create processes to track changes in the business, products and services, and the organizational structure that might lead to new risks ■ Infuse ethics and compliance messages into other company communications ■ Prepare to quickly create internal controls to prevent future violations ■ Treat ethics as integral to the way the company does business

(Continued)

MANDATED ACTIONS OF THE AMENDMENTS TO SENTENCING GUIDELINES FOR ORGANIZATIONS

Area Under Amendment	Mandated Actions	Recommended Steps
		▪ Identify the party responsible for making disclosure to outside parties of the violation ▪ Create a "compliance resume" so that if a violation occurs, the company can prove that it took every reasonable measure to comply with the highest standards of corporate governance

Reprinted with permission from the Corporate Executive Board, Washington, DC © 2006.

Sample Compliance Program Charter

Compliance and Ethics Leadership Council, 2005

CONTENT OF PROGRAM CHARTERS

Program charters are intended for internal stakeholders, providing visibility into the structure and objectives of the program. Charters aid in the management of the compliance and ethics program by clearly defining the following:

- Role of the compliance and ethics office and responsibilities of individual staff
- Reporting relationships of the Compliance and Ethics Officer
- Protocols for development and dissemination of business conduct standards and procedures to stakeholders
- Guidelines for monitoring and auditing of the Compliance and Ethics program
- Guidelines for reporting of business conduct allegations and advice requests (managing a whistleblower program)
- Guidelines for investigating alleged violations
- Role of the Audit Committee of the Board of Directors (or other committee to which the Compliance and Ethics Officer reports)
- Delivery schedule for compliance and ethics training

KEY PRINCIPLES

Organization and Independence

The Compliance and Ethics Officer is accountable to the Chief Compliance Officer and the Audit Committee with respect to the activities performed by the Compliance and Ethics Office. The Compliance and Ethics Office reports to the Chief Executive Officer and shall have direct access to the Audit Committee and shall take directly to the Chairman of the Audit Committee matters of sufficient magnitude and urgency to require immediate attention. As a matter of policy, the Compliance and Ethics Officer will review ethics issues with the appropriate operating head before going to the Audit Committee, unless a conflict of interest situation precludes an objective, unbiased review.

Authority

The Compliance and Ethics Office conducts ethics and compliance programs and activities under the authority of the Chairman of the Audit Committee. Managers at all levels of the Corporation are expected to provide reasonable access to relevant people, information, and records during the course of ethics investigations.

Retaliation

Company has established procedures for the reporting of complaints regarding accounting, internal control, auditing, or other policy or code of conduct matters. These allegations can be reported anonymously. All complaints, whether or not reported anonymously, will be handled in a confidential matter, with disclosure limited to those persons necessary to conduct a full investigation of the alleged violation or to carry out appropriate disciplinary or corrective action.

Reporting suspected violations of policies, code of conduct, or other processes is a benefit to the corporation and expected behavior of all employees. Any form of retaliation against any employee for reporting or participating in the investigation of a suspected violation will not be tolerated.

Requirements of all Employees   All Company employees and employees of Company subsidiaries are required to:

- Understand the Corporation's code of conduct and workplace policies
- Abide by the provisions of the code of conduct and workplace policies
- Participate in required training relative to the code of conduct and other workplace policies
- Provide written acknowledgment of the code of conduct and compliance with its provisions when requested

Responsibilities of Operating Unit Heads   Operating unit heads are responsible for creating an ethical work environment and acting as role models of ethical behavior. Specifically, they are responsible for:

- Cascading communications about business ethics, workplace policies, and corporate values, including their personal message customized to their employee constituency
- Ensuring there is a reliable process in place within their organization to confirm that employees receive required training, receive appropriate communications, understand the code of conduct, and comply with the provisions of the code of conduct and other workplace policies
- Supporting the Compliance and Ethics Office and it agents on ethics investigation activities in a timely manner
- Exemplifying role model behavior when it comes to ethics and other corporate values
- Directing all ethical issues and concerns to the Compliance and Ethics Office in a timely and comprehensive manner. The Compliance and Ethics Office is the only official office of record for ethics files for the corporation. Information to be transmitted to the Compliance and Ethics Office includes:
  - Description of suspected violation, including policy, law, or regulation reference
  - Person or persons involved, if known or available
  - Location where suspected violation occurred
  - Date when suspected violation occurred
  - How suspected violation was observed or identified
  - Investigative or disciplinary actions already taken or underway, if any
- Ensuring that no retaliation occurs against any employee for reporting or participating in the investigation of suspected violations
- Ensuring that their Compliance and Ethics Committee member has adequate management support and resources to fulfill their duties for the organization

Compliance and Ethics Office   The Compliance and Ethics Office has primary responsibility for developing and implementing programs that support an ethical work environment.

- Developing and implementing a worldwide code of conduct and associated compliance program that supports the Corporation's requirement to maintain an ethical work environment
- Developing and implementing code of conduct training materials for the Company employees worldwide
- Ensuring annual written acknowledgment of and compliance with the Company Code of Conduct by all designated senior managers and executives. This acknowledgment must include confirmation of their organizations' compliance.
- Providing channels for employees, suppliers, and customers to report suspected violations and provide ethical guidance. These channels include a toll-free telephone number, e-mail, Internet links, Web page, and internal and external mail address. The option to remain anonymous must be available to individuals reporting suspected violations.
- Overseeing investigations of suspected ethical violations. Investigations are generally conducted using existing internal competencies. Ethics cases can be closed only by the Compliance and Ethics Officer.
- Coordinating the Compliance and Ethics Committee activities to ensure consistency and provide an executive-level forum for discussing emerging trends, issues, and concerns
- Reporting ethics and compliance activities and issues for Company senior management and the Audit Committee to the Board of Directors
- Networking with peer group companies and professional trade associations to understand and adapt best practices

Compliance and Ethics Committee   Senior operational and functional executives comprise the Compliance and Ethics Committee. The Committee works closely with the Compliance and Ethics Office and has primary responsibility for:

- Implementing ethics training and education
- Ensuring consistent enforcement of discipline policy
- Overseeing changes and making recommendations to Company policies
- Evaluating ethics and business conduct issues and trends, to address potential problems pro-actively
- Evaluating the performance of the Compliance and Ethics Office and the effectiveness of the ethics and compliance program and providing

feedback to the Compliance and Ethics Office and the Compliance and Ethics Officer

Additionally, each member is individually responsible for:

- Establishing a formal or informal business ethics and compliance network within his or her respective organization
- Ensuring that all organization-specific policies are consistent with Company values, Code of Conduct, existing laws, and other Company policies
- Attesting that ethics and business conduct training is fully deployed with his or her organization
- Attending all Compliance and Ethics Committee meetings

Governance Board members are not responsible for the intake of ethics violations. All suspected violations should be directed to the Compliance and Ethics Office directly via the Ethics Helpline.

Resources and Communications The Compliance and Ethics Office maintains the Ethics Helpline as a resource on ethics, code of conduct, and workplace policies and a channel for employees and others to report suspected allegations of ethical misconduct. The Helpline is available 24 hours a day, 7 days a week from all locations. According to its charter, the Helpline must:

- Preserve anonymity, if requested by the caller
- Ensure confidentiality of all callers and subjects of allegations
- Provide guidance on questions and inquiries
- Direct allegations and inquiries to the Compliance and Ethics Office in a timely manner
- Treat all callers with respect and dignity

Resources for Compliance Professionals

While this book intends to be comprehensive, due to the enormity of the subject, it is not possible to cover all the relevant content and materials. This book has attempted to convey the underlying principles of an effective compliance program while providing numerous best practices and strategies for success. Still, there is much more information available to discover and apply. There are a number of outstanding resources available to compliance professionals and others with a keen interest in the subject. Detailed below are a number of selected resources to guide the reader. An excellent source of compliance best practices can be gleaned through involvement in professional compliance associations. The Internet also contains many Web sites, publications, articles, and blogs available to the general public.

CORPORATE EXECUTIVE BOARD

The Corporate Executive Board Company (NASDAQ: EXBO) is a leading provider of best practices research and analysis focusing on corporate strategy, operations, and general management. The Corporate Executive Board (CEB) provides its integrated set of services currently to more than 3,700 of the world's largest and most prestigious corporations, including over 80% of the Fortune 500. These services include best practices research studies, executive education seminars, management implementation toolkits, customized research briefs, and Web-based access to a library of over 300,000 corporate best practices. Of special note, the CEB was extremely helpful in providing insight and content for the writing of this book. Their substantial assistance is gratefully appreciated.

"The CEB's mission is to increase the effectiveness of executives and their enterprises by discovering and teaching the membership the best new thinking and strategies from across industry and around the world." The CEB has many different practice areas including financial services, human resources, information technology, corporate finance, operation and procurement, and legal and administrative. Membership is on an annual subscription basis. Within the legal and administrative practice is the Compliance and Ethics Leadership Council that focuses on improving the compliance and ethics programs of organizations worldwide.

Compliance and Ethics Leadership Council

"The Compliance and Ethics Leadership Council (CELC), a membership program of the CEB, serves compliance and ethics executives at hundreds of organizations around the world. The CELC's dedicated team of research, executive education, and member services staff support members on their most pressing problems by helping them learn from the collective experience of their peers." The CELC has access to executive suites and other senior management to understand the strategic, governance, and business challenges impacting legal and compliance departments. This unique perspective allows the CELC to lend unparalleled perspective to research that reflects enterprise-wide concerns.

The CELC uses quantitative and fact-based case study research to provide insights into proven practices from legal and compliance leaders. The case study approach offers significant insight and opportunities for improvement in compliance programs. The CELC has a dedicated staff of analysts and researchers to study the best practices of the world's leading organizations. Members get access to this information to solve compliance and other challenges. An excellent tool afforded members is the member-driven agenda that includes polling of members to determine pressing issues and business challenges. In addition, the CELC hosts a number of member events including senior executive forums, leadership briefings, member-hosted forums, and teleconferences where research and other best practices are shared and discussed.

A searchable archive and resource center provides online access to research and tools on a wide variety of compliance and ethics topics. Included is the most current research on such compliance areas as establishing a compliance and ethics program, measuring program effectiveness, compliance risk management, compliance education and communications, corporate governance, and metrics. Members of the CELC include such companies such as Bank of America, Dow Chemical, IBM, Royal Dutch Shell, Johnson & Johnson, General Motors, and Barclays. For more information on the Compliance and Ethics Leadership Council, please visit their Web site at www.celc.executiveboard.com/Public/Default.aspx.

Compliance and Ethics Program Assessment Wizard™

The Compliance and Ethics Program Assessment Wizard™ is a comprehensive measurement and benchmarking system for compliance and ethics program performance. It is a Web-based, self-assessment of program maturity that assesses an organization's compliance program across eight key elements and 28 sub-elements. The elements and sub-elements align closely with the revised Federal Sentencing Guidelines for Organizations and incorporate expectations of the SEC and European regulators. The Program Assessment Wizard was created by the Corporate Executive Board's Compliance and Ethics Leadership Council (CELC). The results can benchmark a program against peers and external standards and identify areas of strength as well as opportunities for improvement and resource allocation.

The Program Assessment Wizard's eight key elements and 28 sub-elements are as follows:

- Program Structure and Oversight
  - Leadership and Resources
  - Enterprise Oversight
  - Program Objectives
- Standards and Procedures
  - Development
  - Accessibility
  - Applicability
- Compliance Risk Assessment
  - Process
  - Responsibility
  - Prioritization
  - Scope
  - Mitigation
- Training
  - Content
  - Delivery Mechanism
  - Audience
  - Tracking
  - Assessment and Certification
- Communications
  - Content
  - Channels
- Discipline and Incentives
  - Background Checks
  - Performance Review Process
  - Disciplinary Action

- Allegation Reporting and Investigations
  - Allegation Reporting
  - Allegation Tracking and Analysis
  - Investigation Management
- Program Measurement and Monitoring
  - Monitoring Standards
  - Monitoring Ownership
  - Metrics
  - Employee Perception Measures

The CELC developed an Importance Scale from 1 to 5 for the eight elements with 1 as "Very Low Importance" and 5 as "Very High Importance." The CELC also developed a Maturity Scale from 1 to 4 that indicates the maturity level of each of the 28 sub-elements. A Level 1 is "Unstructured" and a Level 4 is "World-Class." The four levels of program maturity were developed using best practices research and through extensive consultation with dozens of member companies.

There are additional benefits to using the Program Assessment Wizard. The CELC will recommend processes, procedures, and organizational structure to address program gaps and enhance program strengths. Their benchmarking is a result of interactions with over 300 companies. They will provide ready-to-use tools, templates, and best practices for program improvements from their archives. It should be noted that an organization must be a member of the CELC in order to receive these benefits. For more information, please visit www.celc.executiveboard.com.

SOCIETY OF CORPORATE COMPLIANCE AND ETHICS

The Society of Corporate Compliance and Ethics (SCCE) is an organization dedicated to the continuous improvement of corporate governance, compliance, and ethics. It is headquartered in Minneapolis, Minnesota and services the growing industry of corporate compliance and compliance officers. As stated on their Web site, the SCCE's Mission is to "champion ethical practice and compliance standards in all organizations and to provide the necessary resources for compliance professionals and others who share these principles."[1] The SCCE offers tools, resources, and training for compliance officers and others involved in developing and maintaining compliance programs. The SCCE also offers a speaker's bureau to provide speakers on compliance related topics at conferences and other training events. Members of the SCCE include Fortune 500 companies such as Colgate Palmolive, Dell, Microsoft, UPS, and Wal-Mart, as well as law firms, compliance service providers, and other businesses. For more information on the Society of Corporate Compliance and Ethics, please visit their Web site at www.corporatecompliance.org/index.htm.

Certified Compliance and Ethics Professionals

With the growing emphasis on corporate compliance, there is an ongoing need for compliance and ethics professionals. Professional certification in the field is an excellent way to advance compliance as well as personal development and growth. The SCCE offers a certification program in compliance and ethics that is administered by the SCCE Certification Board. The Board's mission "is to develop criteria for the determination of competence in the practice of corporate compliance and ethics at a variety of levels, and to recognize individuals meeting these criteria."[2] The Certified Compliance and Ethics Professional (CCEP) is a certification that requires an applicant to fulfill requirements in work experience and continuing education, as well as pass a certification examination.

According to the SCCE, a "CCEP is a professional with knowledge of relevant regulations and expertise in compliance processes sufficient to assist corporate industries to understand and address legal obligations, and promote organizational integrity through the operation of effective compliance programs."[3] The CCEP certification will formally recognize compliance professionals and provide a national standard of requisite knowledge in ethics and compliance. This certification program is another best practice in developing the knowledge, skills, and abilities to further the quality of professionals involved in compliance as well as compliance programs.

ETHICS AND COMPLIANCE OFFICER ASSOCIATION

The Ethics and Compliance Officer Association (ECOA) is a not-for-profit, non-consulting, member-driven organization for individuals responsible for oversight of ethics, compliance, and business conduct programs in their respective organizations. The ECOA was incorporated in 1992 and today has over 1,300 worldwide members. It offers compliance resources and networking to both highly experienced compliance officers and those new to the field. The mission of the ECOA, as stated on its Web site, is "being the leading provider of ethics, compliance, and corporate governance resources to ethics and compliance professionals worldwide" and providing a worldwide network of compliance professionals "for the exchange of ideas and strategies."[4]

Membership in the ECOA is restricted "to those individuals who are recognized by their organization as having the assigned role and responsibility for designing, implementing, and/or administering ethics, compliance or business conduct programs."[5] ECOA members are expected to share their knowledge, experience and best practices with other members to further corporate compliance. Member companies include Alcoa, CA, Inc., Citigroup, General Electric, Lockheed Martin, Microsoft, PepsiCo, and United Technologies. The ECOA conducts training and other educational conferences, forums, webcasts and professional development programs. For more information on the Ethics and Compliance Officer Association, please visit their Web site at www.theecoa.org.

DEFENSE INDUSTRY INITIATIVE (DII) ON BUSINESS ETHICS AND CONDUCT

The Defense Industry Initiative on Business Ethics and Conduct (DII) is as they state on their Web site, a "consortium of U.S. defense industry contractors that subscribes to a set of principles for achieving high standards of business ethics and conduct."[6] The DII was established in 1986 by 32 major defense contractors "who pledged to adopt and implement a set of principles of business ethics and conduct that acknowledge and express their federal-procurement-related corporate responsibilities to the Department of Defense, as well as to the public, the Government, and to each other."[7] The DII provides a whole host of member services including Best Practices Forums, ethics training resources, annual reports of DII activities and other related services. Each DII member company commits to adopt and adhere to the DII's six principles of business ethics and compliance. The principles state that each member shall:

- Have a written code of conduct setting forth the high ethical values expected for all within their organization.
- Train everyone in their organization about their responsibilities under the code.
- Encourage reporting of violations of the code as well as promoting a non-retaliation policy for such reporting.
- Be required to implement internal controls to monitor compliance with federal procurement laws and adopt voluntary reporting of violations of federal procurement laws to authorities.
- Share best practices related to the DII Principles, as well as participate in the annual Best Practices Forum.
- Be accountable to the public.[8]

DII members have worked over the years to make their principles a standard for the entire defense industry as well as for other industries. "Perhaps because of their disciplined approach to ethics and conduct, no member of the DII family of companies experienced the fate of the Enrons, the Global Crossings, the WorldComs, and the like. We cannot know for sure that it is the DII values-based ethical culture that set the DII family above those that failed, but that *ethical culture had to have been a contributing factor* (emphasis added)."⁹ There is an annual assessment for membership that is determined by each member company's total annual company revenues. The DII has grown steadily since 1986 to 74 members at the end of 2006. For more information, visit www.dii.org.

UNITED STATES DEPARTMENT OF JUSTICE

The Department of Justice, as the entity responsible for prosecuting corporate crime on the federal level, sets out the enforcement policies of which all corporate professionals should be aware. The Justice Department, and in particular its Corporate Fraud Task Force, developed these enforcement standards. These policies, particularly as described in the 2003 "Thompson Memo" and the 2006 "McNulty Memo," can be viewed on the Department's Web site. These memos as well as speeches, reports from the Corporate Fraud Task, and other materials can be found in the "President's Corporate Fraud Task Force" and "Publications & Documents" sections of the site. The site also contains links to the text of important laws such as the Sarbanes-Oxley Act, the USA PATRIOT Act, the Foreign Corrupt Practices Act, and SEC rules. The Corporate Fraud Task Force site can be found at www.usdoj.gov/dag/cftf. The McNulty Memo can be read in full at www.usdoj.gov/dag/speech/2006/mcnulty_memo.pdf. The section on the Foreign Corrupt Practices Act containing the law itself and many other informational resources can be found at www.usdoj.gov/criminal/fraud/fcpa.

UNITED STATES SENTENCING COMMISSION

The U.S. Sentencing Commission creates and [manages] the Federal Sentencing Guidelines, legislation which has had a profound and dramatic effect on compliance.

An independent agency in the judicial branch, the Commission principally "establish[es] sentencing policies and practices for the federal courts, including guidelines to be consulted regarding the appropriate form and severity of punishment for offenders convicted of federal crimes."¹⁰ The Guidelines' list of the seven elements of a minimally effective compliance program serves as the baseline for many of the corporate compliance programs in existence. Chapter Eight of the Guidelines covers the sentencing of organizations and the best practices it set forth have been adopted or served as the basis for model compliance programs created by other federal agencies.[11] The Sentencing Commission's site includes the entire Sentencing Guidelines and numerous resources, particularly those pertaining to the Organizational Guidelines, as well as statistical data regarding organizational sentencing practices.

The main site can be found at www.ussc.gov/. The link to the Advisory Group on Organizational Guidelines to the United States Sentencing Commission is www.ussc.gov/corp/advgrp.htm. The Organizational Guidelines themselves and supplemental material can be found at www.ussc.gov/orgguide.htm.

NOTES

1. The Society of Corporate Compliance and Ethics, www.corporate compliance.org/about/about.htm.
2. Certified Compliance and Ethics Professional (CCEP), The Society of Corporate Compliance and Ethics, www.corporatecompliance.org/ CCEP/index.htm.
3. Ibid.
4. The Ethics and Compliance Officers Association, www.theecoa.org/AM/ Template.cfm?Section=Mission&Template=/CM/HTMLDisplay.cfm& ContentID=1819.
5. The Ethics and Compliance Officers Association, www.theecoa.org/ source/Members/cMemberInsert.cfm?Section=Join_the_ECOA&WHE RE_TO_NEXT_SOURCE=../Members/paJoinAddlInfo.cfm.
6. The Defense Industry Initiative on Business Ethics and Conduct, www.dii.org.
7. The Defense Industry Initiative on Business Ethics and Conduct, www.dii.org/Statement.htm.
8. Ibid.
9. The Defense Industry Initiative on Business Ethics and Conduct, 2003 Annual Report to the Public, 1, www.dii.org/annual/2003/Annual Report2003.doc.
10. "An Overview of the United States Sentencing Commission," United States Sentencing Commission, June 2005, www.ussc.gov/general/USS Coverview_2005.pdf.
11. Paula Desio, "An Overview of the Organizational Guidelines," United States Sentencing Commission, www.ussc.gov/corp/ORGOVER VIEW.pdf.

Index

AbTox, Inc., 175, 182–184
Adelphia, *See* Adelphia
    Communications Corporation
Adelphia Communications
    Corporation, 166–168, 216
    compliance failures, 166–168
Airservices Australia:
    company mission and values, 236
    company profile, 235
    confidentiality, 240–241
    control strategies, 242, 248–249
    definition of fraud, 237, 247–248
    fraud awareness, 239–240, 250–253
    Fraud Control Plan, 233–244
    fraud incidents, 237–238
    internal investigations, 241–242,
        249–250
    Managers' Guide for Fraud and
        Corruption Control, 244–253
    risk assessment, 242–243
Allen, William, 73, 75
AML. *See* Anti-money laundering
Anti-money laundering, 131–145. *See
    also* Money laundering
    audit function, 143–144
    compliance programs, 138–143
    criminal sanctions, 137
    enhancements and regulations from
        USA PATRIOT Act, 136–137
    forfeiture, 137–138
    "Know Your Customer," 138, 141
    monitoring, 140
    non-financial institutions, 138
    record-keeping requirements, 135
Antitrust, 49–50
Aristotle, 3
Arizona State University, 20
    W. P. Carey School of Business, 20

Arthur Andersen, 48, 159
Aspen Institute, 15
Asset forfeiture, 137–138
    Asset Forfeiture Fund, 137
    Asset Forfeiture Program, 137
Association of Certified Fraud
    Examiners, 122, 253
Attorney-client privilege, 57–58
    waiver of privilege, 58–59
Audit Committee, 175, 226

Background checks, 185–186
Bank Secrecy Act, 132–133, 139
    origin, 133
    record-keeping requirements, 135
    reporting requirements, 133, 135
    transaction activity, 133
    USA PATRIOT Act enhancements,
        136–137
Barnsley, Jan, 152
Barry, Megan, 223–224
Bay of Pigs, 260–261
Blakely v. Washington, 164
Blue Ribbon Commission on Defense
    Management, The, 50
Board of directors, 175
    fiduciary responsibility, 20, 35, 216
    reports, 197–199
Booz Allen Hamilton, 15
Brown, Shawn, 28–29
BSA. *See* Bank Secrecy Act
Buffett, Warren, 6, 46
Burke, James, 157
Business Roundtable, The, 157

CA, Inc., 1–2, 87–105, 263–265
    Business Practice Officers, 103
    chief compliance officer, 92–94

CA, Inc., (*Continued*)
code of conduct, 95–99
Compliance and Ethics Program
Assessment Wizard, 103
compliance best practices, 104
compliance failures, 264
Defense Industry Initiative, 99
Deferred Prosecution Agreement,
89–92, 105
document retention policies, 100
Gnazzo, Patrick J., 92–97, 99–105,
176, 215
hotline, 95, 100, 102
independent examiner, 89, 92, 105
Kumar, Sanjay, 89–90
McDermott, John, 101
"New CA Way, " 263–264
Ombudsperson Program, 102
remedial steps, 90–92
35-day month, 88–90
tone at the top, 99–100
training, 100
"unfettered access," 93–94
Caputo, Ross, 182–184
Caremark. *See In Re Caremark*
Castillo, Judge Ruben, 184
CELC. *See* Compliance and Ethics
Leadership Council
Certified Fraud Examiner, 187
Certified Compliance and Ethics
Professional, 187
Certified Protection Professional, 187
Chief Compliance Officer, 52, 92–94,
155, 175–177
"Corporate First Responder," 175
importance of, 176–177
prosecution of, 182–184
responsibilities, 175–176
Coca-Cola, 31–33
Code of conduct, 11–12, 63, 96–99,
121, 154–155
benchmarking and evaluation, 172
core values, 171
designing and distributing, 193
integrity as a value, 32

Investigator's Code of Conduct,
187–188
promotion of, 154–155
protecting trade secrets, 32–33
Seaboard Corporation, 63
Code of ethics. *See* Code of conduct
Committee of Sponsoring
Organizations, 211
Commonwealth Fraud Control
Guidelines, 234–235
definition of fraud, 237
Compliance:
anti-money laundering, 138–143
best practices, 128–129, 154–155,
195–196, 200–201
business case, 14
chief compliance officer, 52, 92–94,
155, 175–177
communicating compliance values,
35
consultants, 37, 39
definition of, 8, 150
development of modern compliance,
49–52
effective, 2–3, 8, 9, 28–29, 31–33,
62, 150
ethical lapses, publicizing, 102,
193–194, 207
evaluating program effectiveness, 62,
202–204, 210–211
failures, 48, 54, 55–57
gatekeepers, 34–35, 258
gift policy, 194
global concerns, 127–128
history, 45–53
incentives, 207–208
individuality, 11–12
job descriptions, 177–179
meaningful accountability, 30
obstacles to, 16, 17–19, 21, 40
organizational structure, 178,
180–181
"paper program," 61–62, 76
programs, 61–62, 128–129, 138
red flags, 20
retaliation, 266

side letters, 102
training, 40–41, 191–193, 195
Compliance and Ethics Leadership
Council, 8, 103, 203, 266
Compliance and Ethics Program
Assessment Wizard, 103, 203
Compliance Emergency Preparedness
Kit, 211, 213–214
Comprehensive Crime Control Act of
1984, 137
Computer Associates. *See* CA, Inc.
Connor, Laura, 131, 148
Cook, Jay, 46, 48
Cooper, Cynthia, 265
Copeland, Howard, 153
Copeland, Dr. John D., 149–162
Corporate first responders, 175
Corporate crime, 53–54
culpability, 60–61
defense, 53–54
enforcement, 54
Corporate Executive Board, 103
Corporate governance, 124
Latin America, 124–125
value of, 13, 15
Corporate regulation, 47
Congressional intervention, 47–50
New Deal, 48–49
historical patterns of, 45–49
Presidential influence on, 47–49
COSO. *See* Committee of Sponsoring
Organizations
Coughlin, Thomas, 55–57
Cox, Christopher, 174
Croft, Bob, 26–27
CTR. *See* Currency Transaction Report
Cuban Missile Crisis, 261
Culture of compliance, 266
Currency Transaction Reports, 133,
135, 143

Defense Industry Initiative, 51, 99
Deferred Prosecution Agreement,
89–92, 114, 117
Delaware Court of Chancery, 73
Dewey & LeBoeuf, 166

DII. *See* Defense Industry Initiative
Director liability, 76–77, 161–162
Discipline, 155, 205–206
DOJ. *See* United States Department of
Justice
DPA. *See* Deferred Prosecution
Agreement
Drucker, Peter, 30
Duke University Lacrosse case, 257
Dunlap, Al, 158
Durham County, North Carolina
District Attorney's Office,
257–258

Ebbers, Bernie, 53
ECOA. *See* Ethics and Compliance
Officers Association
Enron, 19–20, 48, 53, 159, 215
code of conduct, 3, 151, 171
Enterprise Risk Management, 100, 211
ERM. *See* Enterprise Risk Management
Ethics, 3–4
ethical behavior, 150, 152
ethical culture within the New York
City Police Department, 5–6
"ethics fad," 4
link with retention and productivity,
15–16
warning signs of ethical collapse, 20
Ethics and Compliance Officers
Association, 94
Ethisphere Magazine, 98–99
Executive compensation, 10–11
Executive leadership, 174–175
*Executive Roadmap to Fraud
Prevention and Internal Control*,
34, 54

Fabiano, Pedro, 121–129
Fastow, Andy, 215
FATF. *See* Financial Action Task Force
FBAR. *See* Report of Foreign Bank and
Financial Accounts
FBI. *See* Federal Bureau of Investigation
FCPA. *See* Foreign Corrupt Practices
Act

FDA. *See* Food and Drug
    Administration
Federal Bureau of Investigation, 28–29,
    31, 88
Federal Sentencing Guidelines for
    Organizations, 3, 9, 12, 52–54, 77,
    163
    Caremark, 73, 77
    Chapter 8, 163
    compliance standards and
        procedures, 165–166, 170–173
    criminal conduct and remedial action,
        170, 205–206, 208–209
    culpability score, 9
    effective compliance, 71, 165
    mitigating factors, 9–10, 12, 71,
        164–165
    organizational leadership, 168–169,
        173–178, 180–181
    performance incentives and
        disciplinary action, 170,
        204–208
    program effectiveness, 169, 196,
        201–204
    prohibited persons, 169, 185–188
    Seven Steps, 52, 75, 154–155,
        164–165, 168–170
    training and communication, 169,
        191–196
    2004 Amendments, 52, 164
Feeney, Thomas F.X., 166
Financial Action Task Force, 144
Financial Crimes Enforcement
    Network, 135
    IRS/FinCEN Form 8300, 138
FinCEN. *See* Financial Crimes
    Enforcement Network
Fisher, Alice S., 115–117
Fonda, Henry, 258, 265
Food and Drug Administration,
    182–184
Foreign Corrupt Practices Act, 37, 72,
    107–108, 115, 122, 128
    audits, 119
    books and records provision, 108,
        123

code of conduct reference, 98
compliance consultants, 116
cultural implications, 127
Department of Justice opinion
    procedure, 116
disclosures, 115–116
disgorgement of profits, 121
due diligence, 117
effective compliance program,
    118–119, 121
enactment, 50, 108
enforcement, 120, 123
facilitating payments, 88, 127
foreign issuers, 122, 127–128
investigations, 111–113, 117–118,
    120
Fraud:
    corporate, 53, 55–56
    defense contracting, 50
    investigations, 55–56, 63, 88–89,
        101
    prevention, 244, 253–254
    prosecution for, 205–206
    zero tolerance for, 205
Freakonomics, 207
FSGO. *See* Federal Sentencing
    Guidelines for Organizations

Gatekeepers, 34
General Electric, 50, 117
Gnazzo, Patrick J., 92–97, 99–105,
    176, 215
Greenspan, Alan, 30
Groupthink, 260–261

Hackett, Susan, 176
Hammer, Armand, 159
Hanson, Kirk O., 222
Healthcare Industry Group Purchasing
    Association, 224–225
Hewlett-Packard, 4, 50
    civil settlement with California
        Attorney General, 262
    compliance enhancements, 263
    spying and pretexting scandal,
        261–263

HIGPA. *See* Healthcare Industry Group Purchasing Association
Hoak, John, 262–263
Hotlines, 75, 95, 102, 201–202
   aversion to, 126
   confidentiality, 102, 201–202
   non-retaliation, 202
   restrictions, 213
Howard, Michael, 234
HP. *See* Hewlett-Packard
Hunt, J.B., 153

"Icarus Effect," 10
"Icaran" risk factors, 10–11
In Re Caremark, 62, 72–75
   board responsibility, 73–76
   compliance program, 74–75
   director liability, 76–78
   duty of care, 72–75
   duty of loyalty, 77
   role of ethics, 77
Infosys Technologies, 174
Insull, Samuel, 48–49
Integrity, 26, 96–97
Investigations:
   government, 59
   internal investigative unit, 186–187
   investigator's code of conduct, 187–188
InVision Technologies, Inc., 117
Invitrogen Corporation, 81
Isdell, Neville, 32

Jennings, Marianne, 20
Johnson & Johnson, 157–158
   baby oil case study, 158
   credo, 157
   tone at the top, 157–158
   Tylenol product tampering, 157

Kennedy, President John F., 260–261
   Bay of Pigs invasion, 260
   importance of open debate, 261
Kennedy, Robert, 261

Kinder Lydenberg, Domini & Company, 160
King David, 259–260
Knapp Commission, 7–8
"Know Your Customer," 138, 141.
   Also see Anti-money laundering
Kumar, Sanjay, 89–90
"KYC." *See* "Know Your Customer"

Lauer, Stephen A., 212
Lay, Ken, 16, 19–20
Lockheed Martin, 121
LRN, 15
Lucier, Greg, 81
Lucky CEOs Study, 30, 33–34
Lucky Directors Study, 34

Mail Fraud Statute, *See* United States Mail Fraud Statute
Malcolm Baldrige National Quality Award, 207, 220
Management:
   Deterring management misconduct, 206
   role in fraud prevention, 224
Market Value Added, 13
Markkula Center for Applied Ethics, 222
McDermott, John, 101
McNulty Memo, 54, 58–62, 121
   analysis of, 58–59
   charging factors, 59–60
   cooperation with prosecutors, 59
   criminal culpability, 60–61
   "paper program," 61
   sentence reduction, 59, 61–62
McNulty, Paul, 58
"Meaningful accountability," 30
Meilstrup, David, 131, 148
Merck, 158
   River blindness case study, 158
Metcalf & Eddy International, Inc., 117–120. *See also* Foreign Corrupt Practices Act
   effective FCPA compliance program, 118–119

Money laundering, 131–133. *See also*
Anti-money laundering
Black Market Peso Exchange, 132
convictions, 134
definition, 132
drug trafficking, 132
foreign statutes, 144–145
integration, 132
layering, 132
placement, 132
red flags, 141–143
Monitoring, 140
Monsanto Corporation, 120
Montedison, S.P.A, 122–123
Moritz, Scott, 37
Murphy, Joseph E., 42, 214–215
MVA. *See* Market Value Added

NASDAQ, 72, 95
foreign issuers, 124
National Institute of Standards and
Technology, 220
NCCT. *See* Non-Cooperative Countries
and Territories
New York City Police Department, 5–8
history of corruption within, 7–8
*Police Student's Guide: Introduction
to the NYPD*, 6
reforms efforts, 6
New York Stock Exchange, 72, 95
foreign issuers, 124
policy on financial risk, 100
Nicomachean Ethics, 3
Nifong, Mike, 257–258
NIST. *See* National Institute of
Standards and Technology
Non-Cooperative Countries and
Territories, 144
Nye, Vince, 262
NYPD. *See* New York City Police
Department

Occidental Petroleum, 159
OFAC. *See* Office of Foreign Assets
Control

Office of Foreign Assets Control, 37, 83
Oil States International, Inc., 122
OSI. *See* Oil States International, Inc.
Oxley, Michael, 82

Packard Commission, 50–51
Packard, David, 50
PATRIOT Act. *See* USA PATRIOT Act
PCAOB. *See* Public Company
Accounting Oversight Board
PepsiCo, 31–33
Petroleos de Venezuela, S.A., 122
Postal Inspectors. *See* United States
Postal Inspection Service
Premier, Inc., 207, 220
audit committee, 226
awards and incentives, 229
background, 220–222
best practices, 227–229
code of conduct, 224–225
communications, 225–226
compliance officer, 223–225
compliance program, 224–229
ethical practices and standards
report, 222–223
hotline, 225, 228
program assessment, 226
training, 225
winning the Baldrige Award, 220
Pretexting, 4, 261–262
Principles of Corporate Governance,
157
Principles of Federal Prosecution of
Business Organizations. *See*
Thompson Memo and McNulty
Memo
Professional Certified Investigator, 187
Prophet Nathan, 259
Program Assessment Wizard, *See*
Compliance and Ethics Program
Assessment Wizard
Public Company Accounting Oversight
Board, 78

RadioShack, 185
Reagan, President Ronald, 50

Redflex Traffic Systems, 28–29
Report of Foreign Bank and Financial
   Accounts, 135
Report of the National Commission on
   Fraudulent Financial Reporting,
   The. *See*
   Treadway Commission
Rigas, John J., 166–167
Rigas, Michael, 167
Rigas, Timothy, 167
Riley, Robert, 182–184
Roosevelt, President Franklin Delano,
   48–49
Roosevelt, President Teddy, 47
   State of the Union speech, 47–48
Russell, Greg, 237

SAR. *See* Suspicious Activity Reports
Sarbanes, Paul, 82
Sarbanes-Oxley Act, 3–4, 38, 46, 52,
   53, 72, 78–79, 108
   adoption by private companies, 153
   costs of implementation, 79–82
   criticism of, 79
   director responsibility, 153
   financial expert on board, 215
   financial reporting, 153
   impact on business, 80–82
   Section 302, 123
   Section 404, 79–81, 123
   Section 906, 124
Schlesinger, Jr., Arthur, 261
Schnitzer, Sam, 109
Schnitzer Steel Industries, Inc., 109–114
   Deferred Prosecution Agreement, 114
   FCPA violations, 110–113
   history, 109–110
   impact of Sarbanes-Oxley Act, 111
   prosecution of, 112–114
   remedial efforts, 113–114
Scott Paper, 158
Seaboard Corporation, 63
Seaboard Criteria. *See* Securities and
   Exchange Commission
SEC. *See* Securities and Exchange
   Commission

Securities and Exchange Act of 1934, 49
Securities and Exchange Commission,
   4, 49, 63–64
   enforcement activity, 5, 120
   Seaboard Criteria, 61, 64–66
Seven Signs of Ethical Collapse, 20
Seven Steps, *See* Federal Sentencing
   Guidelines for Organizations
Share Our Strength, 160
Sherman, Marc, 131, 148
Sherman Antitrust Act, 50
Side letters, 102
Skeel, David A., 10
"Skunk in the Room," 258, 264–265
Soderquist Center for Leadership and
   Ethics, 149–150
Soderquist, Don, 152
Speaking up, 265–266
Spying, 4, 261–262
SSI International Far East, Ltd., *See*
   Schnitzer Steel Industries, Inc.
SSI International, Inc., *See* Schnitzer
   Steel Industries, Inc
St. Thomas, University of, 16
   Center for Business Ethics, The, 16
Stamboulidis, George, 59
Stock Options:
   backdating, 30, 33–35, 161
   companies probed, 36–37
Stone v. Ritter, 77
Sullivan & Cromwell, 88
Sunbeam, 158
Suspicious Activity Reports, 134–135,
   141–143
Swainson, John, 96, 105

Third-party risk, 108
Thompson Memo, 54, 57, 121
Titan Corporation, 120–121
Tone at the top, 25–26, 35, 38
   absence of, 34
   creating, 99
   definition of, 26, 156
   demonstration of, 28–33, 40–43,
   153, 157, 159
   measurement, 27, 99–100, 160

Training, 40–41, 100, 152, 169,
191–193
Treadway Commission, 51–52, 211
12 Angry Men, 258, 265
Tylenol, 157
Tyson Foods, 151,159–160
compliance program, 151
compliance training, 152
tone at the top, 159
Tyson, John, 159

United States Attorney's Office:
District of Oregon, 112
Eastern District of New York, 88–89
United States' Federal Sentencing
Guidelines. *See* Federal Sentencing
Guidelines for Organizations
United States Department of Defense,
51
United States Department of Justice, 8,
53–54, 57–59, 63, 120
asset forfeiture, 137
cooperation with, 59
FCPA enforcement, 120
money laundering, 133
United States Department of the
Treasury, 133
United States Mail Fraud Statute, 47
"United States person," 135
United States Postal Inspection
Service, 101

Postal Inspector, 166
United States Sentencing Commission,
163. *See also* Federal Sentencing
Guidelines for Organizations
United States v. Booker, 164
United States v. Fanfan, 164
United States v. Kay, 120
United Technologies Corporation,
92
USA PATRIOT Act, 37, 72, 107, 131,
135–136
anti-money laundering program,
137
asset forfeiture, 137–138
criminal sanctions, 137
regulations, 136
USSC. *See* United States Sentencing
Commission

Values, 156
corporate, 56
communication of, 35
Verschoor, Curtis C., 13

Wal-Mart, 55–57, 152
Wall Street Journal,
The, 211
Westinghouse, 50
Whistleblowers, 207, 265
Wooh, Si Chan, 114
WorldCom, 53, 265